IMAGES
of America

ELLENVILLE

On the Cover: "American Beauties," seen here in front of the newly opened Wayside Inn on Liberty Square in Ellenville, won first prize in the 1908 Ulster County Fair Coaching Day Parade in the category "Four Horse Summer Boarders Float." Carrie Clark, who assisted parents Joseph and Alice Clark with operating a boardinghouse in Ellenville, organized the float. Onboard are young women—Ellenville's "beauties"—decorated with roses. (Courtesy of Ellenville Public Library & Museum.)

IMAGES
of America

ELLENVILLE

Henry "Bucky" Green and
Ellenville Public Library & Museum

ARCADIA
PUBLISHING

ISBN 978-1-4671-2369-3

Published by Arcadia Publishing
Charleston, South Carolina

Printed in the United States of America

Library of Congress Control Number: 2014959341

For all general information, please contact Arcadia Publishing:
Telephone 843-853-2070
Fax 843-853-0044
E-mail sales@arcadiapublishing.com
For customer service and orders:
Toll-Free 1-888-313-2665

Visit us on the Internet at www.arcadiapublishing.com

To our community

Contents

ACKNOWLEDGMENTS

Writing this book was a team effort and, ultimately, a community collaboration. Notes, files, ephemera, and images donated to the library over the years began that effort, as did the dedicated work of the library staff and volunteers who organized, indexed, and labeled these items. Town of Wawarsing historian Katharine T. Terwilliger left an incredible legacy of notes, clippings, and references, along with her published writings. Pat Clinton left valuable notes and articles. Past library directors, including Dorothy H. Sanderson and Marion M. Dumond, left wonderful legacies. All of this formed the foundation for the book now in your hands. Unless otherwise noted, all images are from the collections of Ellenville Public Library & Museum (EPL&M). To learn more, or to access our local history collections, please contact us at (845) 647-5530 or epl@rcls.org, or visit our website at www.eplm.org.

The support of the museum advisory board and board of trustees is greatly appreciated. Thanks are due to current library director Pam Stocking for saying yes. Museum advisory board member Debbie Stack was instrumental to the book's early stages. Thanks go to former director Marion M. Dumond for fulfilling the directive she was given when hired—to create a local history museum. Her advice and personal support were invaluable. The efforts of library staff were indispensable, especially those of the late Marion Ehrhardt, whose knowledge of the community and museum resources helped get the project off the ground. The contributions of library digital archivist Sandy Marsh were extraordinary, from formatting images to researching and writing captions. Rita Helgesen was tireless in searching for information and sharing her knowledge. We could not have done it without you.

Thanks go, as well, to Pam Kuhlmann, avid historic postcard collector and author of *Wawarsing* (an Arcadia Postcard History Series book), and Jeff Golliher for their assistance with caption writing. Finally, we want to acknowledge our families and friends. For their support, enthusiasm, and patience, we are truly grateful.

—Bucky Green,
Town of Wawarsing Historian

—Lynne "Asha" Golliher,
EPL&M Outreach Librarian

Introduction

Located at the foot of the Shawangunk Mountains, Ellenville reflects the colorful history of many towns and cities across America; industry and community flourished with improvements in travel, communication, and modern technology. Primarily farmland and forest in the Colonial Revolutionary era, Ellenville began to grow in earnest in the early 1800s. What we know today as Route 209 is, in fact, one of the oldest "sanctioned" (by the king and queen of Holland) public roads in the United States. Route 209 was first used by Native Americans and later by Spanish and Dutch settlers. Route 209, variably known as the Old Mine Road, the Minisink Trail, the Kings Highway, and the Queens Highway, was the lifeline for early settlers and commerce, especially mines for lead and other treasures hidden deep within the mountain ridge it follows. Eventually, Ellenville would also be on the routes of the Delaware & Hudson (D&H) Canal and Ontario & Western (O&W) Railway. When Route 52—an east-west route coming from the Hudson River—intersected Route 209 in Ellenville, the village then had two very popular courses for travel. Ellenville has long been at the center of industrial, civic, and community life in the town of Wawarsing, New York.

In many ways, the story of Ellenville began in 1823 when Charles Hartshorn arrived in this small community, known then only as Fairchild City, to try a criminal case at the Hoornbeek Tavern. He liked the area so well that, after the trial was completed, he decided to make it his home. He purchased a small business and realized that the so-called city needed a post office. In preparation of the formal petition for the post office, a name had to be chosen. After much discussion, it was decided that Maria Hoornbeek's sister, Ellen Snyder, who was visiting at the time, would lend her name; hence the village was called Ellenville.

Ellenville experienced a period of sustained growth with the building and operation of the D&H Canal in the mid-1800s. The D&H Canal, built by the Wurts brothers to transport coal from mines in northern Pennsylvania to the Hudson River, helped people open their eyes to new possibilities for commerce. The canal offered a convenient means to transport other raw materials and finished products besides coal. The first major industry was the Ellenville Glass Factory, and many others found this area an ideal location as well. In turn, it was these industries—pottery, tanning, knife making, and a foundry, to list only a few—that helped to grow the village.

As a direct result of the D&H Canal and the industrial development that followed, the population of Ellenville transformed from mostly Dutch settlers to a wide range of Irish, German, and Italian residents. It was this period that attracted many businessmen and new residents to Ellenville. People who had previously lived in large communities and had prior experience with running a growing municipality were drawn to the opportunities here. With this diversified community came many varied houses of worship and civic groups. In the 1850s, the prominent Dutch Reformed church and Methodist church found themselves in need of new structures to serve their expanding congregations. Soon after, Catholics, Lutherans, and Episcopalians established their first churches. In 1856, Ellenville was formally incorporated as the only village in southern Ulster County.

After the end of the Civil War, Ellenville suffered the economic hardship shared by the whole nation. New forms of transportation and modern technology once again played prominent roles in renewing Ellenville as a strong community. This is especially evident in the arrival of the railroad in 1872. In the latter part of the 19th century, many of Ellenville's most beautiful Victorian and Queen Anne homes were built. As Ellenville's population grew in size, so did an interest in having a well-rounded community life. Three fire departments were organized, all very active in the village; they had sports teams and bands and displayed their equipment in wonderful, well-attended parades. The proper education of children was also a major concern of the people of Ellenville. Education development can be traced from a small schoolhouse on Market Street to a brick school on Main Street and then to the creation of the Pine Grove School, which served families on the east side of the canal. Private schools were also located in the village; one of them, known as the Post Academy, became the site of Ellenville's first high school.

The railroad was mainly responsible for the fact that Ellenville and the surrounding region became a very popular resort area. Many larger resorts had humble origins as small farms and boardinghouses. With the growth of the resort industry came numerous fine stores to Ellenville, which made the village popular among tourists and residents, who recognized it as a successful community.

The pages that follow share only a glimpse of what life was like in years past. They offer a sense of what it was to be part of this community at a time when the nation was growing and transforming and meeting the many challenges and successes that cultivated genuine civic pride. Based on the historic collections at Ellenville Public Library & Museum, the period covered herein is from the mid-1800s until 1940. To represent the history of Ellenville in this way was an exciting journey, not only of fact-finding but also of recreating a sense of place from ephemera, newspaper articles, anecdotes, and images. With this glance into the past, we hope to rekindle the vision that founding father Charles Hartshorn once had as he stood at what is now Liberty Square, looked toward the Shawangunks, and imagined what would become the village of Ellenville.

One

Where People Lived

What is known as the village of Ellenville today began as a group of four humble buildings near the intersection of Market and Canal Streets. Among these was a small tavern owned by Nathan Hoornbeek. Following the arrival of Charles Hartshorn in 1823 and the building of the D&H Canal in 1828, many businessmen moved to Ellenville and built stately homes. Alfred Preston of the glass factory laid out the major streets, which were named for popular citizens or familiar nearby locations. Charles Hartshorn, who bought the Hoornbeek Tavern, eventually replaced it with a large home on Canal and Liberty Streets. The Hartshorn residence was always available for civic and community gatherings—including a portion of his lawn that was donated to the village and eventually became Liberty Square. The Hartshorn home itself became the site of the Hunt Memorial Building. In 1913, land was purchased and developed by the New England Land Company of Hartford; this would become what is known today as Green Acres. Initially, this development included only four streets: Hillcrest Avenue, Clifford Street, Nevins Street, and Multon Street. Later, it referred to the large housing development on the former site of the John Burlison farm. This chapter includes only a portion of the wonderful and gracious homes that made up some of the residential areas of Ellenville.

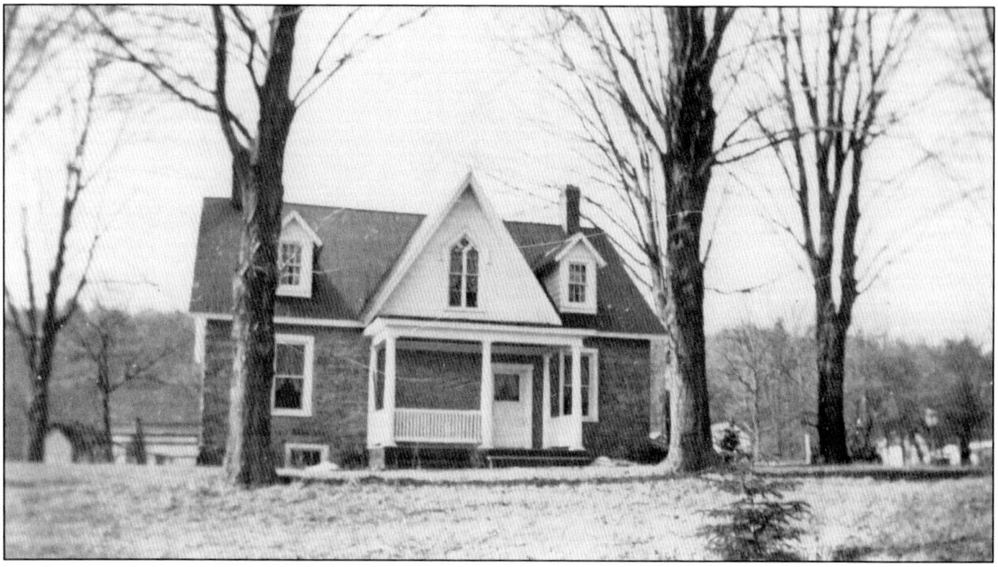

Built around 1725, presumably by the Bevier family, this is the oldest house on the south end of Ellenville. Located on the former Minisink Road (now Country Club Road) prior to the Revolutionary War, this area was considered the frontier with few houses between here and the Susquehanna River. Prominent businessman E. Gordon Jansen bought this home in 1932 and removed stucco siding, repointed the stones, and restored many original features.

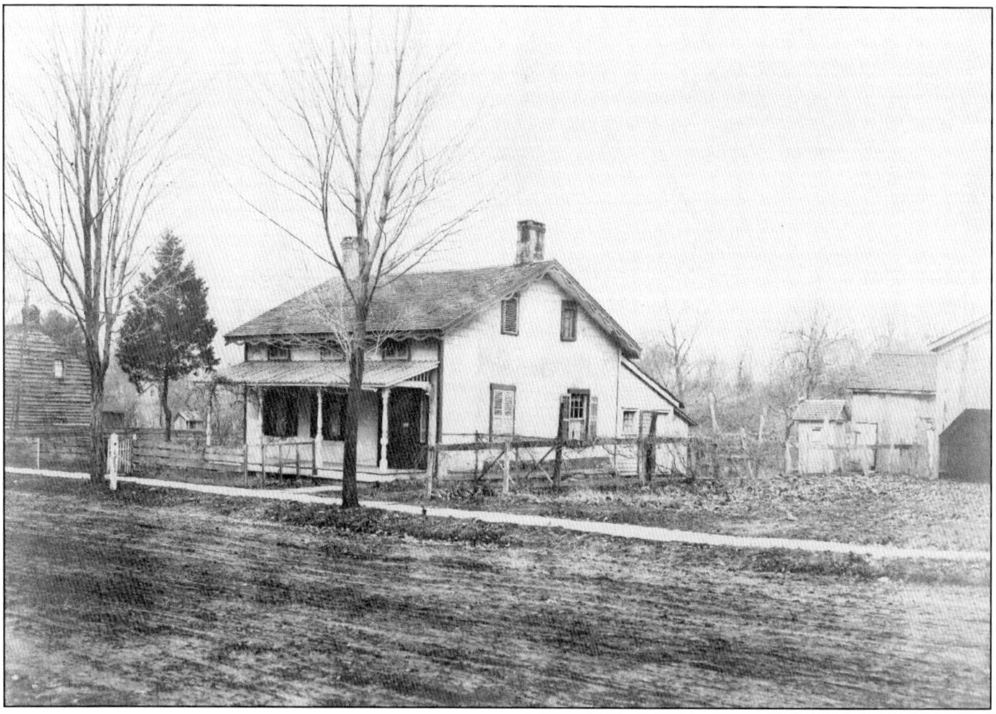

Little has changed since the Blumenauer and Hernberg families lived at this early home in the village of Ellenville at 45 Warren Street, dating back to around 1850. Drusilla Burger lived here for many years; her daughter, Marge Hornbeck, was a longtime administrator of volunteer services at Ellenville Community Hospital.

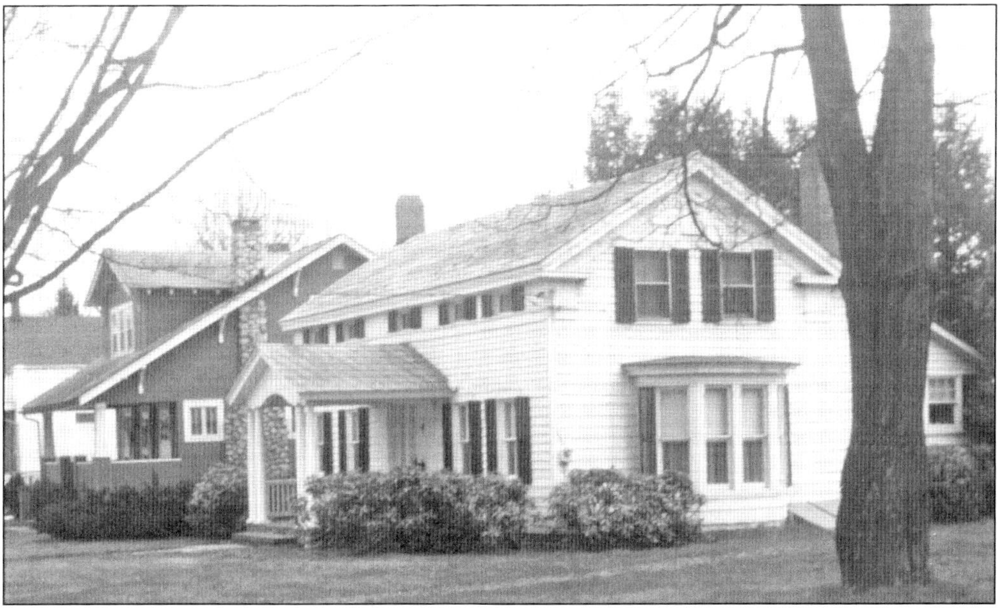

The Martha Betts home was on an 80-acre farm in an area once considered outside of the village. After her husband died, Betts ran the farm and raised five children there. The Betts family lived here from 1839 until the 1970s. Longtime residents would know this property as the Tietjen house; Mae Tietjen was Martha's great-granddaughter. It is currently the site of a Rite Aid store on Route 209.

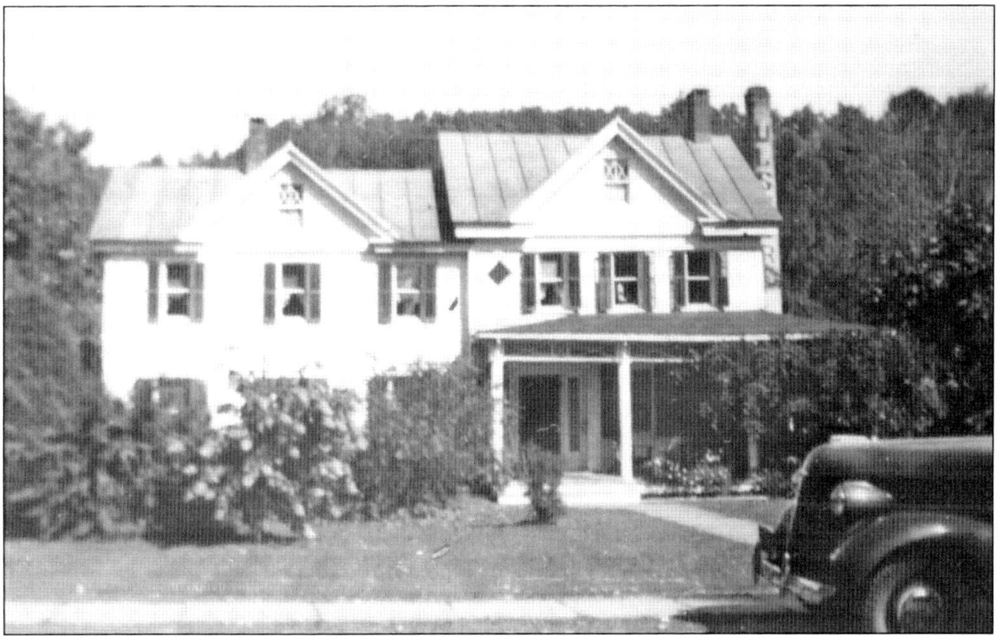

Built in the early 1830s by Levi Kimble, who operated the Red Mill gristmill on Cape Avenue, this home is thought to be the oldest wood-frame house in the village. Located at 24 Canal Street, it was purchased in 1917 by Alfred VanGorder. His daughter, Helen, and son-in-law, Edward Traphagen, also lived here. Traphagen was the head of building and grounds for the Ellenville Central School District.

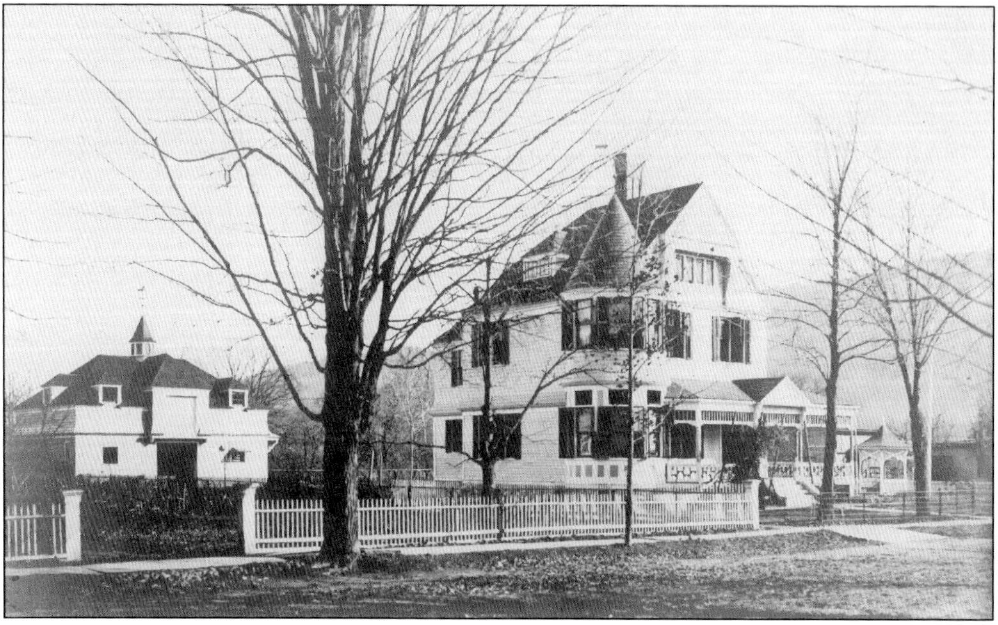

Police captain Robert O. Webb built this home for his second wife, Mary Sohmer Webb, of the Sohmer & Co. piano manufacturing family. Sohmer & Co. marketed the first baby grand pianos. The Webbs summered here at the home of J.W. Rodes; enjoying the beauty of the area, they built this Maple Avenue house in 1884. It later became the home of the Cunningham and then Joseph F. Grable families.

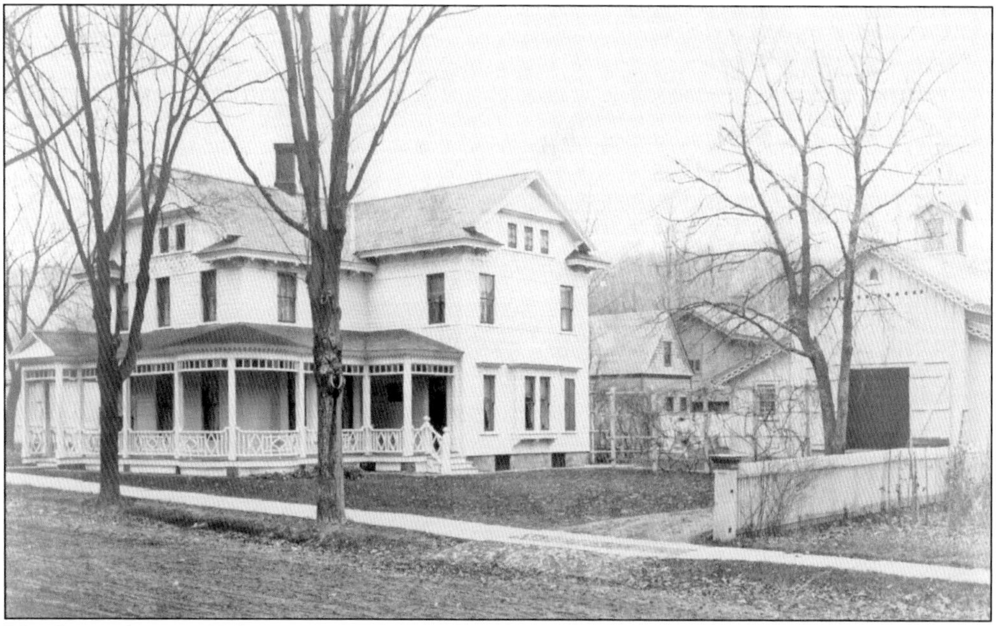

The former home of John Gosman DuBois, who came to Ellenville with his brother Orlando in 1871, still stands at 36 Center Street. The brothers ran DuBois Brothers Hardware on Canal and Main Streets, where the Sterling Bank is now. Next to the Hebrew Aid Society Synagogue, the building would later be the location of the Jewish Agricultural and Industrial Aid Society and then the home of Rabbi Herman Eisner.

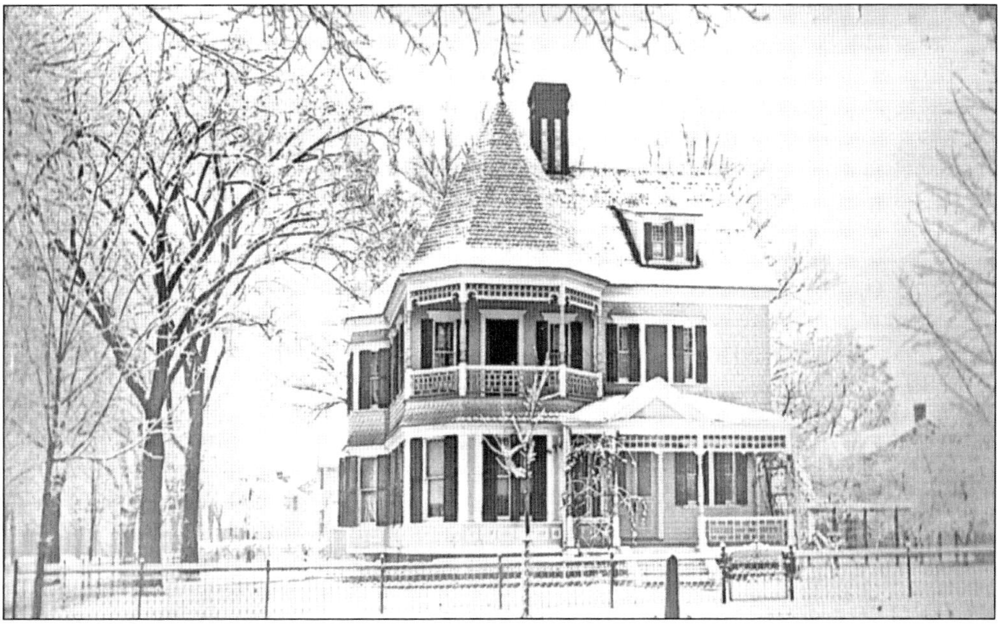

William H. Deyo built the Queen Anne home pictured above at the corner of Maple Avenue and Maiden Lane in the late 1800s. The renowned Alfred Grimley built this house as well as the home of Deyo's son George, on the corner of Childs and Canal. In 1920, George and John C. Johnson (Deyo's son-in-law) tragically died within three days of each other; simultaneous wakes were held in the formal and family parlors. Daughter Lilah Johnson inherited the house in 1923; it still stands. Notice the hitching post in front. The photograph below shows Deyo in his office at the lumber company, which he ran with his partner Edwin J. Bailey. (Above, courtesy of Debbie Stack.)

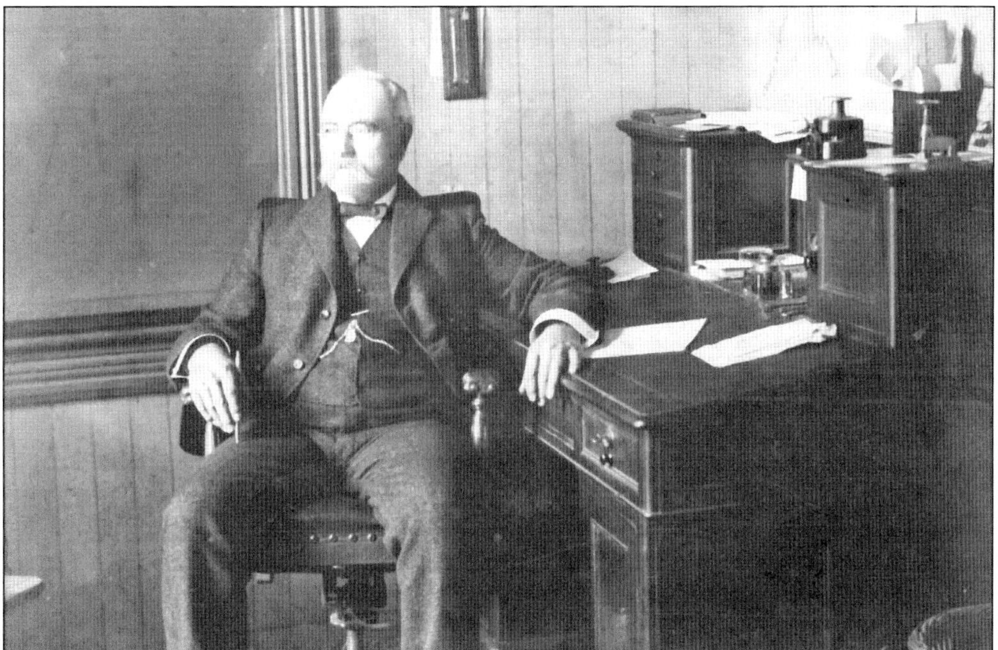

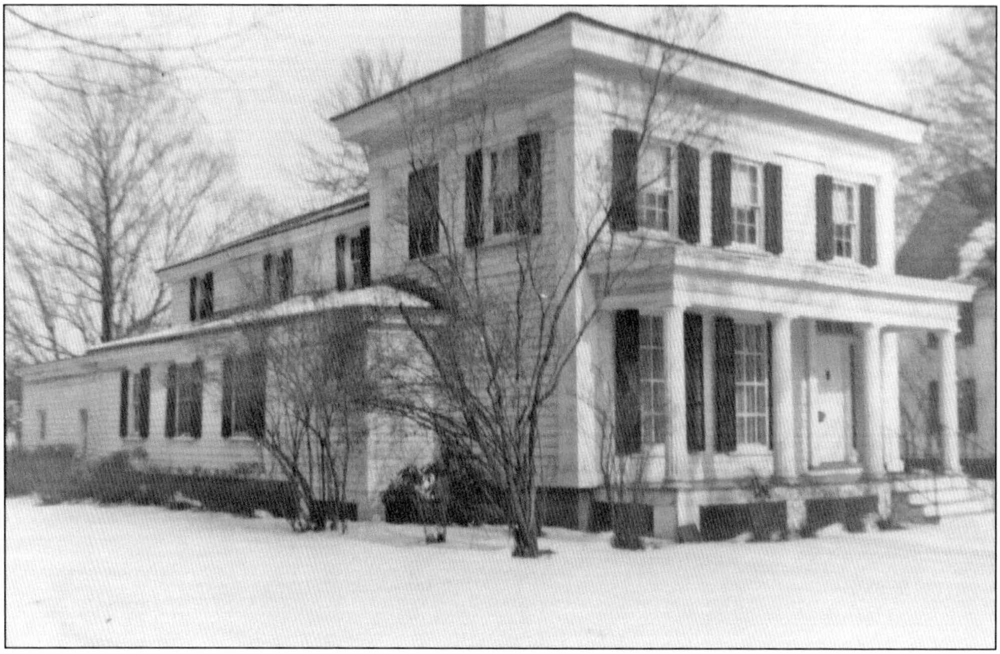

John Bartlett built this Greek Revival home on Maple Avenue around 1852, although it is recognized for his son, nationally renowned organist and composer Homer N. Bartlett. The original property ran to the Ulster fairgrounds, now the athletic fields of Ellenville Central School. The street immediately behind it is now Bartlett Street. In 1924, William L. Douglas, a partner in Rose & Douglas, bought the house, which still stands.

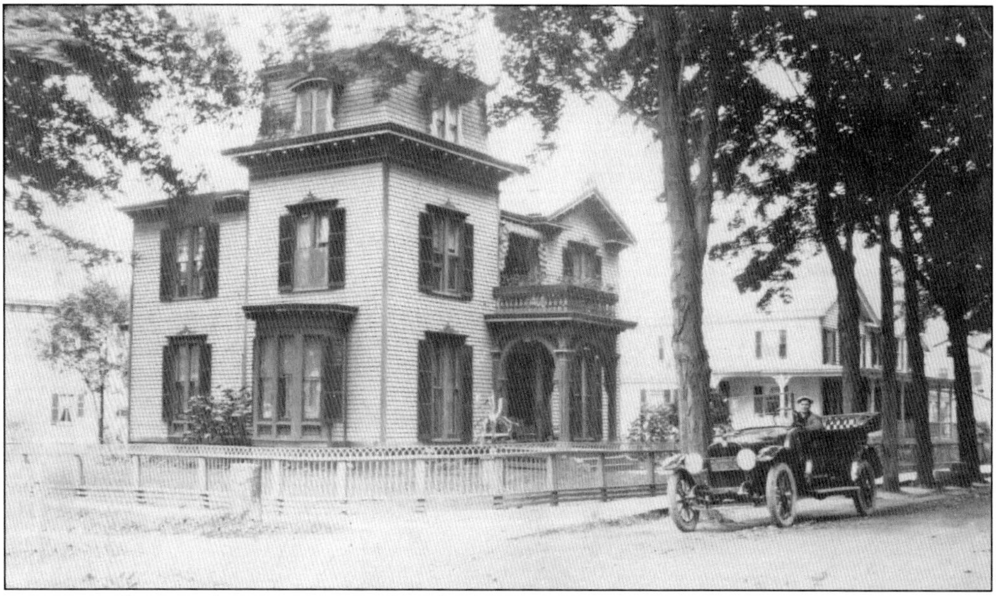

Constructed in 1868 by George A. Dudley, this home was destroyed by fire in 1870 and subsequently rebuilt. The fact that fire companies could not supply enough water to save this house prompted the village to bring piped water to every building in Ellenville. Ellenville Savings Bank bought the property in 1953 for its new building; the house to the right served as the bank's drive-through until the new building was completed. It is now the site of M&T Bank.

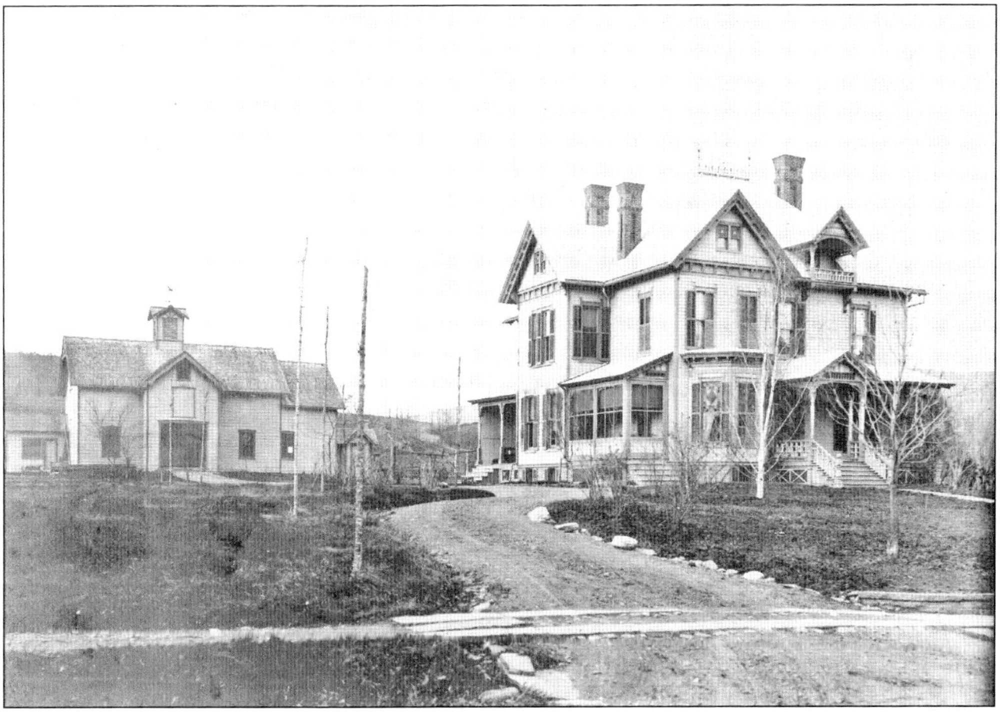

George B. Childs, secretary-treasurer of the Ellenville Savings Bank, built this Victorian home in 1887 on South Main Street (Route 209). His daughter Aimee B. Childs and son-in-law William C. Rose (of Rose & Douglas Hardware) also made their home here. The house still stands today.

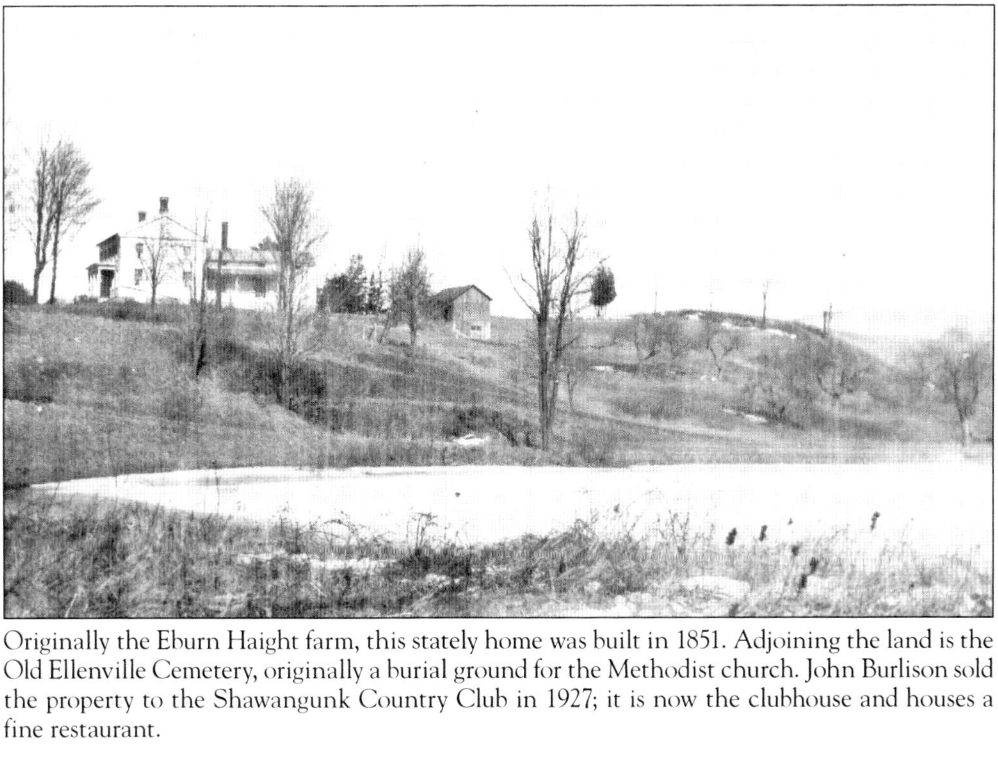

Originally the Eburn Haight farm, this stately home was built in 1851. Adjoining the land is the Old Ellenville Cemetery, originally a burial ground for the Methodist church. John Burlison sold the property to the Shawangunk Country Club in 1927; it is now the clubhouse and houses a fine restaurant.

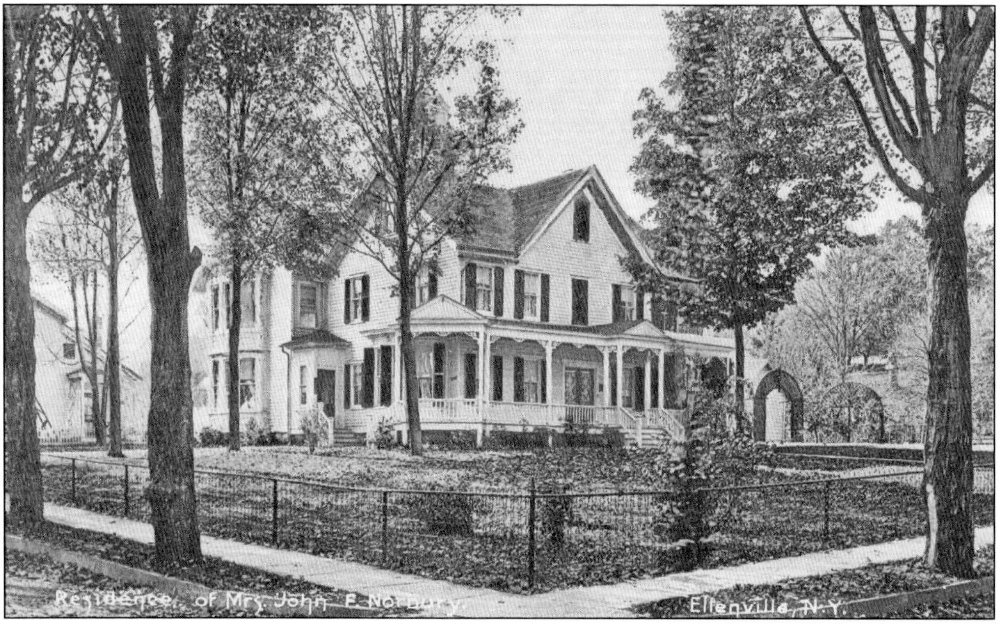

Sarah S. Norbury lived on the corner of Warren and Park Streets for many years. Born in Greenfield, New York, in 1835 to a Quaker family, she helped restore the Greenfield Quaker Meeting House. Norbury was an active member of several local and national organizations. The door on the left led to what later became the apartment of Alice Moffit, who served as Ellenville village clerk from 1938 to 1966.

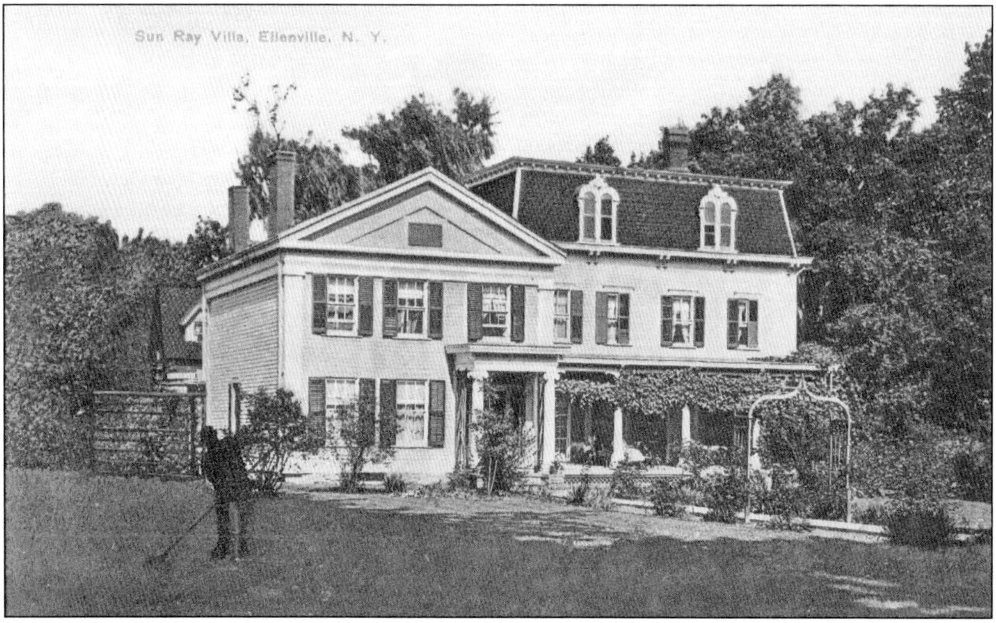

Located at Yankee Place and Canal Street, this home was occupied by prominent businessmen Alvan B. Preston of Ellenville Glass Factory (who built it); pharmacist Isaac Corbin; and Alfred Gaskell, superintendent of Sun Ray Beverage Corporation. Sun Ray bought the building in 1907, calling it Sun Ray Villa. In 1919, the Silverman brothers, who operated a Canal Street clothing store, purchased it. Presently, town house apartments occupy this site; Spectrum Services is next door.

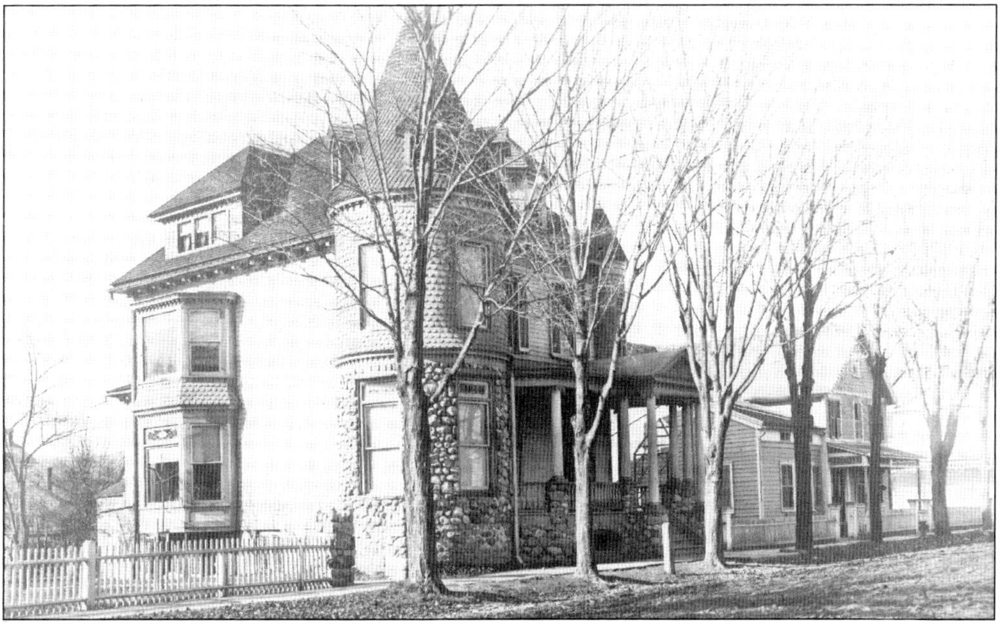

American Legion George Cook Post No. 111 was located in this Canal Street building for many years; the post purchased it from Bertha Demarest, who worked as an assistant librarian at Ellenville Public Library. It was formerly the home of her father, Benjamin Bevier Demarest, a leading citizen and deacon at the Dutch Reformed church. This site is now the location of Ellenville Senior Housing on the east end of Canal Street.

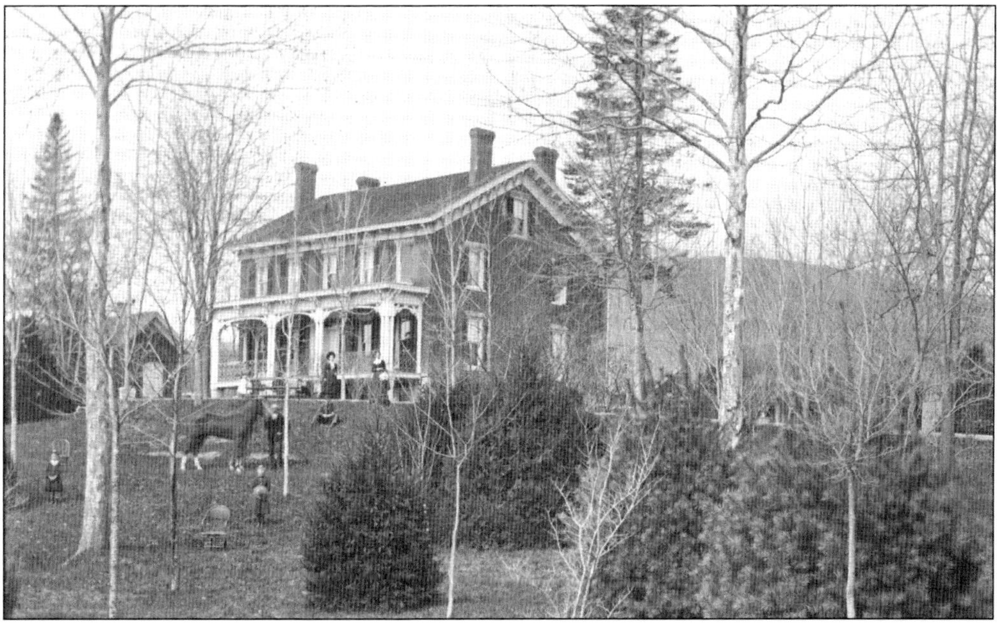

Built of Leurenkill brick in the early 1830s by Willett Griffen, this Center Street home was on a farm running from Warren Street to East View Heights. Dr. William Scoresby purchased it in 1868 and practiced here with his nephew, Dr. James Eastgate. A respected physician and surgeon, Scoresby also served as trustee and president of the village; he was later elected to the New York Senate. In 1924, this building became the Veterans Memorial Hospital.

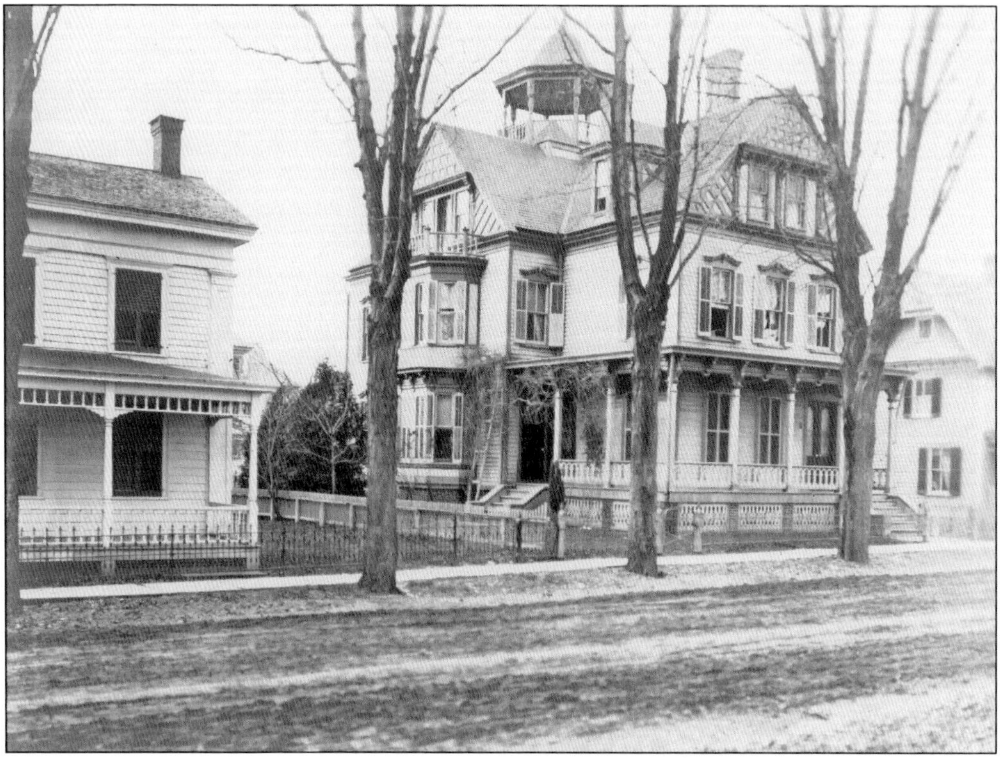

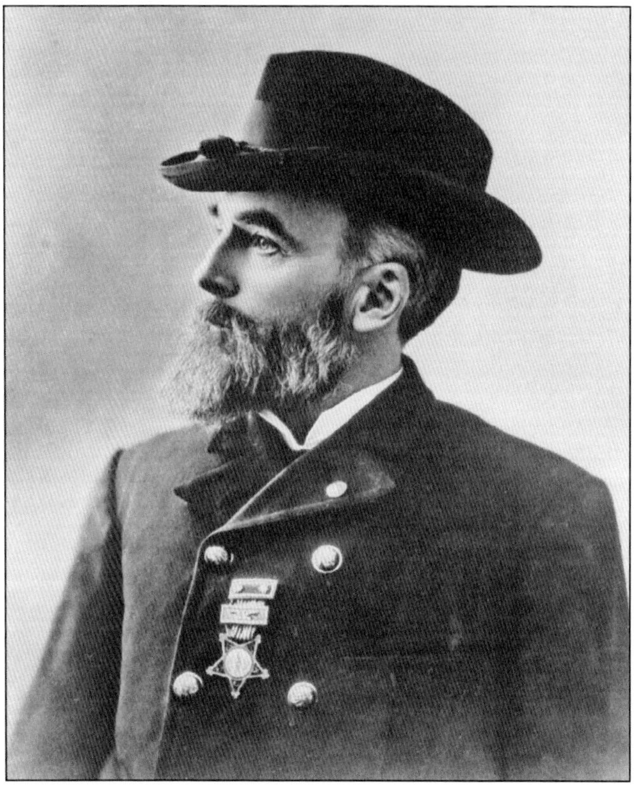

The home of Maj. Dwight Divine on Canal Street is an exemplar of Victorian architecture. Divine helped organize Company C of the 143rd New York Volunteer Infantry at the outbreak of the Civil War. He later served as a trustee of the Ellenville Savings Bank. In 1876, he took control of the Ulster Knife Company and helped it grow into a nationally recognized business. His daughter, Dr. Alice Divine, lived here until her death in 1950; she was a pioneering woman physician known for her generosity and kindness. Sol and Evelyn Albert, proprietors of Albert's Bakery on Canal Street where Gaby's Restaurant is now, later purchased the home and raised their family there.

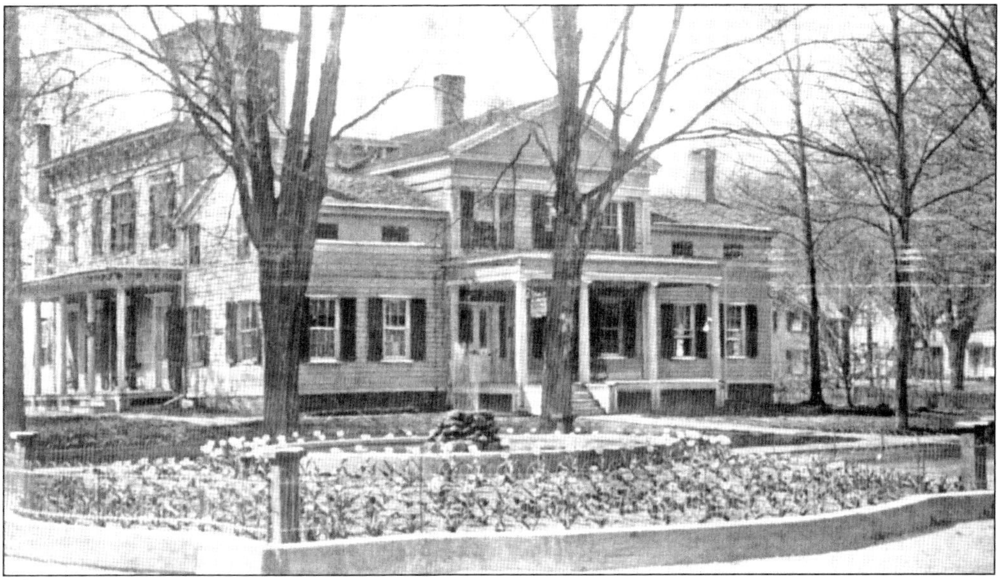

The Hoornbeek Tavern, one of four early structures, stood where Charles Hartshorn would build this stately home. Hartshorn was the first postmaster for the village post office that he helped establish, and he became the first president of Ellenville. The Hartshorn home was always a community gathering place; for a time, the Women's Aid Society had its headquarters here. After Hartshorn's death in 1875, a portion of lawn with a fountain was given to the village; this became Liberty Square. The Hunt Memorial Building is now on this site.

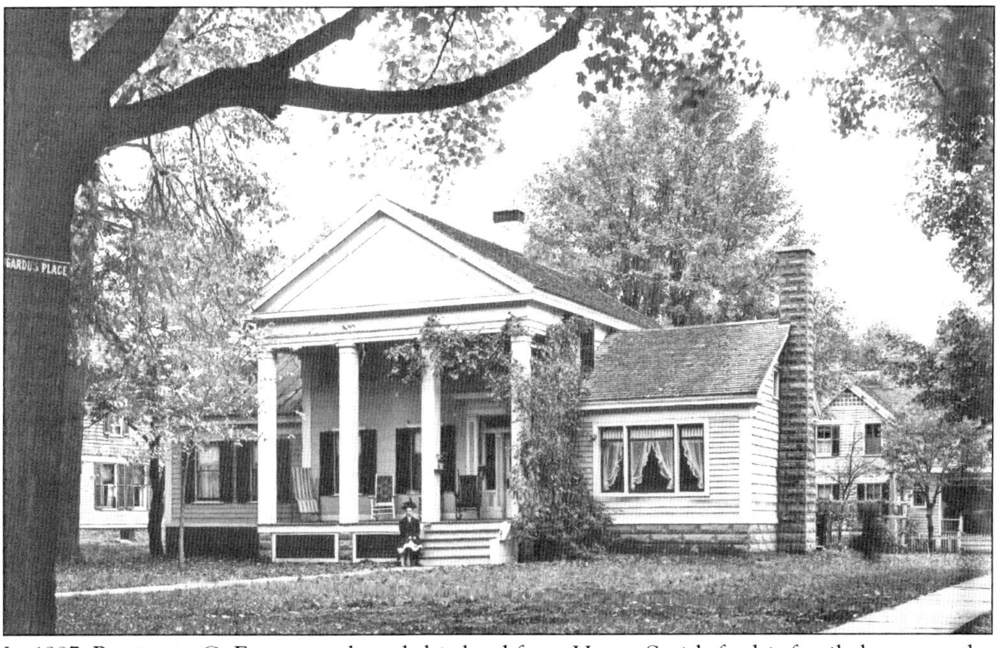

In 1897, Benjamin C. Eaton purchased this land from Henry Smith for his family home on the corner of Bogardus Place and Liberty Avenue. The Eatons were prominent Ellenville citizens and members of the Reformed church. They ran a shoe store on Canal Street and partnered in a liquor business and a drugstore. Mildred H. Eaton, active in the Ellenville Girl Scouts, was the last resident in this house. The building was torn down in 1938 for the new Ellenville Post Office.

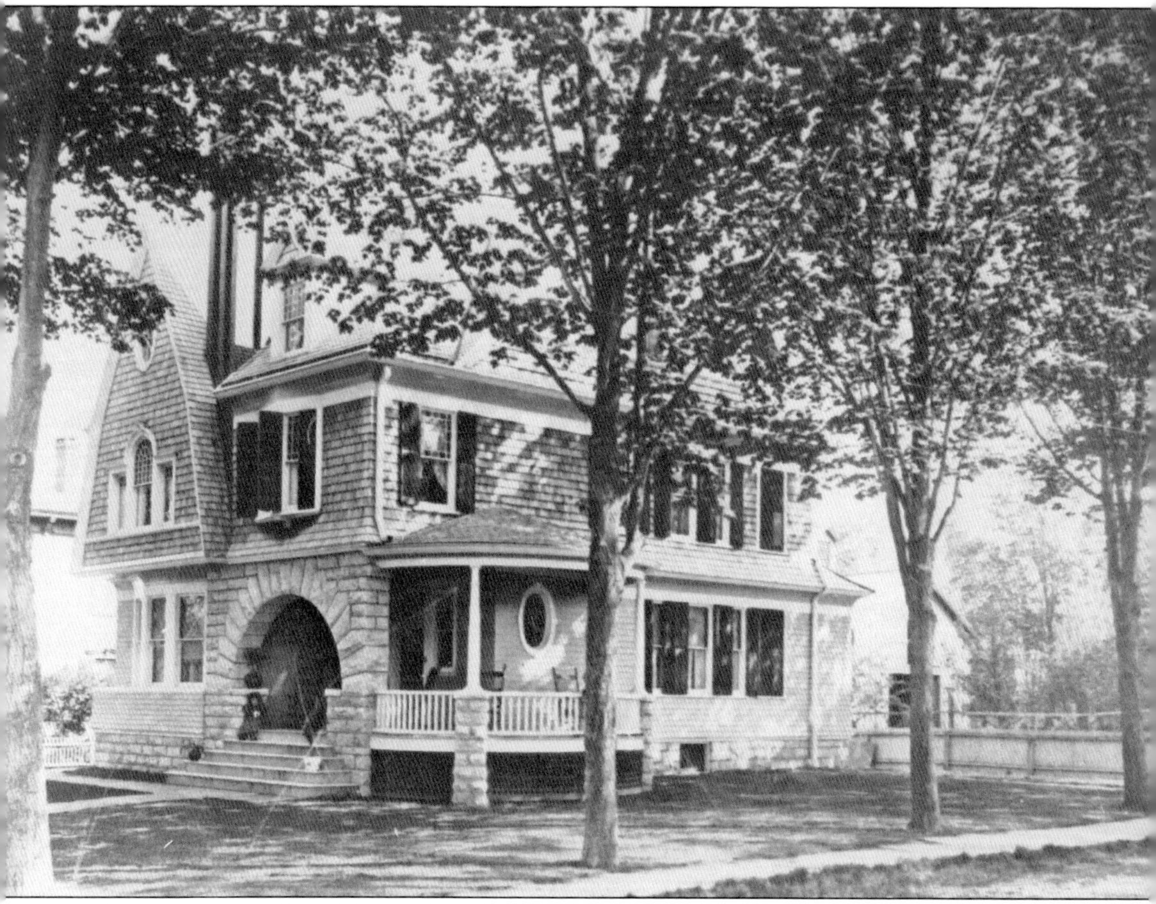

Known as Terwilliger House, this 1895 Queen Anne Victorian home houses EPL&M's local history collections. Named for Town of Wawarsing historian emeritus Katharine T. Terwilliger, the building was acquired by the library in 1980 through the generosity of the Resnick family. It was built by Alfred Grimely in 1895 for George Deyo. Deyo served as both town clerk and supervisor of the Town of Wawarsing, as well as treasurer of Ulster County. He was one of the building commissioners appointed to erect the Eastern New York Reformatory, where he later served as warden. Deyo was also a trustee of the Ellenville Public Library. When Deyo died in 1920, his family moved into the house, selling it to Ellenville pharmacist Frank Campbell in 1925. The house accommodated "roomers" during the 1930s–1940s, although it continued to be owned and occupied by at least one member of the Campbell family until the late 1970s.

Two

On the Canal and Railroad

New means of transportation can change communities and lives. That is what happened in Ellenville when the D&H Canal and railroads arrived. Before the late 1820s, people had to walk or use horses, donkeys, mules, and oxen to get from place to place. Weather and road conditions could make this difficult and time consuming and restricted the distance that could be traveled easily. In 1828, when the D&H Canal opened, no one quite realized the impact it would have on this small farming community. By the late 1830s, Ellenville had added an iron foundry, production pottery, glasswork factory, and other manufacturing industries to its array of thriving businesses.

In 1871, the New York, Ontario & Western (O&W) Railway ran a new branch line from Summitville to Ellenville. The D&H Canal and O&W Railway ran side by side for almost 30 years. It soon became clear, however, that the railroad was the superior means of transportation both for freight and passenger service. The railroad helped develop and promote a new resort industry in the area, and by 1902, the Ellenville branch was expanded to reach as far as Kingston. Here is a glimpse of what it was like to have these two major means of transport come together in Ellenville.

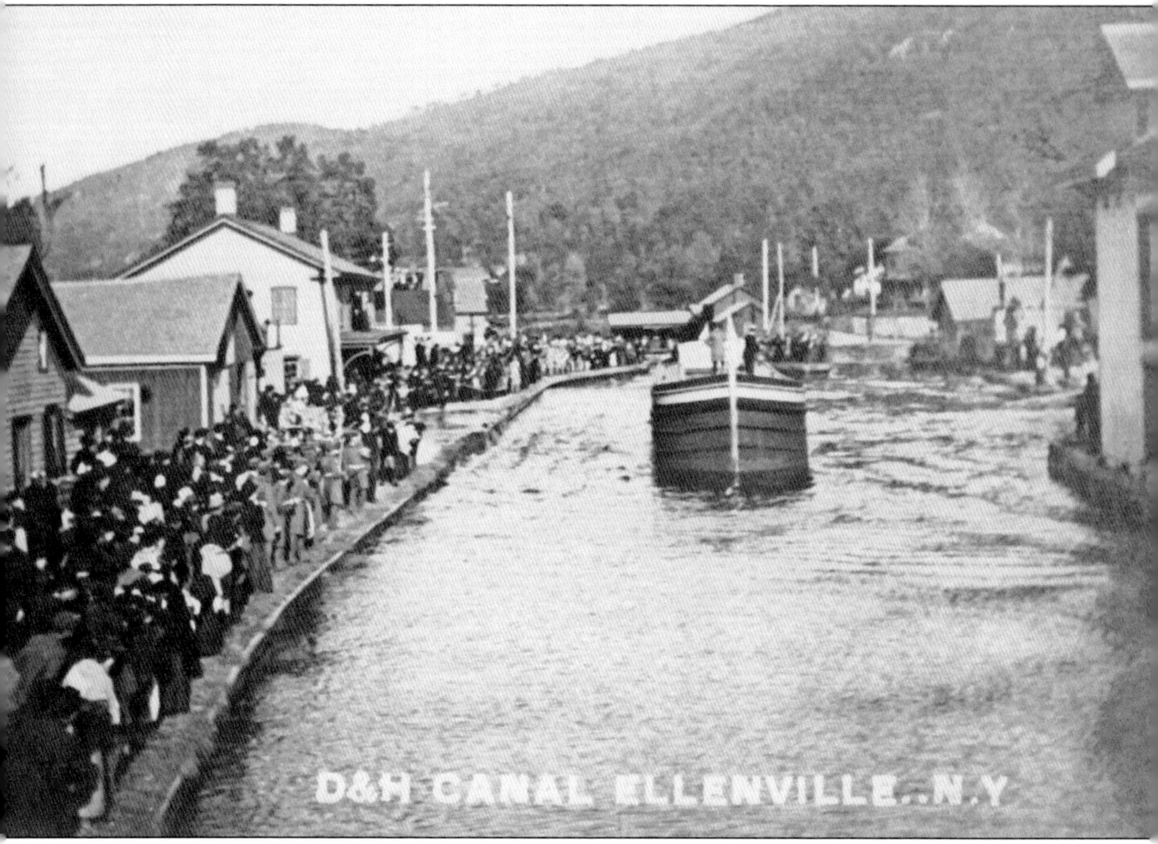

Owned by Dan Hoornbeek, the *Paupau* (also known as *PauPac* and *Paw Paw*) was one of the last canalboats to be built in Ellenville. Large crowds gathered near and across from the Hoar dry dock to celebrate the occasion of its launch in 1895; the wake can be seen to the right of the boat. The story is told that a bottle of water was used to christen the *Paupau*, as Hoornbeek was a prohibitionist. Much of the lumber used in boatbuilding was from the Shawangunk Mountains; the Hoar dry dock was one of the largest boatbuilders on the D&H Canal. This is a northern view of the canal, with the Shawangunks in the background.

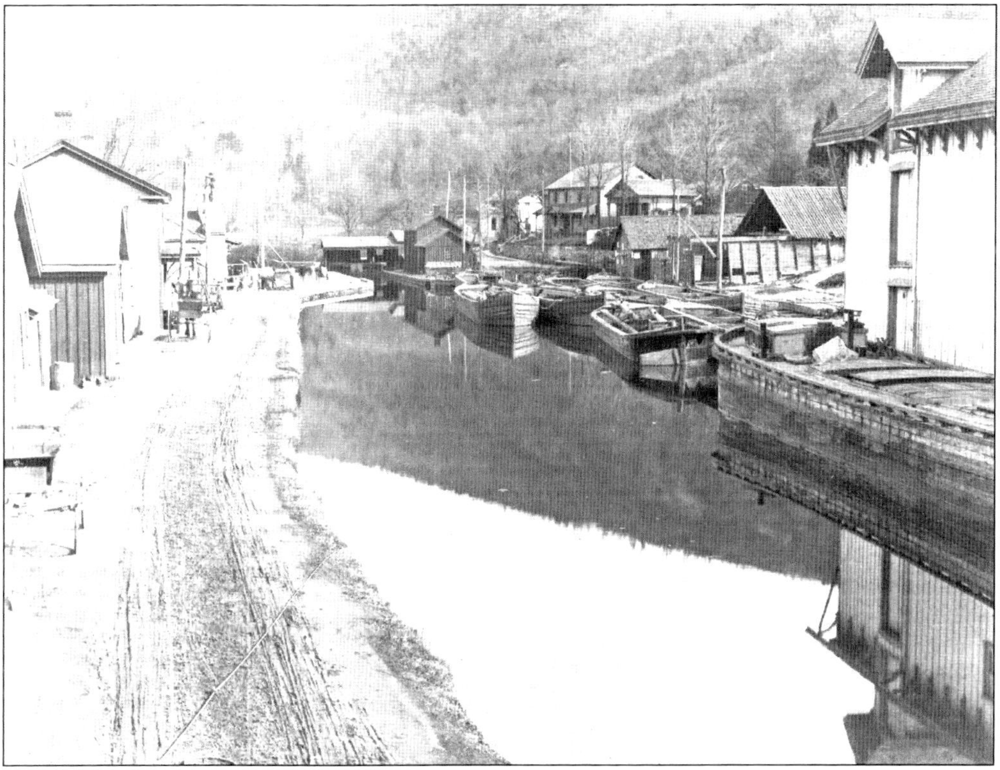

In this view looking north from Center and Canal Streets, the Hoar home and Hoar dry dock can be seen on the right. The above photograph shows loaded boats waiting their turn to pass through Lock 31 in the early morning. They are headed towards Kingston for their trip down the Hudson River. The below image shows a loaded boat sitting low in the water. The front of the canal office building, to the right of the Hoar home, can be clearly seen here along with people looking toward the camera. This building has been preserved and was relocated to Berme Road and Canal Street in 1974.

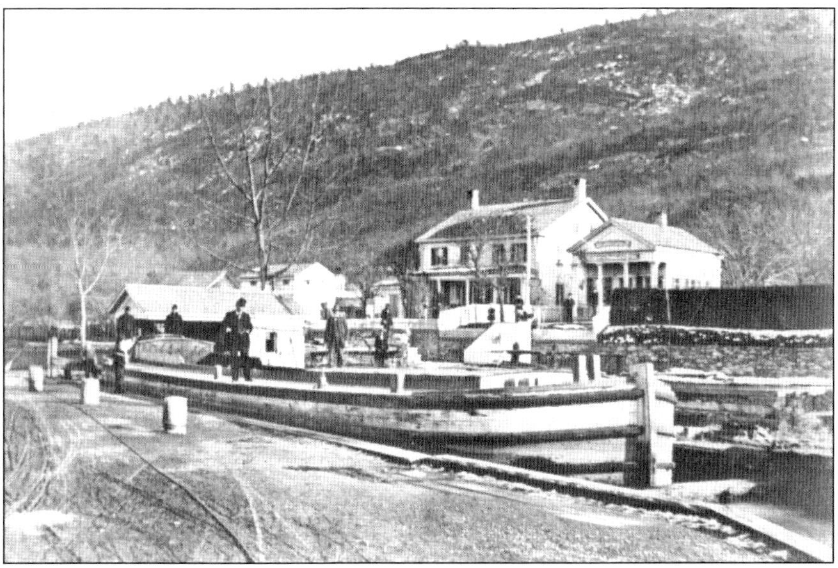

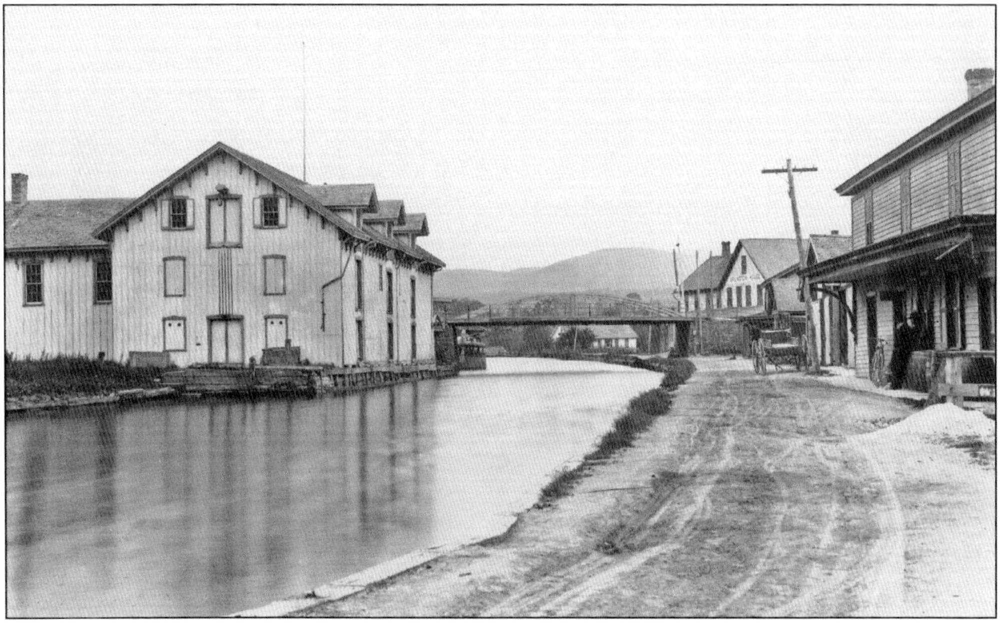

These photographs of the D&H Canal show Lock 31 between Canal and Center Streets. The above image faces south, and the image below faces north. In the above image, the Arlington House (background) and VanWagener's store (foreground) are on the right. Both views show the Center Street bridge and the Hunt & Donaldson warehouse. A bridge was necessary because the canal ran through Center Street; the first bridge was wooden but was replaced with an iron bridge. The latter bridge collapsed into the canal bed along with horses, men, and a load of stone. A third and final bridge was removed when the canal was filled in. Hunt & Donaldson was an essential wholesale and retail business along the canal.

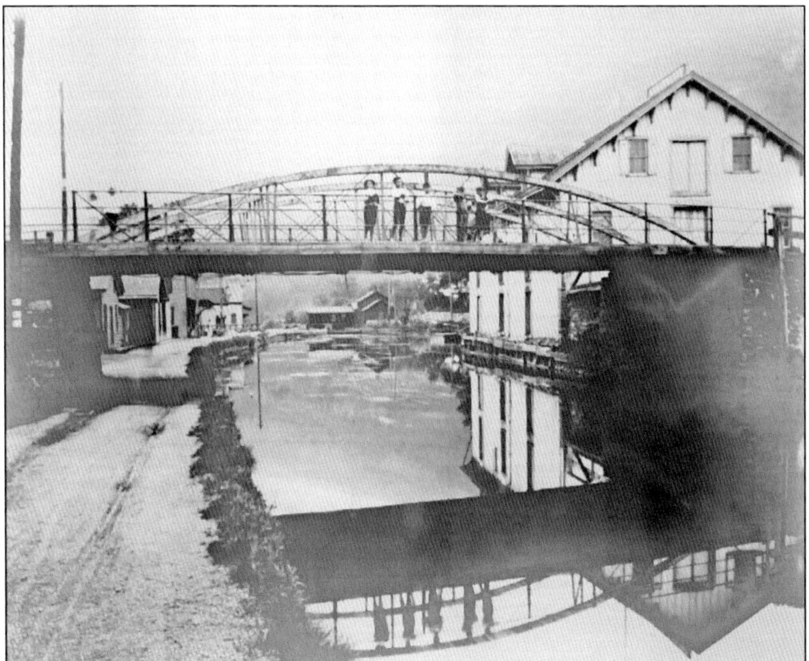

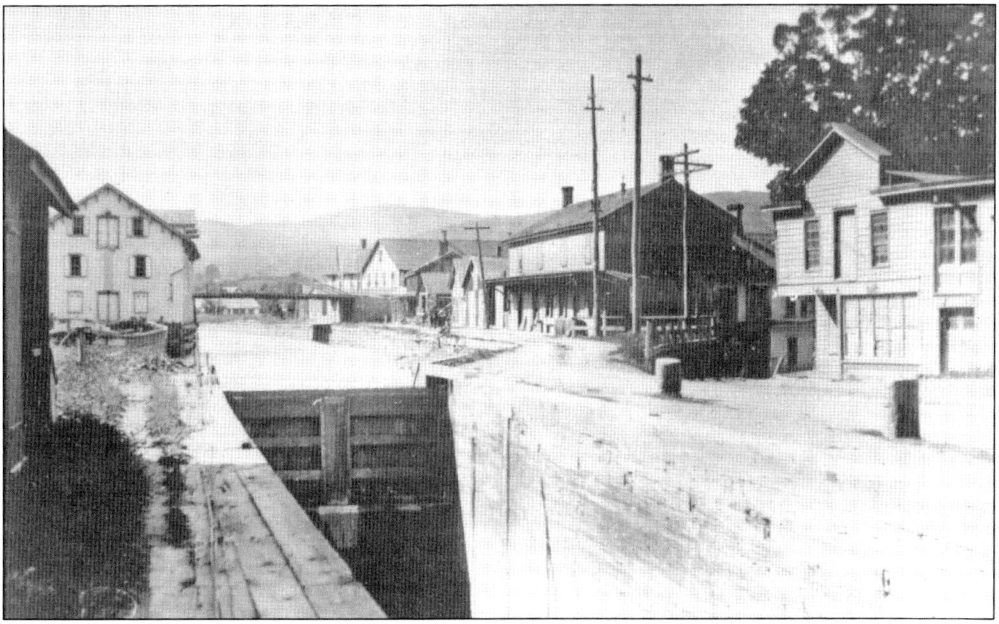

These views between Canal and Center Streets both face south. The Hunt & Donaldson warehouse is on the left, the VanWagener store is on the right, and Arlington House is in the back. In the above photograph from around 1880, Lock 31 stands empty, with the Center Street bridge crossing the canal. The c. 1920 photograph below shows the canal after it was filled in, creating what is now Towpath Road. The Hunt & Donaldson warehouse, Arlington House, and VanWagener store remained, along with the railroad extension (running from the warehouse to the Deyo Lumber and Coal Company) in place. The Center Street bridge was no longer needed and was taken down.

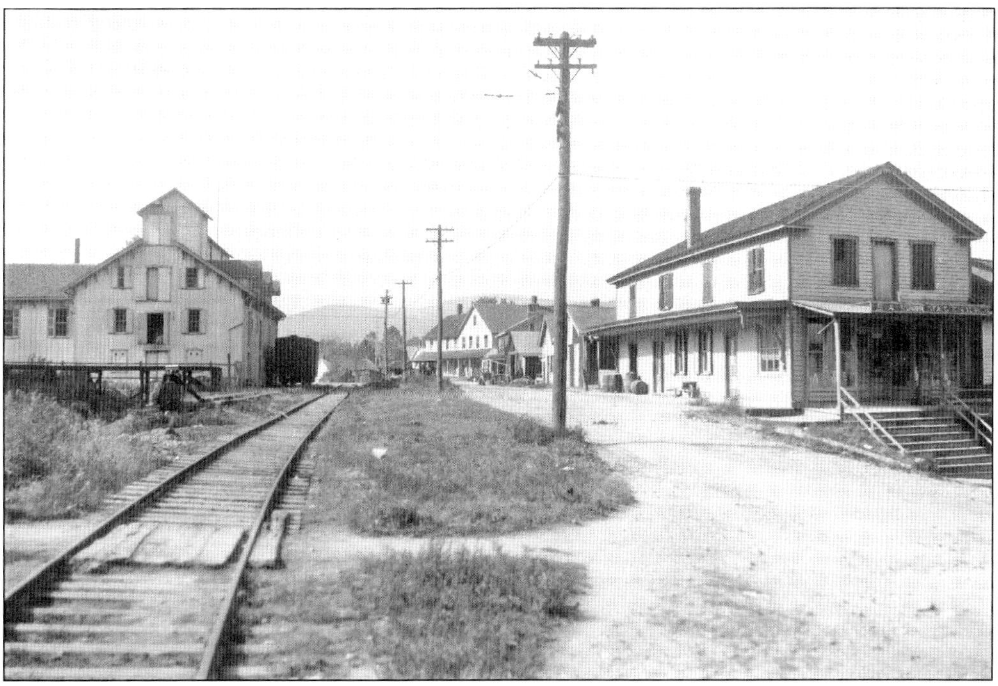

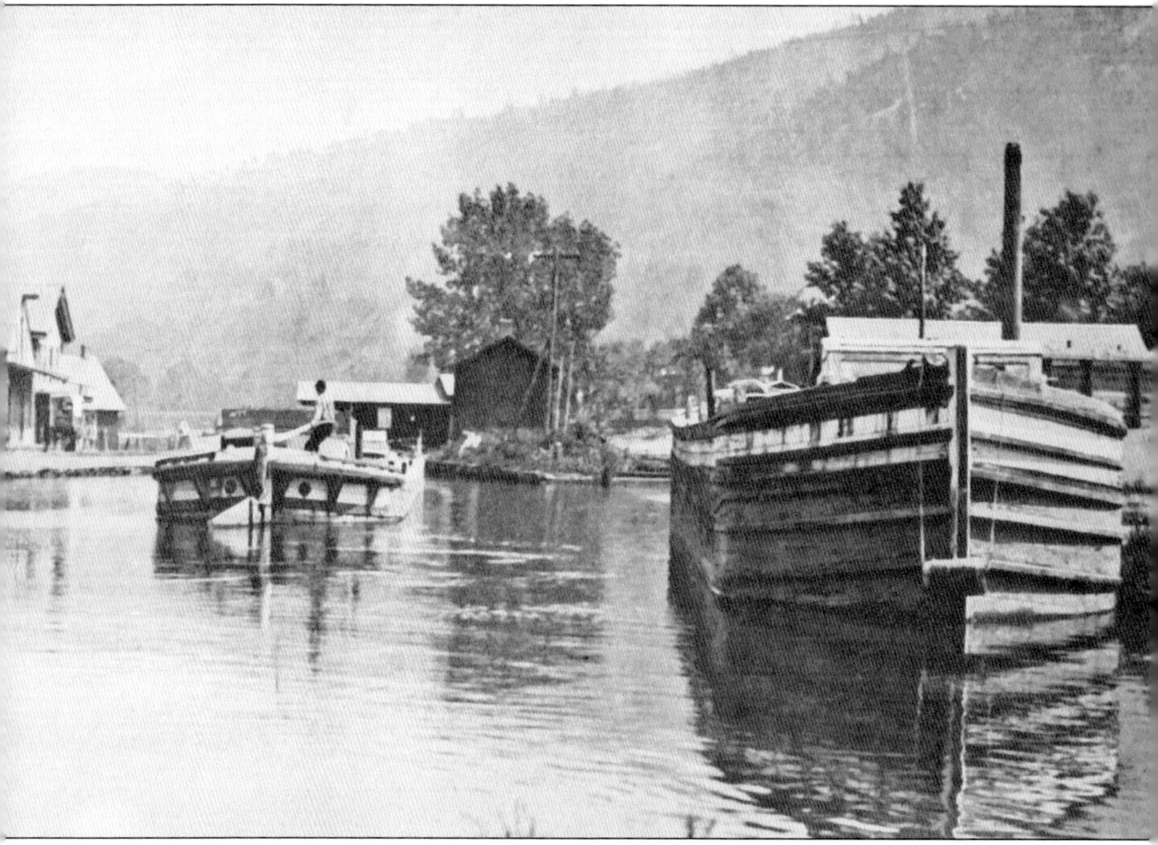

This unique scene clearly shows the difference between a light and a loaded boat. The boat on the right is a light, or empty, boat; it is floating high on the water. The boat on the left is loaded down with cargo and sits lower in the water. Behind the light boat is the George Hoar Sand Mill. The large masonry chimney of the Ellenville Canning Factory can be clearly seen, and in the center of the photograph is the D&H Canal office, run by George Kimble. Kimble was a leading citizen of Ellenville and a D&H Canal superintendent. One of Ellenville's fire departments is named for him.

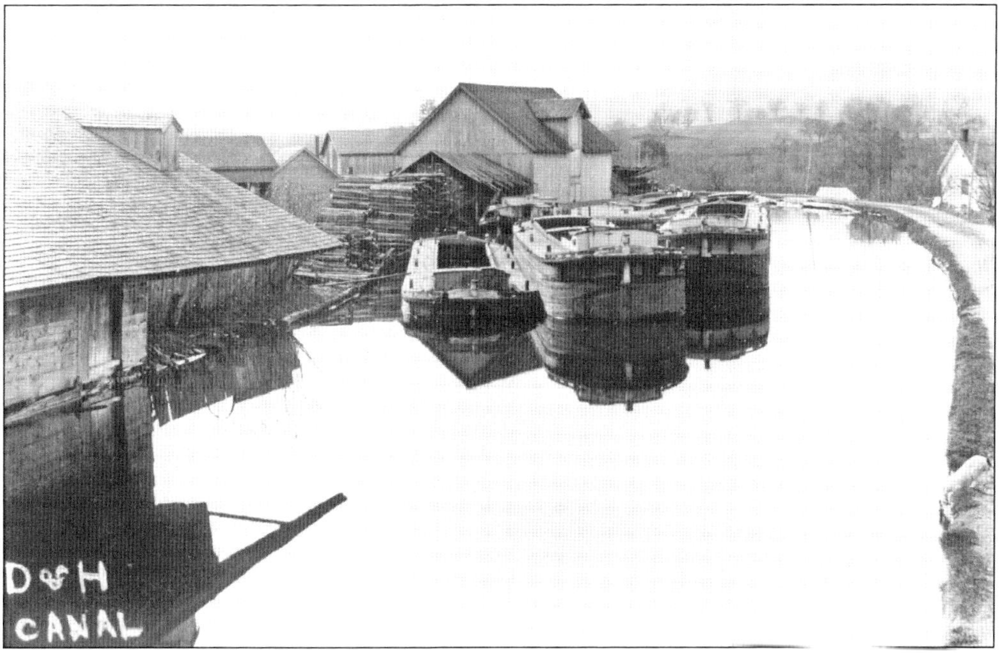

Taken from a Center Street vantage point, this photograph captures a southern view of warehouses and barns along the canal. The central light boat is flanked by heavy, or loaded, boats. The warehouse on the left with its low, overhanging roof was a favorite of local boys; scaling the building from the ground side, they would slide down the roof into the canal for a summertime swim.

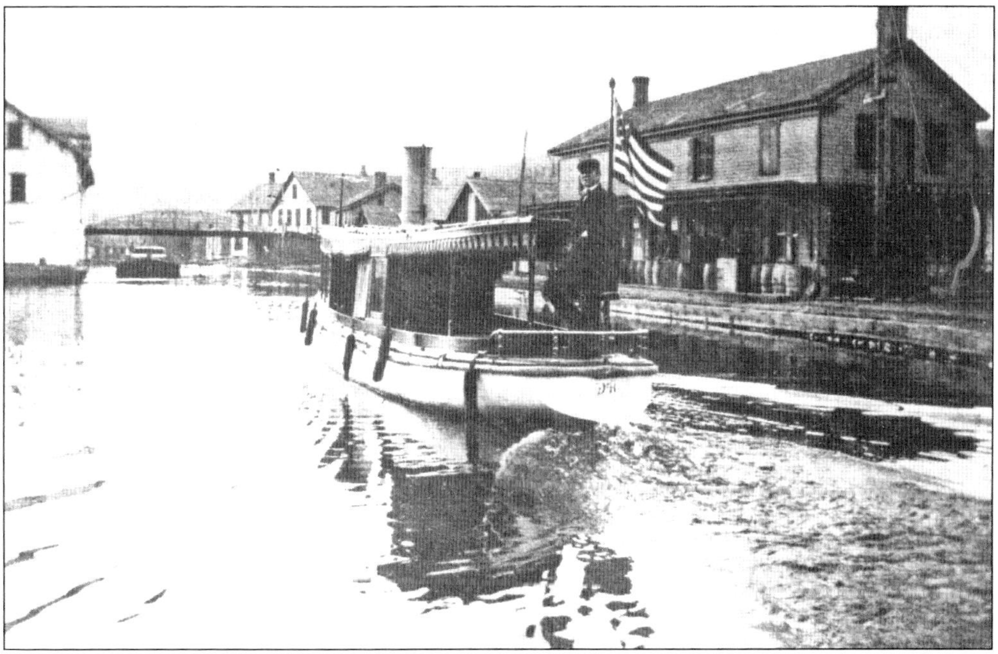

The paymaster traveled the canal, collecting fees from canal agents en route. Here, his boat is traveling north; the D&H Canal office is on the right, and the Hunt & Donaldson warehouse is on the left. Just past the Center Street bridge in the distance is the popular Arlington Boarding House.

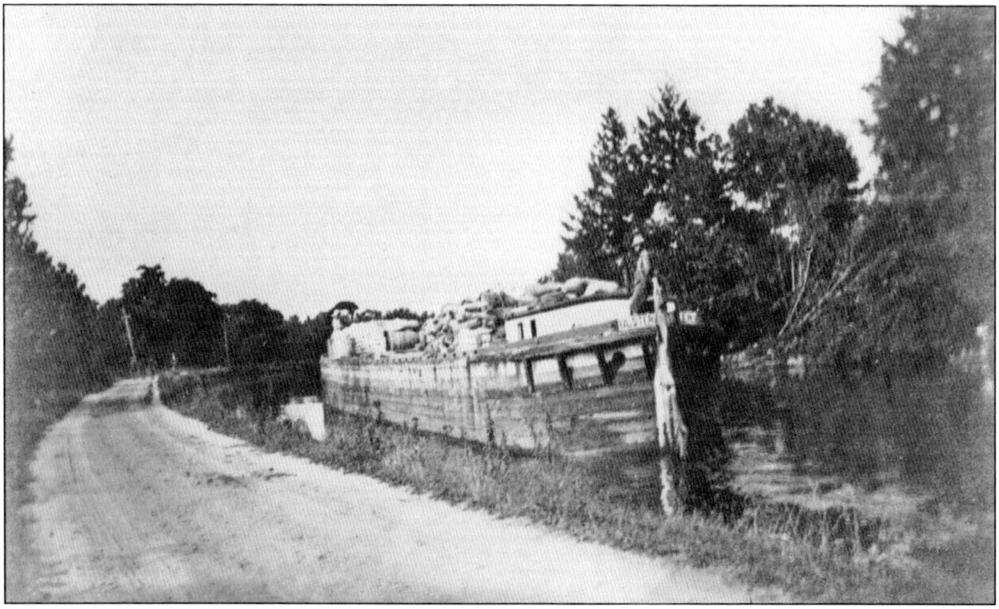

The *Ulster Queen* was a freight boat owned by Hunt & Donaldson, who were referred to as "outside the boat operators" because their canalboats did not carry coal. The retailers and wholesalers dealt in provisions as varied as flour, groceries, salt, lime, cement, and phosphates— but no coal. Hunt & Donaldson boats floated relatively high on the canal compared to boats loaded with 10 tons of coal.

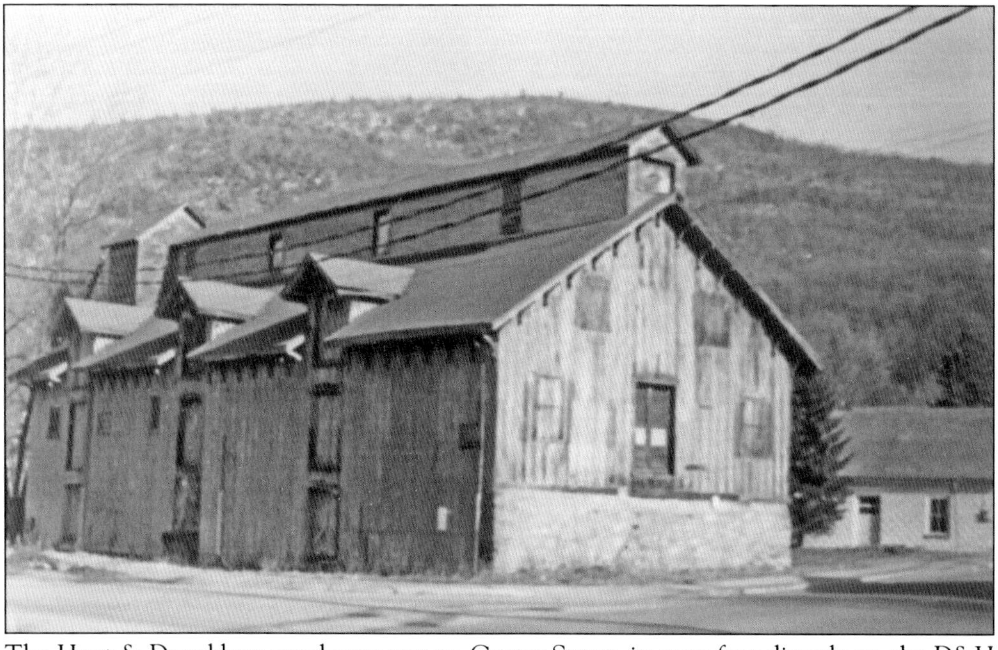

The Hunt & Donaldson warehouse was on Center Street, its west face directly on the D&H Canal, where goods could be easily unloaded. The warehouse is shown here after the canal closed and was filled in. Later a feed and grain store, it was used as a warehouse by many businesses; it stood vacant for years before being razed. This Hunt & Donaldson building existed for over 150 years.

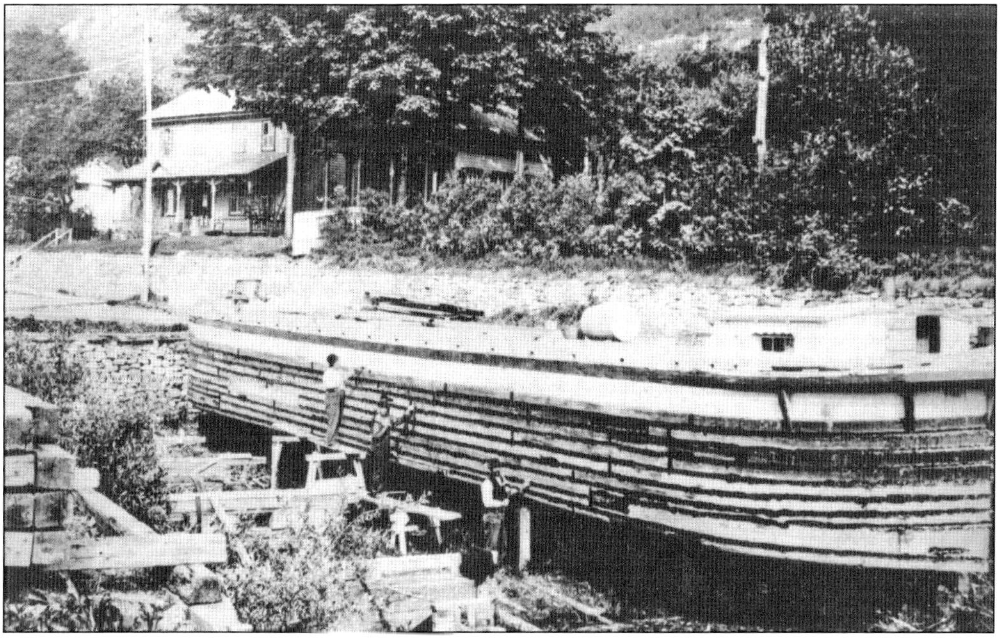

These men are "corking the seams" of a canalboat at the Hoar dry dock. To insure that boats were watertight, hot tar was laid over the seams. After filling the dock with water and floating the craft in, large beams were laid underneath. When the dock was subsequently drained, the crew had full access to the boat. The George Kimble House is in the background.

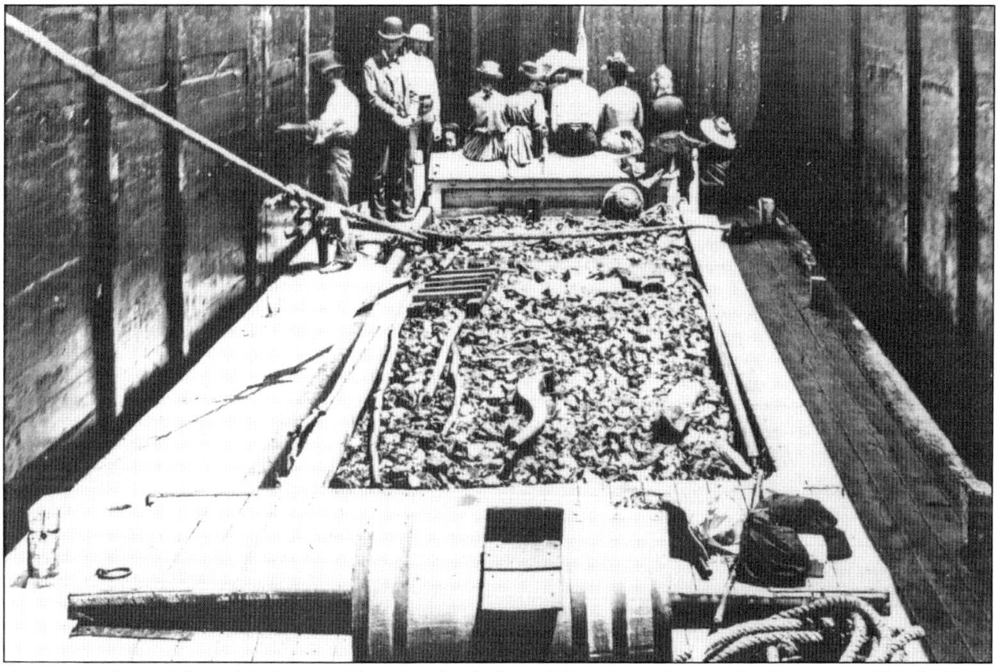

A group of picnickers hitches a ride on a loaded coal boat waiting at the bottom of Lock 31 in Ellenville. The attendant will open the gates, slowly raising the water level (which must have added to the adventure), allowing the group to travel by canal to one of the many picnic groves located nearby.

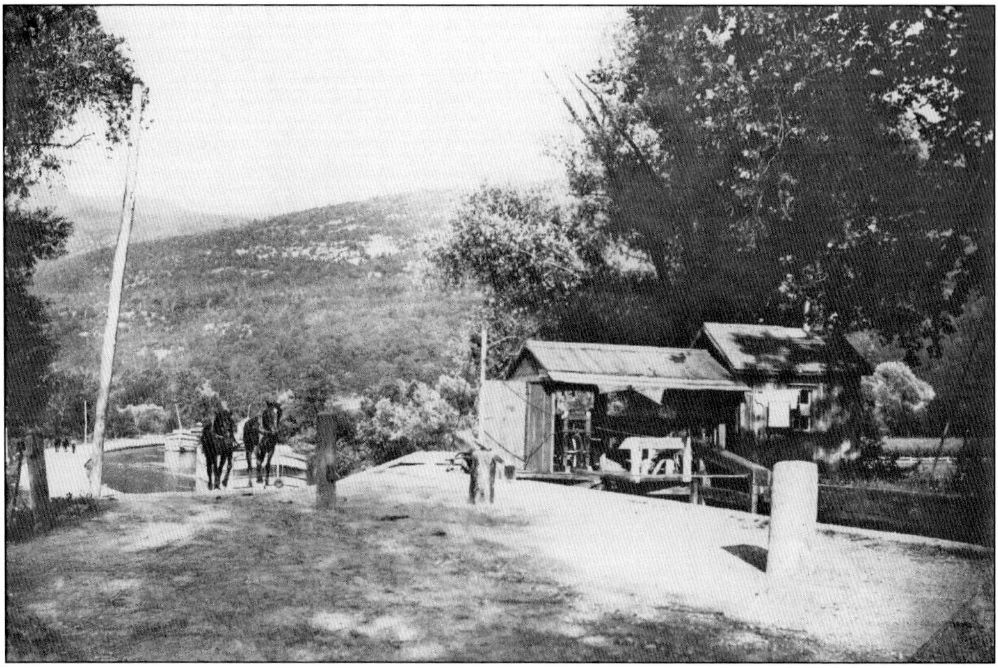

Known as Sam Taylor's Lock, Lock 32 was approximately one mile south of Ellenville. This team of horses, with a boat in tow, waits to enter the lock and continue south. Although mules were widely used on the canal, horses also towed boats. Tom Quigley's saloon and store, which operated until the close of the canal in 1898, was located at Lock 32. The Shawangunk Mountains are in the background.

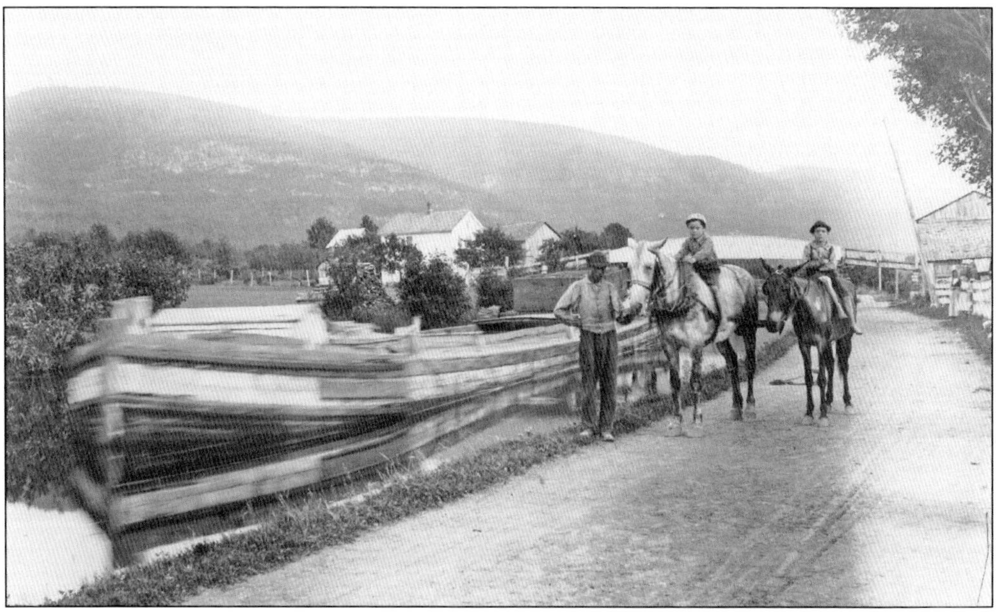

Canalboats were towed by mules or horses led by hoggees, often children, along a trail called the towpath. The bridge in the background was not only for pedestrians; it enabled the towpath to change sides along the canal. This heavy boat is at Sam Taylor's Lock south of Ellenville; the towpath is on the east side. As the canal enters Ellenville, it will be on the west.

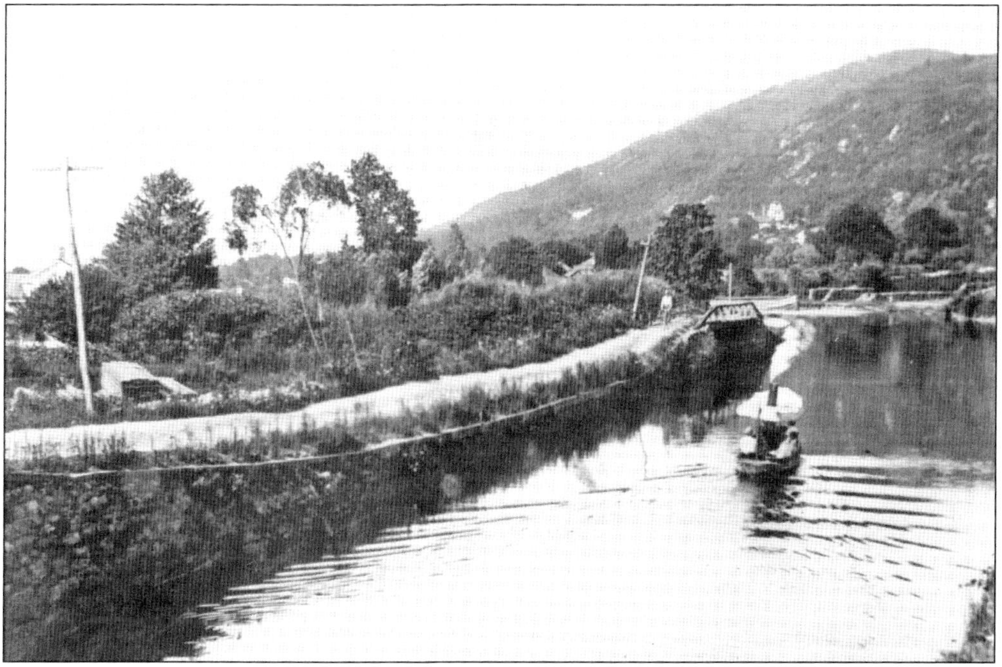

These northern views of the D&H Canal show how close the canal ran to the Shawangunk Mountains. The Kuhlmann Brewery is in the background. The above photograph is of a pleasure yacht, which was an uncommon boat on the canal. A cyclist can be made out riding along the towpath. The below image shows a light canalboat on the right, traveling south. To the left is a loaded coal boat traveling north. Laundry is drying in the wind, and there is a sheltering canopy for shade on this boat; many canalboat captains brought their families along as they made the trip from Honesdale, Pennsylvania, to Edyville, New York.

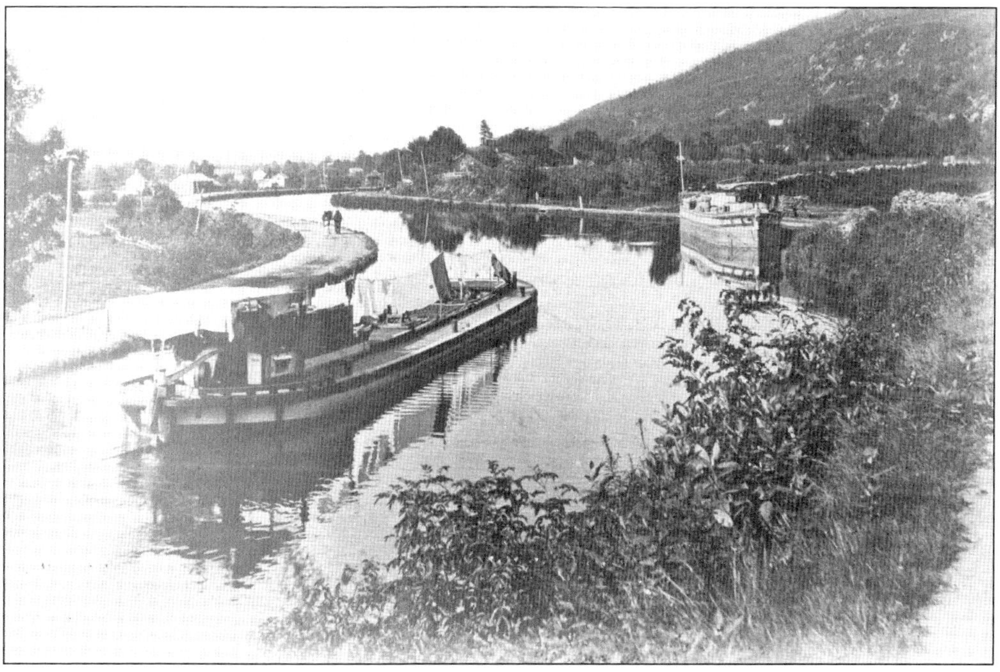

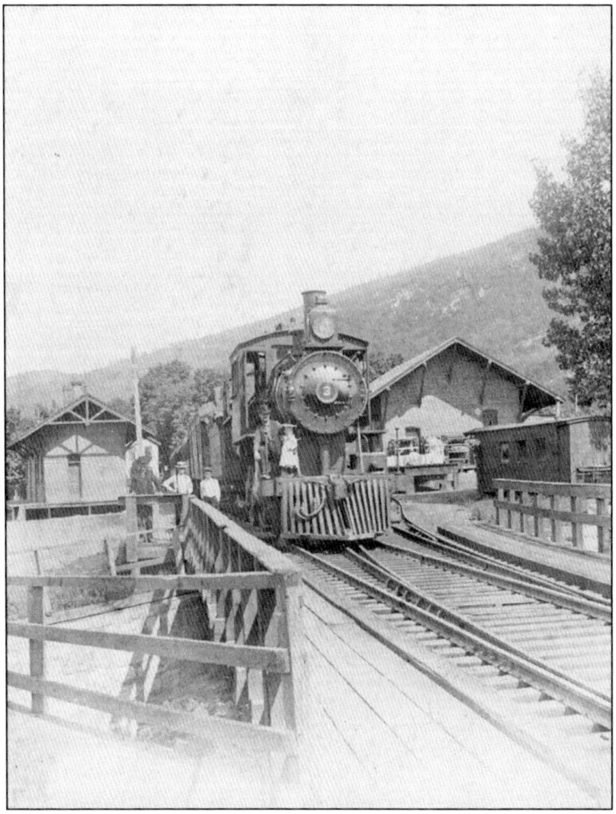

On January 16, 1871, the first passenger train left Ellenville at 5:00 a.m. with 25 citizens on board. A branch line of the New York & Oswego Midland Railroad ran from Summitville to Ellenville. The debate on where the station was to be placed was decided when the majority of citizens objected to having the tracks cross over their main streets. The first station was located in a warehouse just south of Center Street on Railroad Avenue, now known as Clinton Avenue. Soon after starting service, the station was moved to a small, wood-frame building nearby, which was later replaced with a brick station. This station had separate waiting rooms for men and women. A southbound locomotive is in the image below.

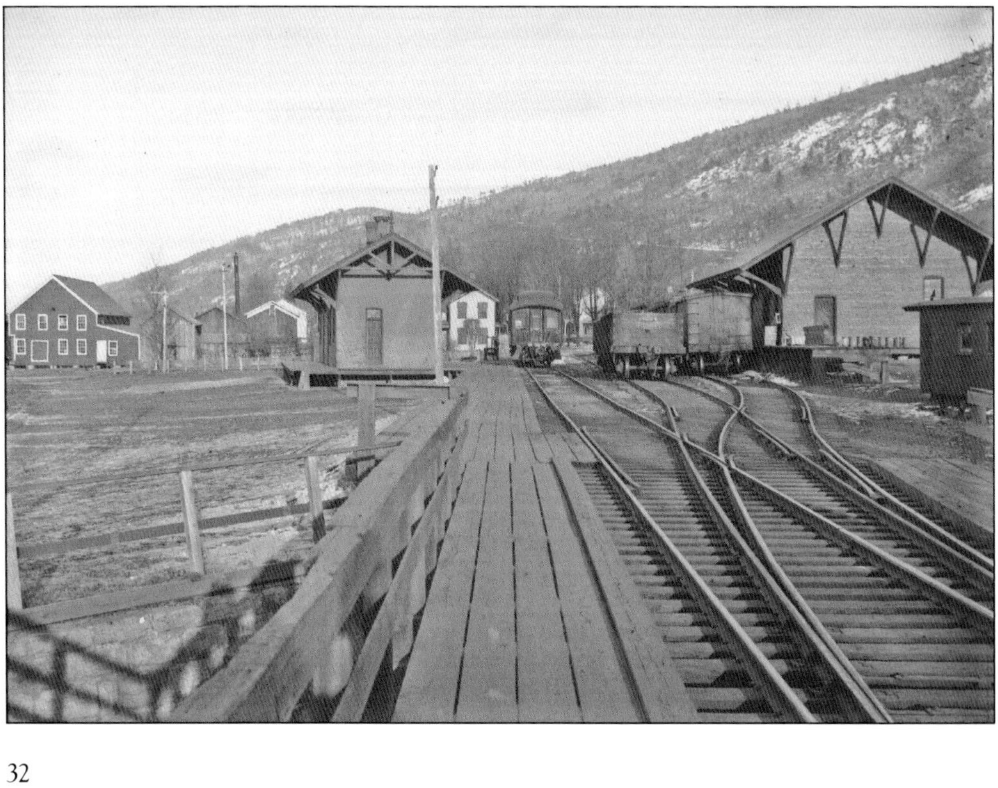

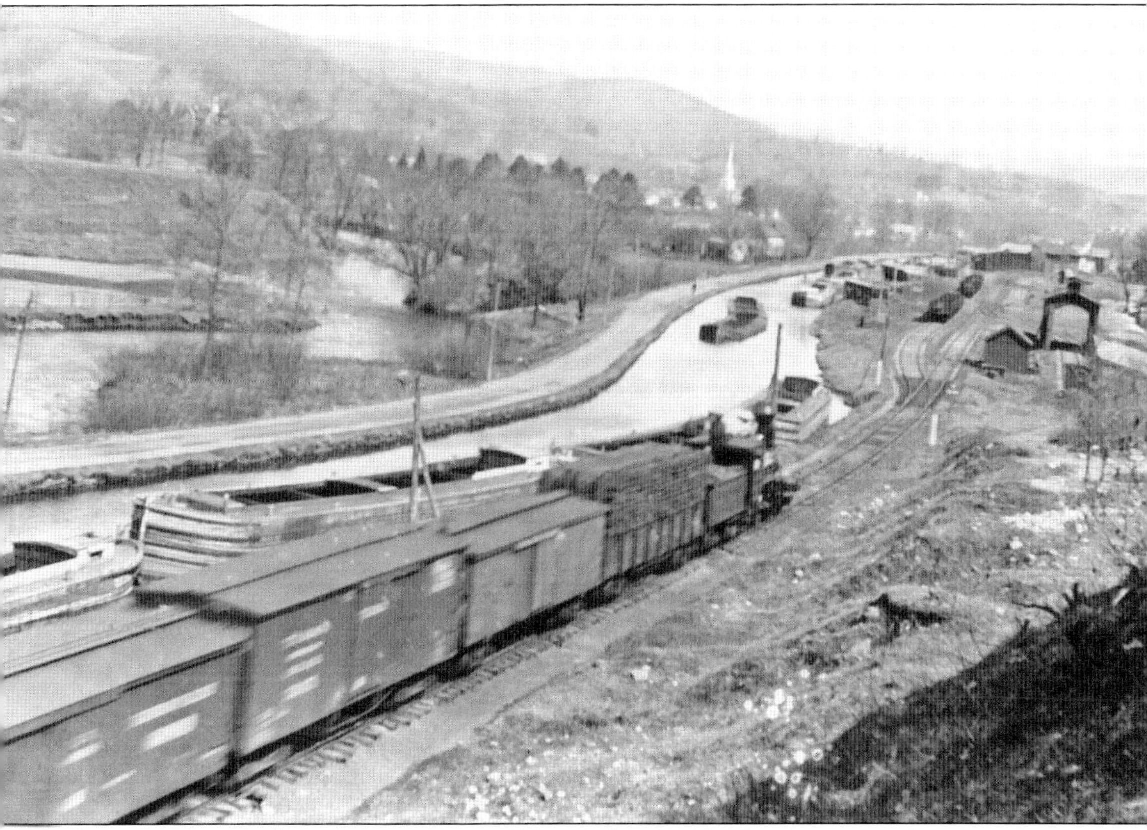

The D&H Canal and the railroad ran parallel to each other for almost 30 years, beginning in 1871 when the railroad arrived here. The canal helped build the village of today by offering transportation of merchandise to and from this area and increasing trade. When the railroad offered this same service at cheaper rates, along with passenger service and year-round operation, the canal's days were numbered. In addition, the railroad serviced many major cities and was not restricted to the canal's 108-mile-long path. It was sad, but no surprise, when the canal ran its last boat in 1901.

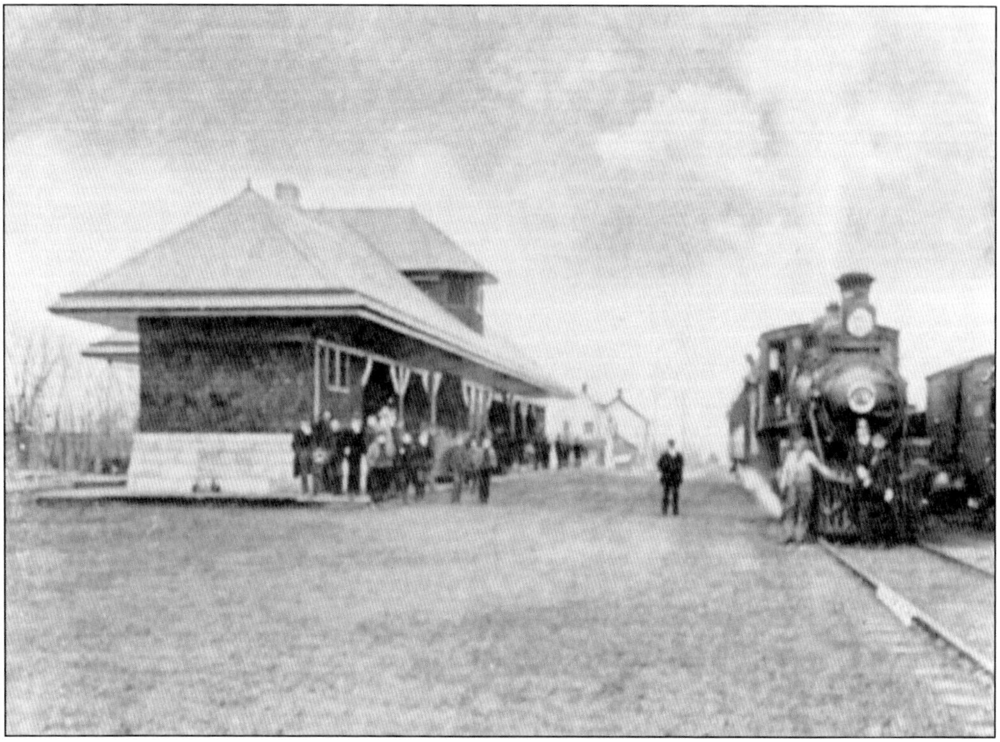

The conductor and engineers pose by this southbound train at the new station in Ellenville just north of Canal Street. Residents north of Ellenville had hoped the railroad would extend all the way to Kingston. By 1902, all right-of-ways had been acquired, and the D&H Canal bed filled in, making way for the first train to Kingston on December 22, 1902.

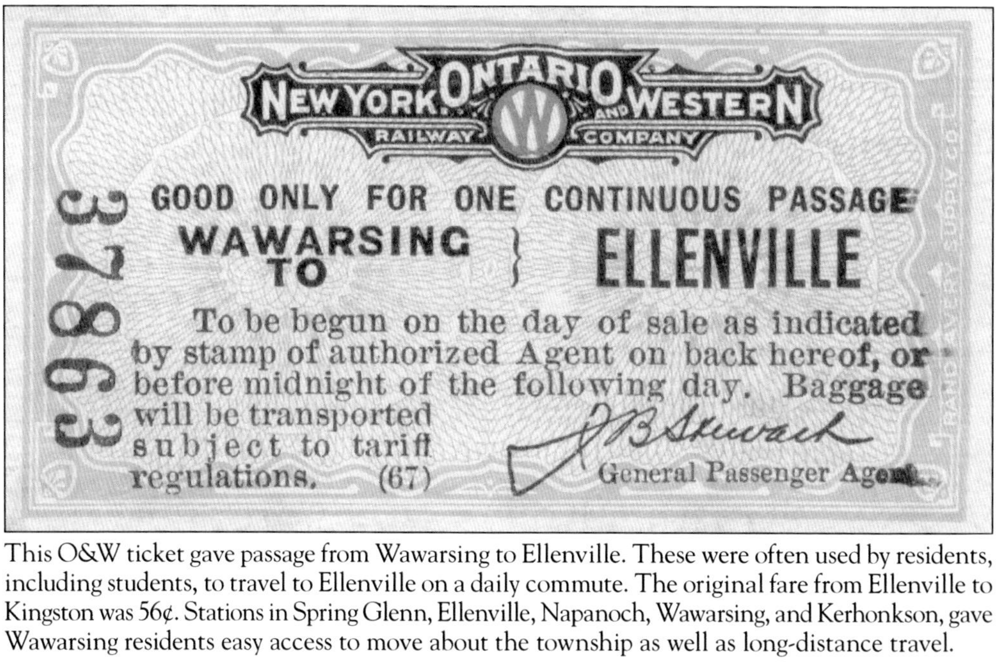

This O&W ticket gave passage from Wawarsing to Ellenville. These were often used by residents, including students, to travel to Ellenville on a daily commute. The original fare from Ellenville to Kingston was 56¢. Stations in Spring Glenn, Ellenville, Napanoch, Wawarsing, and Kerhonkson, gave Wawarsing residents easy access to move about the township as well as long-distance travel.

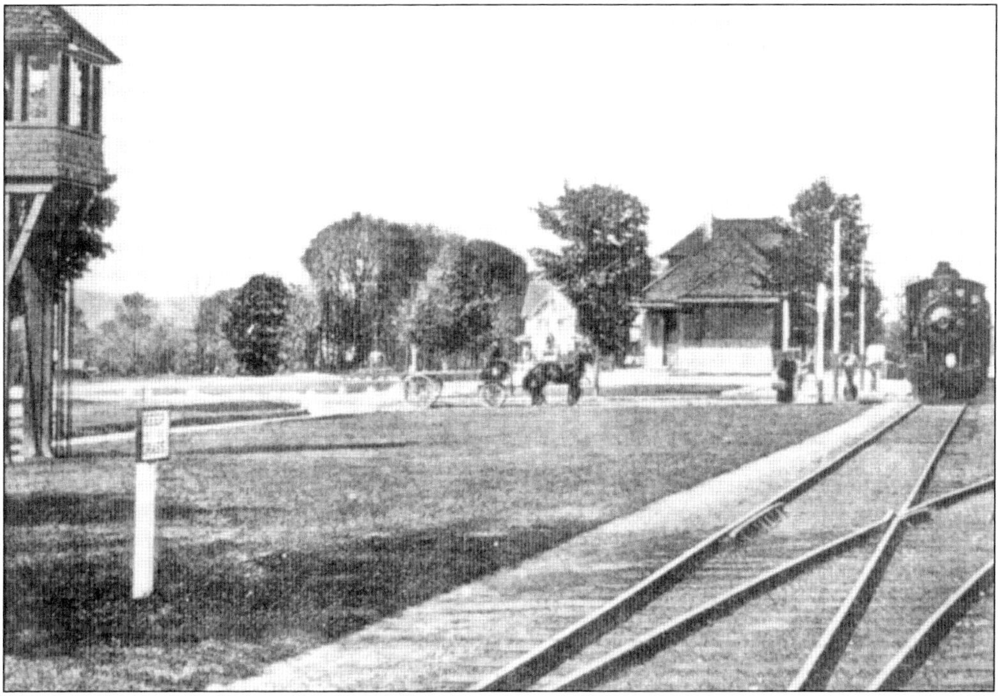

Since the railroad first came to Ellenville in 1871, safety was a major concern of the village and its residents; they were adamant that tracks not cross over main streets. After the village board reached an agreement in 1901, a signal tower and safety gates were installed and maintained by the O&W Railway near its new station. When O&W completed its extension to Kingston in 1902, tracks crossed Center and Canal Streets.

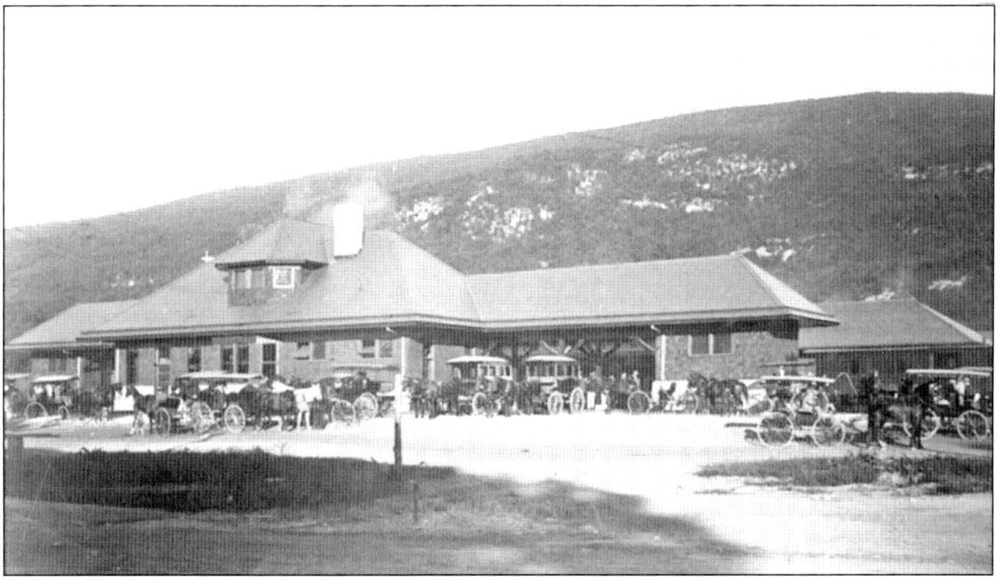

It was common for the area's hotels and boardinghouses to send vehicles to meet their guests. Here, the O&W train station on the east end of Canal is surrounded by carriages and taxis. Teamsters with buckboards would follow, transporting passenger trunks and luggage. Top Shelf Jewelry is located in this old rail station today.

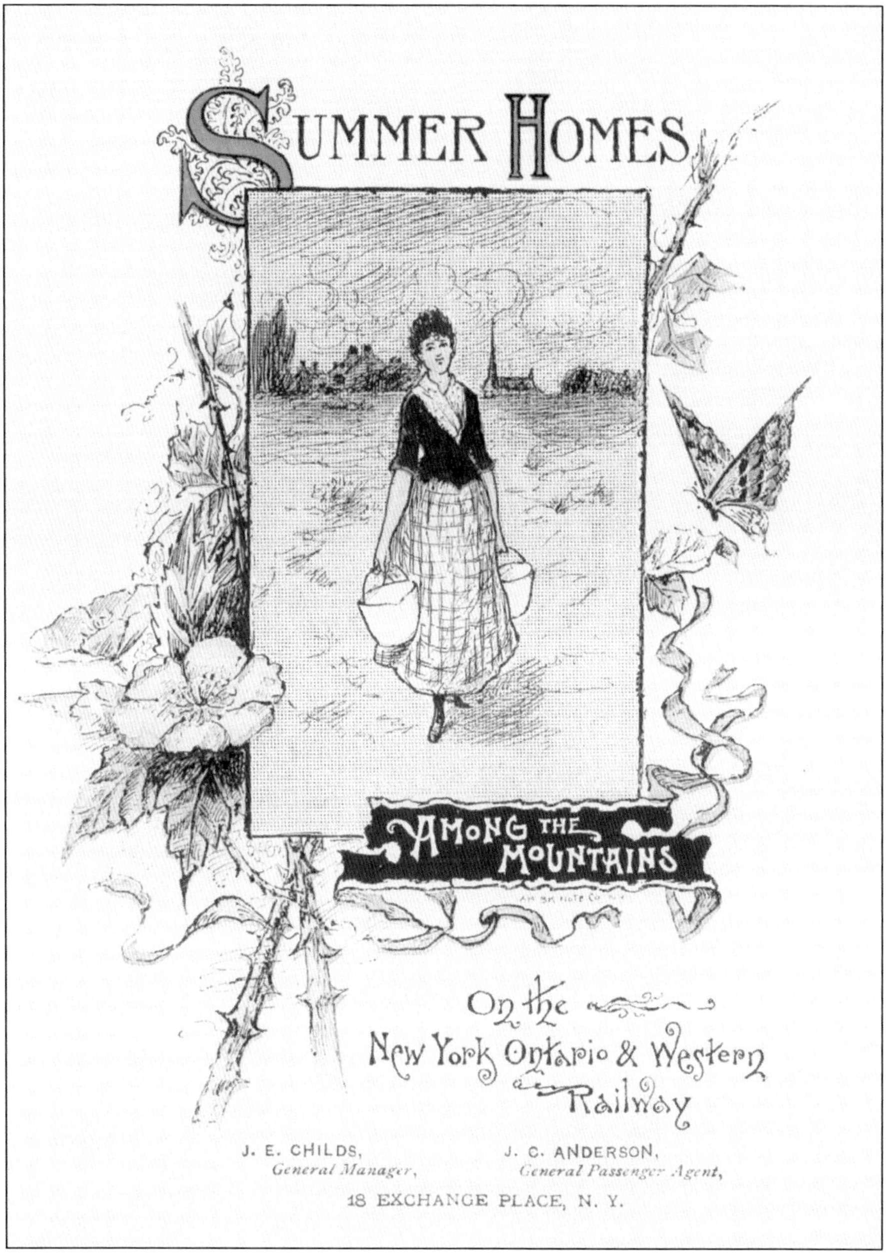

The O&W Railway provided services to local communities beyond transportation. Before the advent of the telephone and telephone directories, O&W published the *City Directory*. Revised annually, it included listings of businesses and residences along the railroad route. The publication *Summer Homes* served several purposes; along with travel information—ticket costs and train schedules—the booklet included hotel and boardinghouse listings, with photographs, advertisements, and details arranged by O&W station stops. Descriptions of the area served to draw visitors to the "exquisitely lovely valleys . . . gem-like lakes . . . quiet nooks," benefiting locals and tourists alike. These publications contributed to Ellenville becoming a popular resort community. The words "No Hebrews or dogs" that accompanied some listings are an unfortunate reminder of the harshness of social prejudice.

Three

Where People Worked

Within the first two decades of the operation of the D&H Canal, the power of water from Beerkill and Sandburg Creeks as well as other vital natural resources transformed Ellenville into the area's largest manufacturing and retail community. Represented here are a few of the numerous businesses and industries that existed at the beginning of the mid-1800s—mining and agriculture; lumbering and tanning; glass, pottery and knife making; wood crafting; canning; and hospitality. A wide range of commerce brought with it the many requirements of a large retail and business center. Merchants—including blacksmiths, pharmacies, haberdasheries, photography studios, tailors, clothing shops, retail dry goods, grocery stores, and home-run "cottage industries"—sold numerous products and offered many services. This chapter exemplifies the industrial and retail areas of Ellenville from the mid-19th to early 20th centuries.

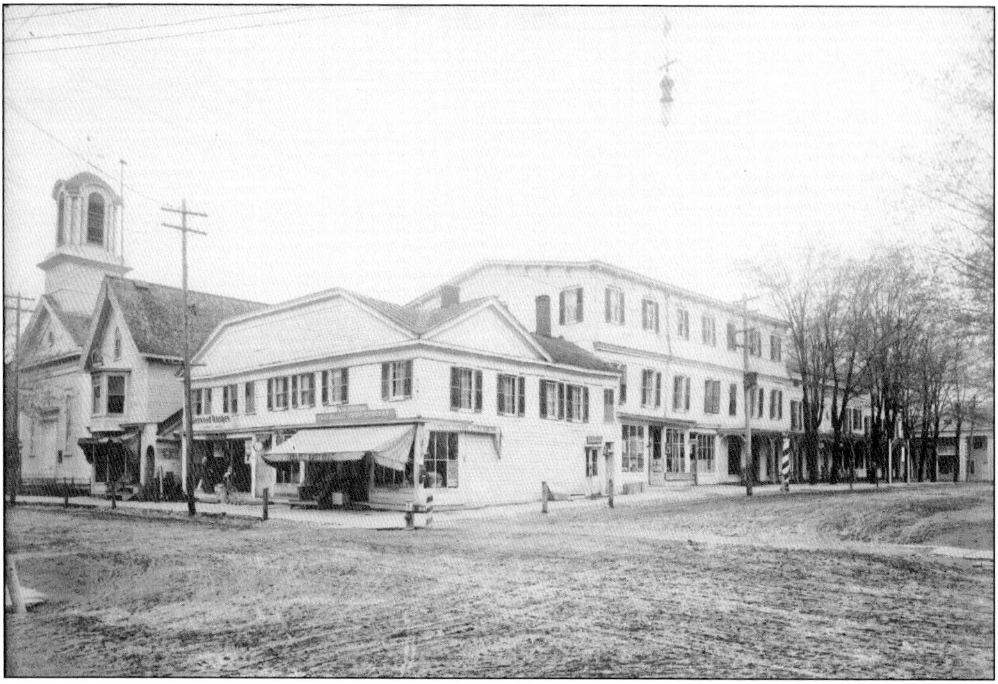

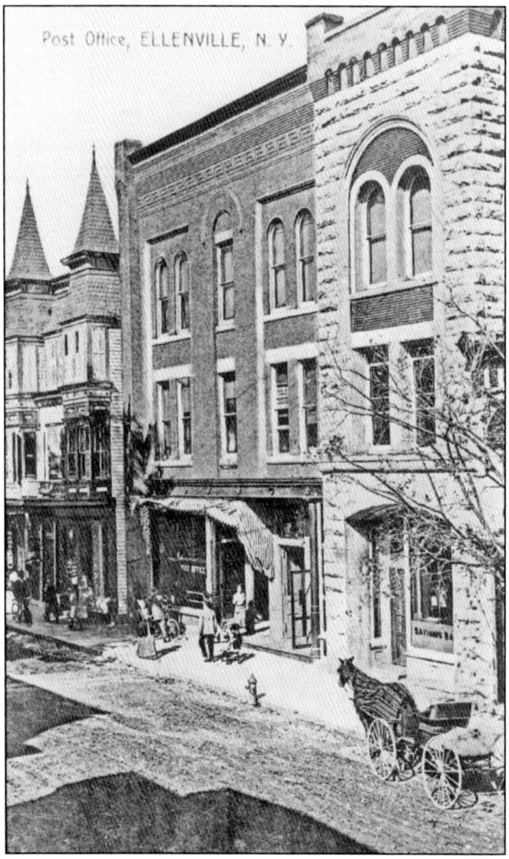

Mitchell House ran from Canal to Center Streets. This photograph from around 1890 shows George Hornbeck's Grocery between the Methodist church and Mitchell House; the Scoresby fire department met upstairs. Continuing on Canal, in the Mitchell House is Frank Rose's Hardware, Steve Mance's Watch and Jewelry, and on the corner, the Ellenville Cash Grocery. On the Main Street side were a piano store, a sewing machine shop, and a barbershop.

In 1889, William C. Rose and Richard T. Childs bought a hardware and tin shop from Beers & Co. Called Rose & Childs, it is pictured here on the far left in the 1890s. Rose and Childs dissolved their partnership in 1910, selling to Edwin J. Bailey Sr. In 1911, Rose repurchased the business, and in partnership with long time employee William L. Douglas, formed Rose & Douglas, which operated until 1976. The Ellenville Savings Bank, formed in 1896, was on the far right; it moved to Liberty and Main in 1954. The Ellenville Post Office was in the building in the center.

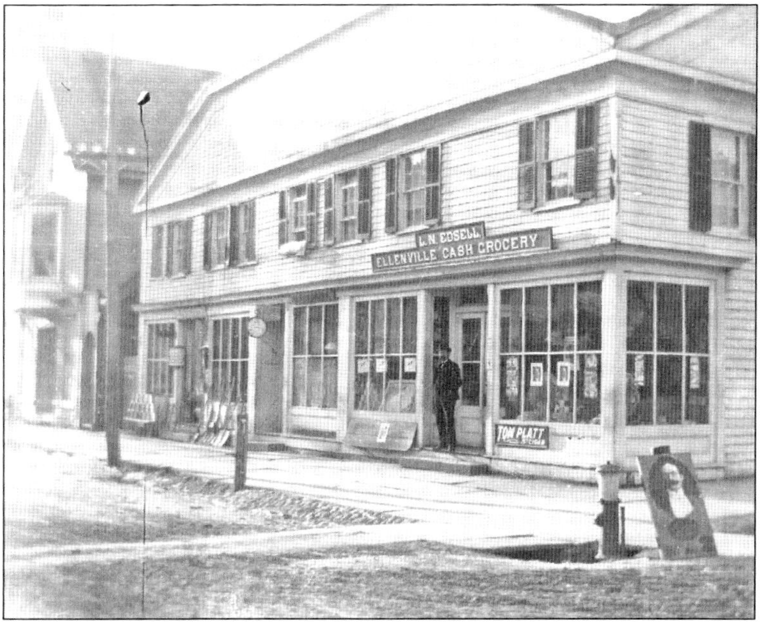

Brothers George D. and Lewis N. Edsell operated Ellenville Cash Grocery in the Mitchell House on Canal Street. They advertised in the Ellenville Business Directory of 1914 as being the sole agent for Chase and Sanborn's Teas and Coffees and as offering "staple and fancy" groceries and a delivery service. The store closed in 1917. Note the bed linens airing on the second floor of the hotel.

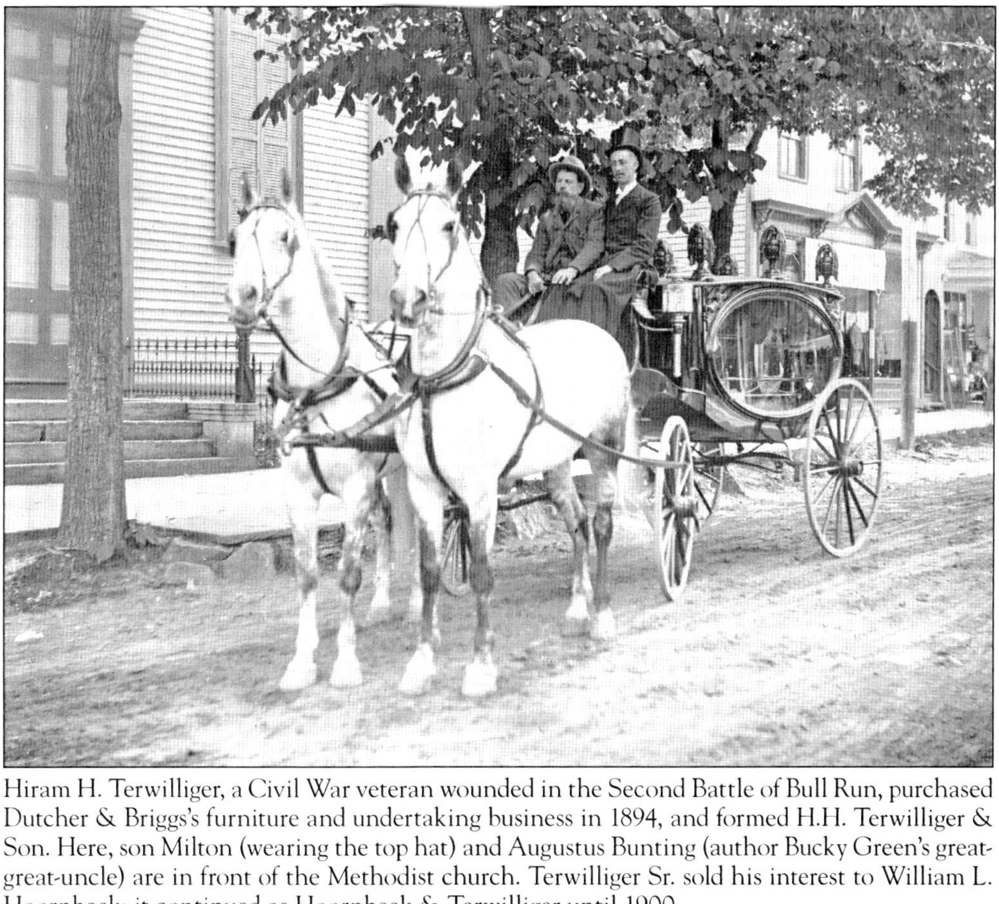

Hiram H. Terwilliger, a Civil War veteran wounded in the Second Battle of Bull Run, purchased Dutcher & Briggs's furniture and undertaking business in 1894, and formed H.H. Terwilliger & Son. Here, son Milton (wearing the top hat) and Augustus Bunting (author Bucky Green's great-great-uncle) are in front of the Methodist church. Terwilliger Sr. sold his interest to William L. Hoornbeek; it continued as Hoornbeek & Terwilliger until 1900.

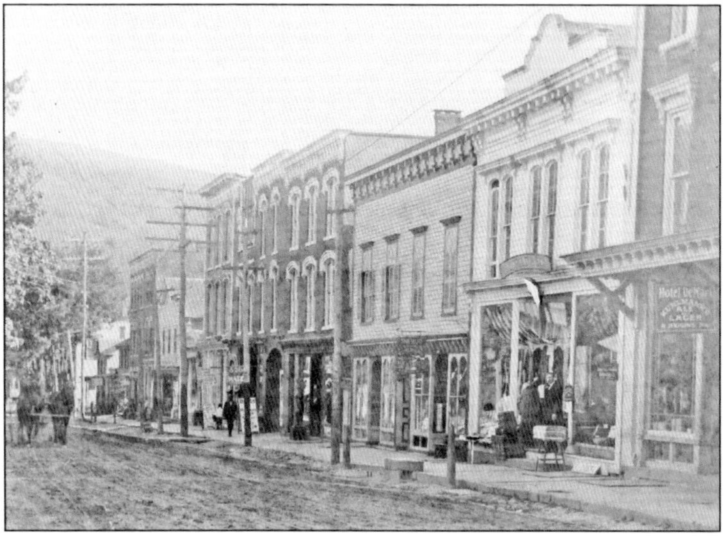

This view of lower Canal Street shows the dry goods store of N. Leopold & Son between the Hotel DeMart and "the Hub" tavern. Signs indicate that both establishments served ale and lager made by Kuhlmann's Brewery. When Nathan Leopold died in 1901, he had been in business here for around 50 years. His son Samuel continued the business under the same name.

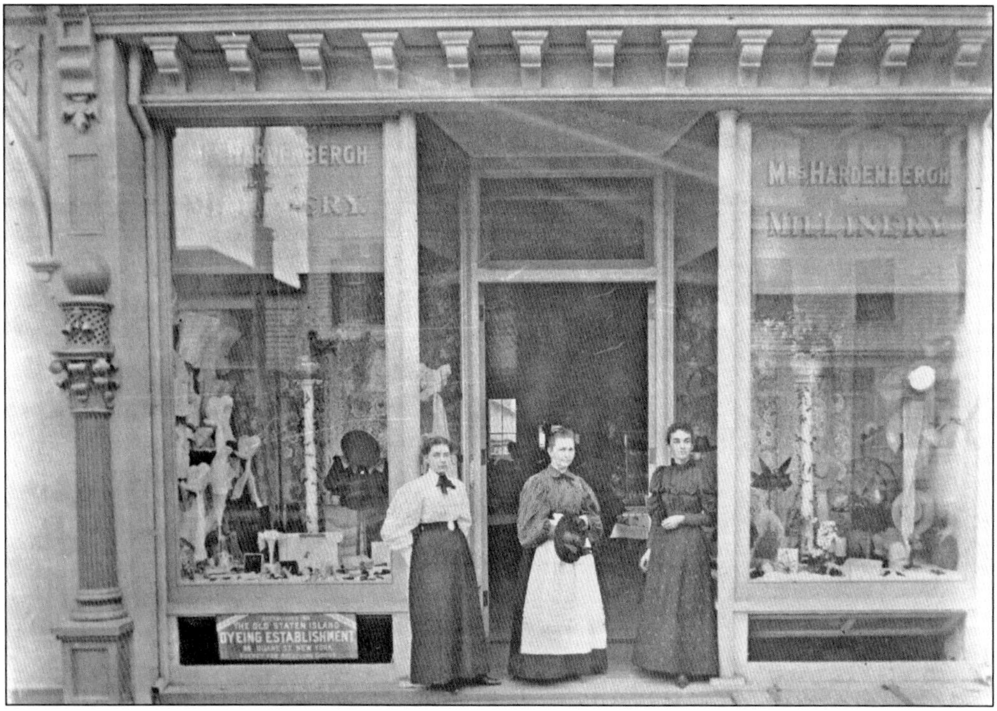

This 1906 photograph is of the Hardenbergh Millinery storefront in the Masonic Building on Canal Street. Emily Fischer Hardenbergh had been in business since the 1890s. Her brother, Scoresby fire chief Charles G.A. Fischer, was her business partner. Both had previously worked for Leopold & Son. She always carried "the finest and latest fashions for sale." An 1890 Ellenville directory promises "Repairing and Trimming Quickly and Neatly Done."

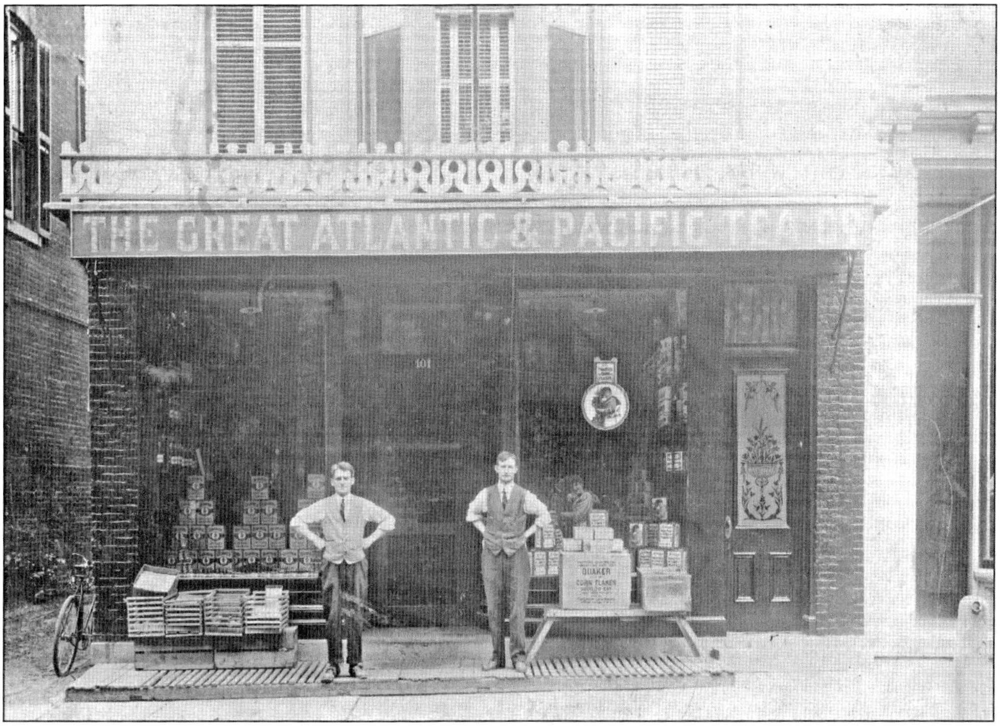

The Great Atlantic & Pacific Tea Company (A&P), the oldest supermarket chain in America, began in New York City in 1859. The company was in Ellenville by 1890 and had three Canal Street locations over the years. The above photograph was taken at 101 Canal Street. Until 1912, goods were delivered by horse drawn wagon. A&P offered a wide range of items, many with its own label. In 1936, it was the first grocery store to offer self-service shelving. From left to right, Edward Dowling and Tracy Schoonmaker pose in front of the store where exterior windows display Quaker Flakes (left) and Kellogg's Corn Flakes (right). The interior image below reveals four brands of canned beans and pork, including Campbell's and A&P, on sale for less than 10¢ each. "New-Laid" Sunnybrook eggs and other farm products were also available. Both images are from around 1910; Matthews Pharmacy is at this location now.

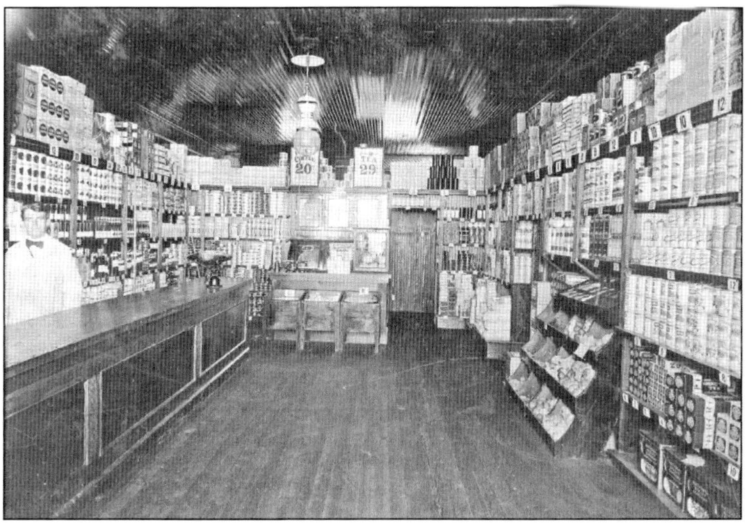

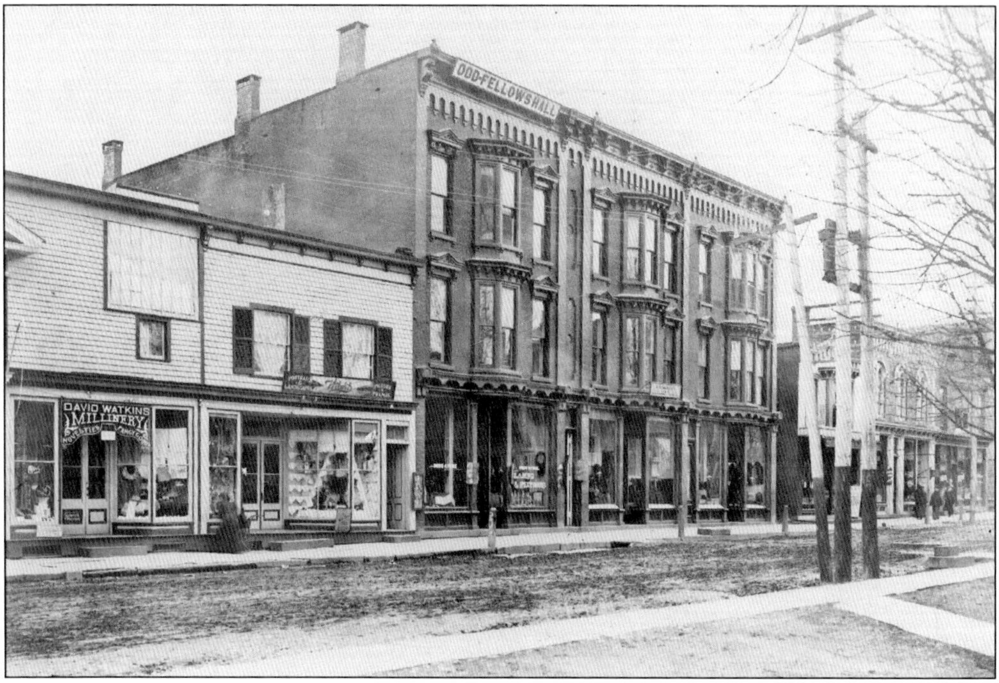

In 1848, Albert Corbin came to Ellenville from Fishkill, New York, establishing a pharmacy. He was joined by brother Isaac in 1860 to form the firm of A&I Corbin. Above is the three-story building known as the "Corbin Brick Block," built by Isaac on Canal Street in 1875. When Albert relocated to Pennsylvania, Isaac continued the pharmacy here. The building also housed the Wilkinson & Denson dry goods store, the Odd Fellows Hall (a fraternal organization), and the YMCA. A nephew of Corbin, Arthur Gridley Smith, became a partner in the firm in 1883 and was named sole proprietor after Corbin's death. In 1936, a fire burned buildings along Canal Street, including those shown to the left above, but was stopped by the so-called brick block from continuing further. The photograph below is of the drugstore interior.

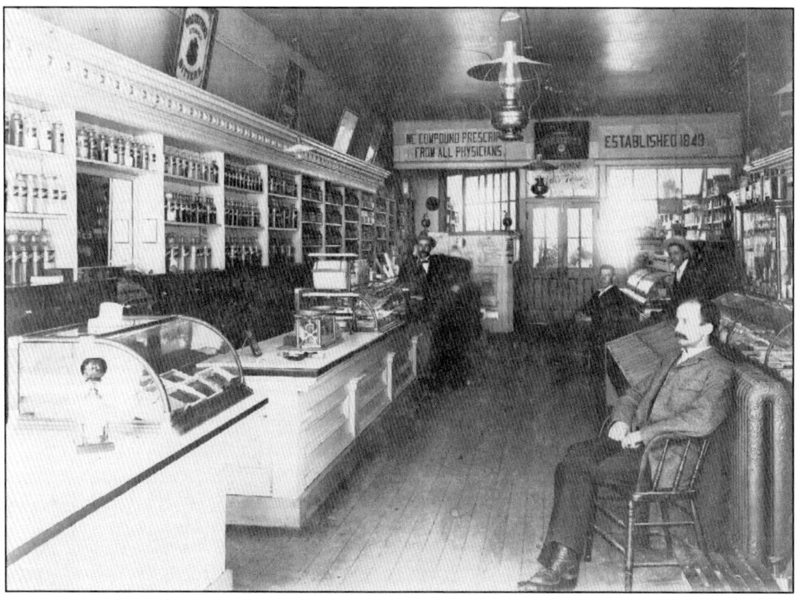

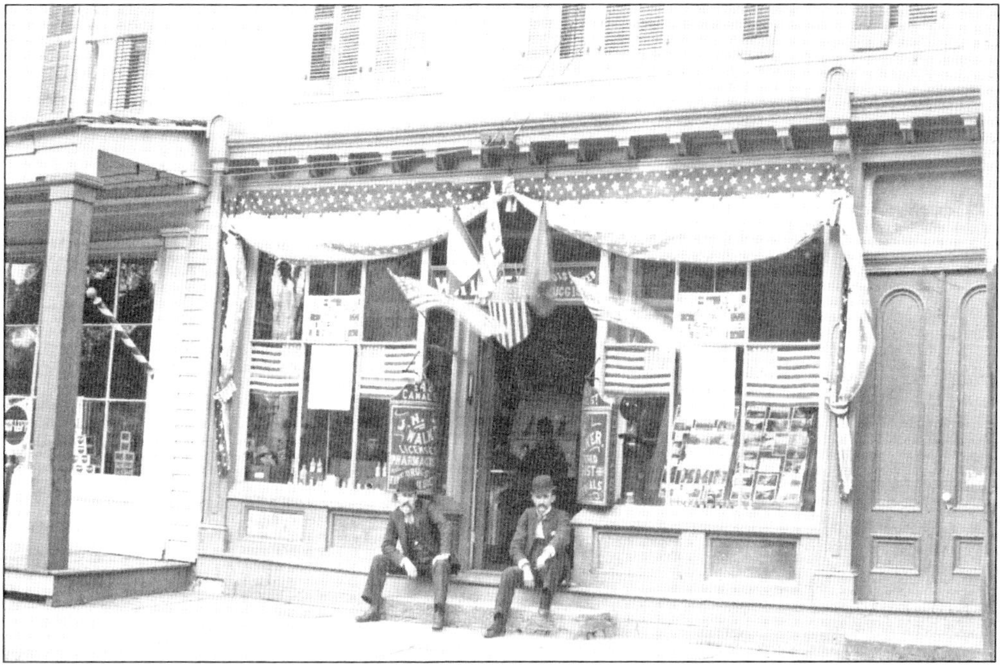

Located at 140 Canal Street in the "Terwilliger House Block" adjacent to the hotel of the same name, this pharmacy was opened in 1888 by Edgar Bevier. The following year, the business was purchased by J.N. Walker and Ralph H. Eaton, becoming Eaton & Walker. Walker continued as sole proprietor until 1894, when the building was purchased by Arthur G. Smith, a druggist previously established in the Corbin Brick Block across the street. The photograph above shows the exterior (possibly decorated for a parade). Below is the interior; note the advertisements for Cascarets Candy Cathartic. Believed to be the first medicine marketed as candy beginning in 1894, this product was a popular alternative to castor oil as a laxative. Humphreys Specifics were also sold here; Frederick Humphreys founded a company in 1844 offering homeopathic remedies for a multitude of ailments for both human consumption and veterinary use.

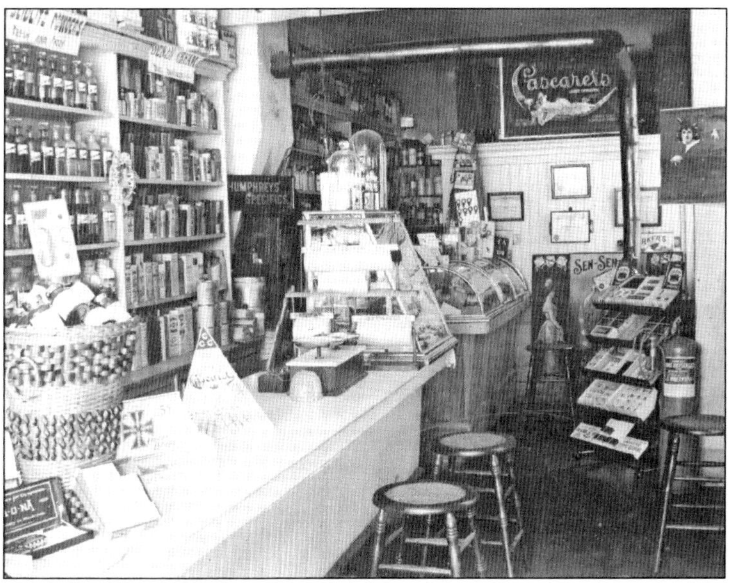

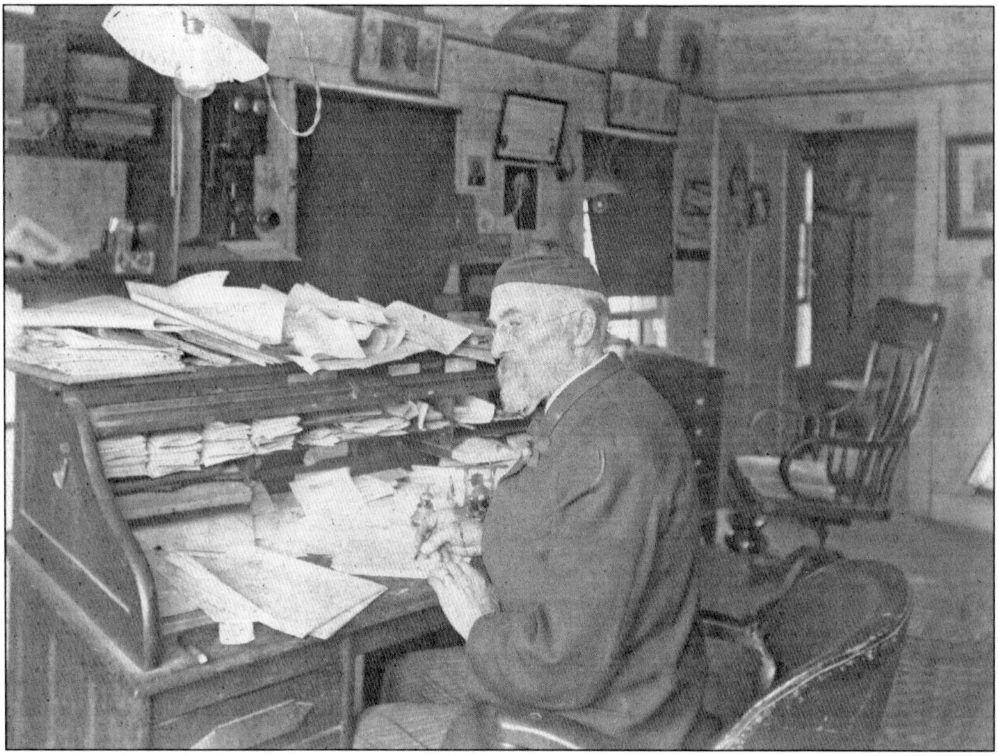

The *Ellenville Journal* was started in 1849 by Richard Baxter Taylor as a Republican newspaper. In its early years, it was located at 84 Canal Street, above the businesses of Potter and Campbell. Sylvester M. Taylor, nephew of Richard, is pictured at his desk at the *Ellenville Journal* in 1906. He came to Ellenville in 1851 when his uncle became editor and publisher of the *Journal*. In 1857, Sylvester became editor. The Taylor family remained involved with the publication in various capacities for generations.

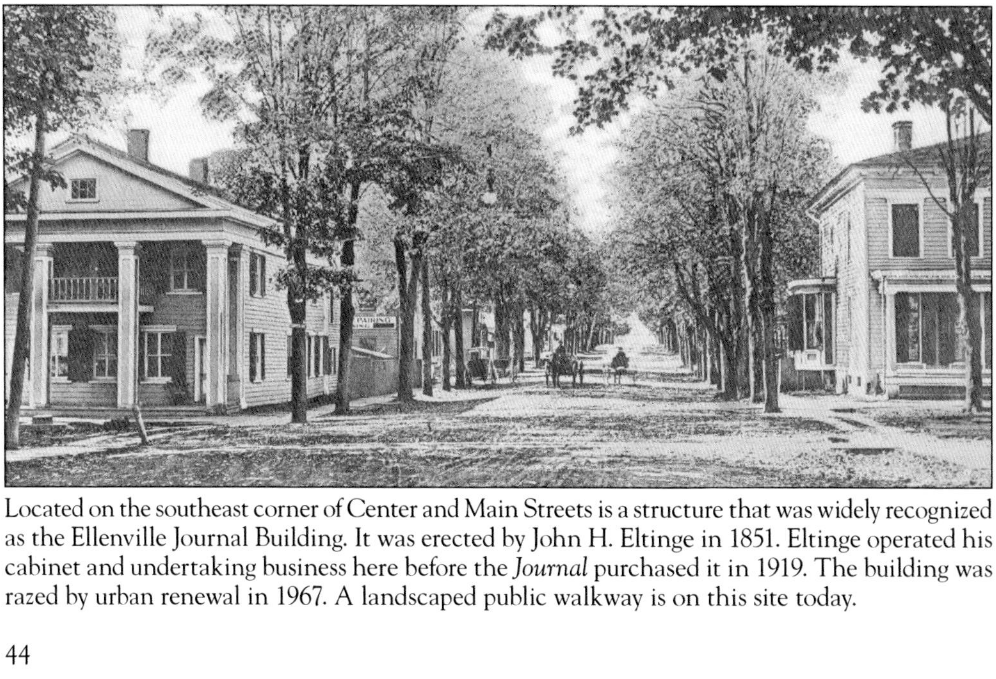

Located on the southeast corner of Center and Main Streets is a structure that was widely recognized as the Ellenville Journal Building. It was erected by John H. Eltinge in 1851. Eltinge operated his cabinet and undertaking business here before the *Journal* purchased it in 1919. The building was razed by urban renewal in 1967. A landscaped public walkway is on this site today.

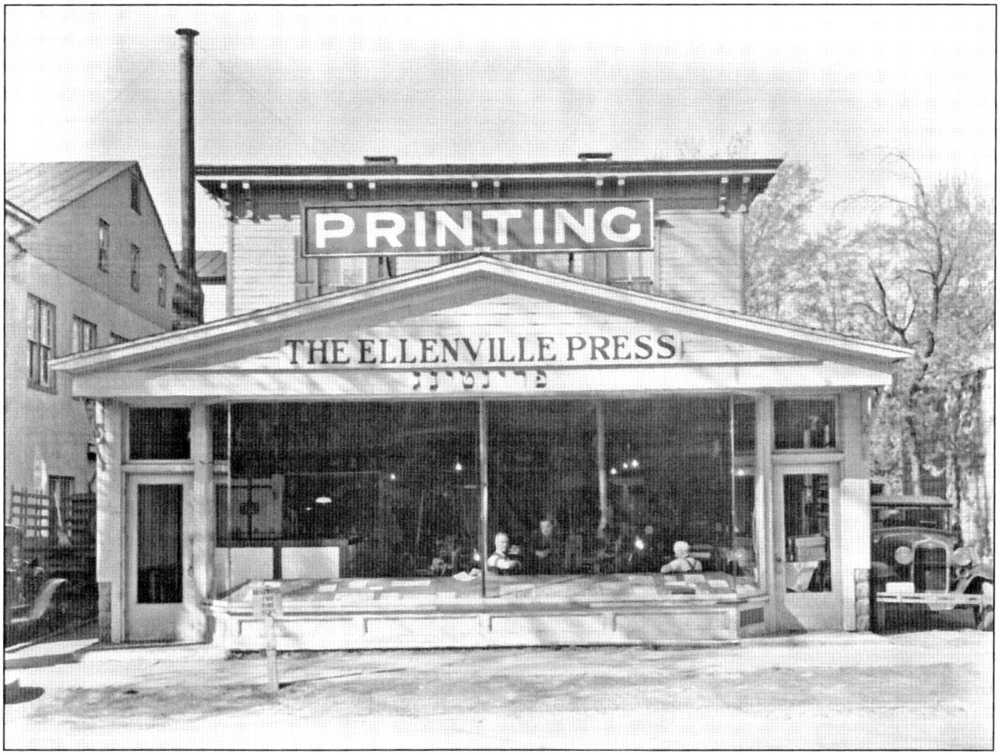

Founded in 1870 by Thomas E. and Gilbert H. Benedict, the *Ellenville Press* was a Democratic newspaper. In 1886, Thomas was appointed public printer of the United States by Pres. Grover Cleveland. Irving McNally acquired the paper in 1933, moving it to 67–68 Canal Street. While ownership changed hands many times, the Benedict and McNally families were involved for decades.

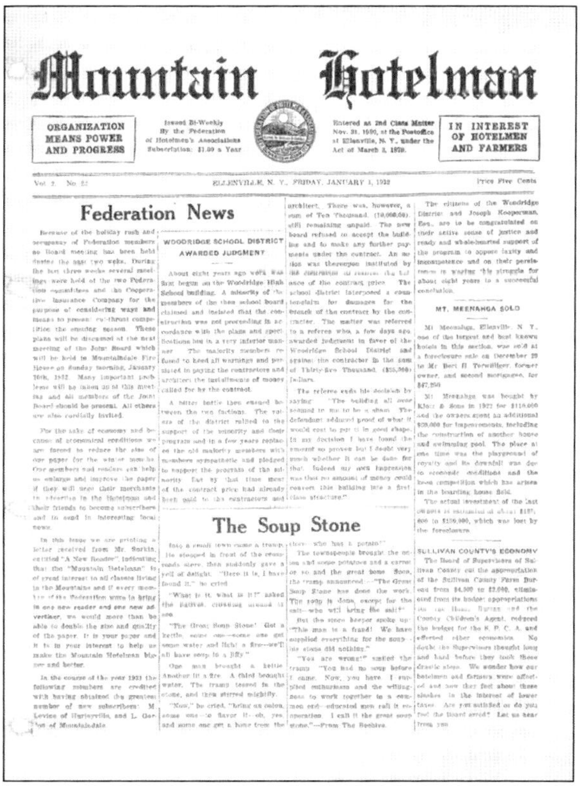

Mountain Hotelman

ORGANIZATION MEANS POWER AND PROGRESS

Issued Bi-Weekly By the Federation of Hotelmen's Associations Subscription: $1.00 a Year

Entered as 2nd Class Matter Nov. 21, 1930, at the Postoffice at Ellenville, N. Y., under the Act of March 3, 1879.

IN INTEREST OF HOTELMEN AND FARMERS

Vol. 2. No. 22 — ELLENVILLE, N. Y., FRIDAY, JANUARY 1, 1932 — Price Five Cents

Federation News

WOODRIDGE SCHOOL DISTRICT AWARDED JUDGMENT

MT. MEENAHGA SOLD

The Soup Stone

SULLIVAN COUNTY'S ECONOMY

The *Ellenville Press* also printed outside jobs. One such newspaper was the *Mountain Hotelman*, a famous biweekly published "in the interest of hotelmen and farmers" by the Federation of Hotelmen's Associations of Sullivan, Ulster, and Adjoining Counties. In 1932, an annual subscription cost $1. The paper was printed in both English and Yiddish; McNally learned to typeset Yiddish.

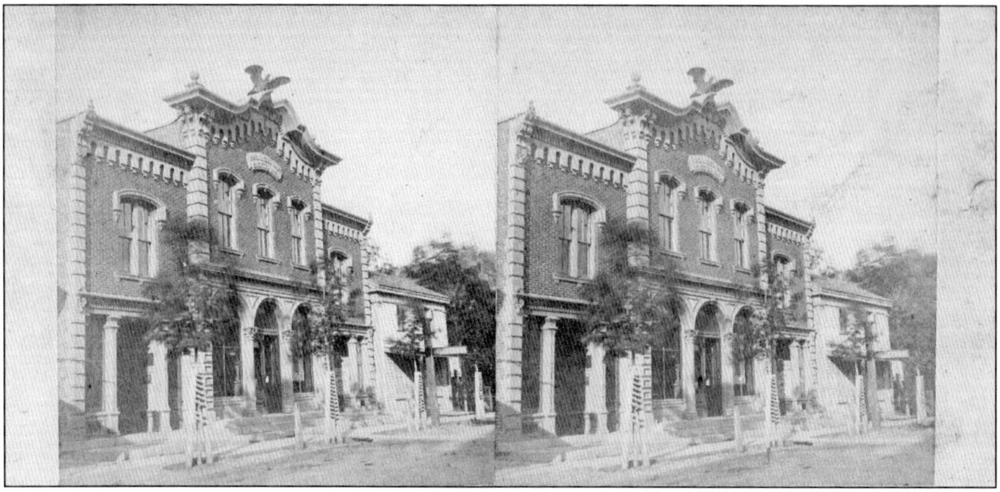

Constructed in 1868 as the new offices of the First National Bank, this building still stands on Canal Street, the present location of Sprague and Killeen, Inc. Organized in 1863, First National was originally located on the northwest corner of Center and Market Streets. In 1928, the name changed to the First National Bank and Trust Company of Ellenville, New York. The bank later moved to the corner of Canal and Main Streets. Seen below are cashier Frank B. Hoornbeek (left) and bank president R.M. Eugene Clark. The above images were made for a stereopticon.

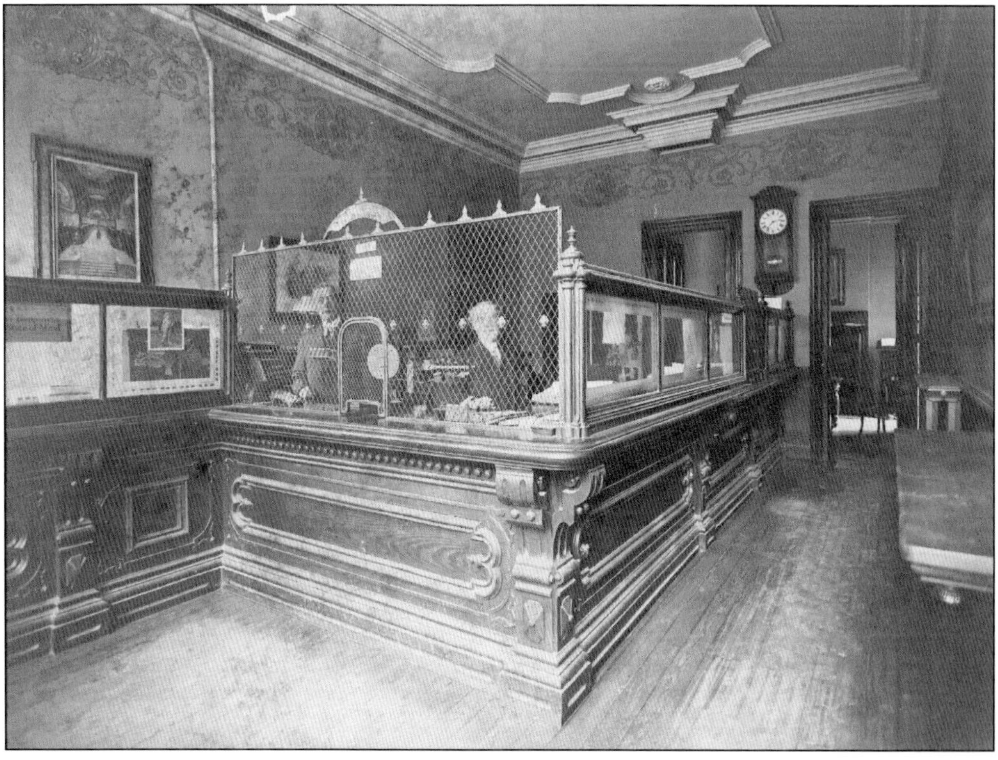

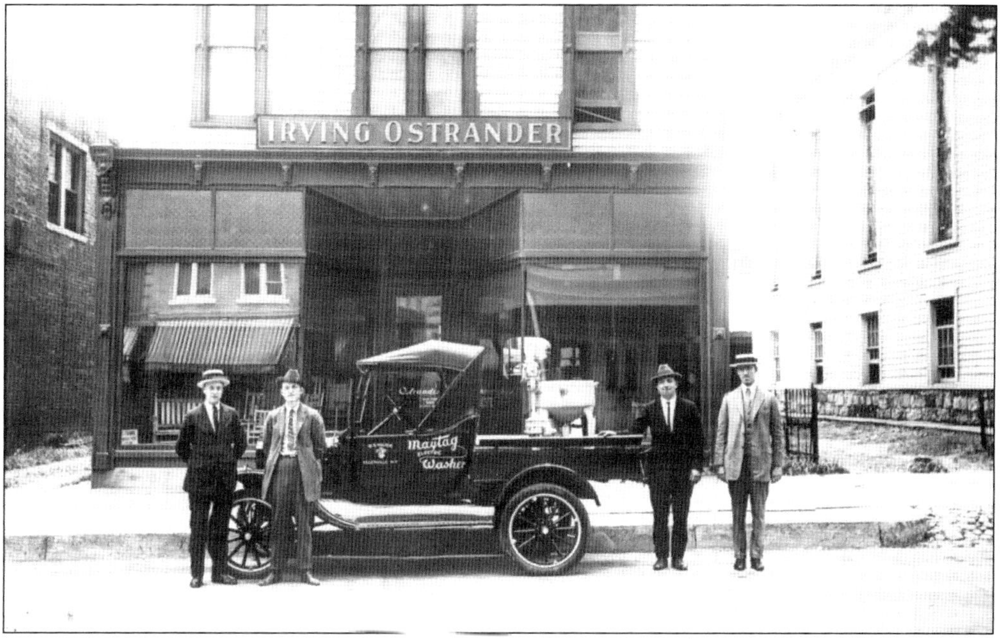

Photographed in front of Irving Ostrander's furniture and undertaking business on Canal Street is a 1930s Ford pickup truck with convertible top. In the truck bed is an early wringer washing machine by the Maytag Company. "R.S. Walker, Ellenville, N.Y." is on the driver's side door; the 1940 census lists Russell Walker as an electrical engineer.

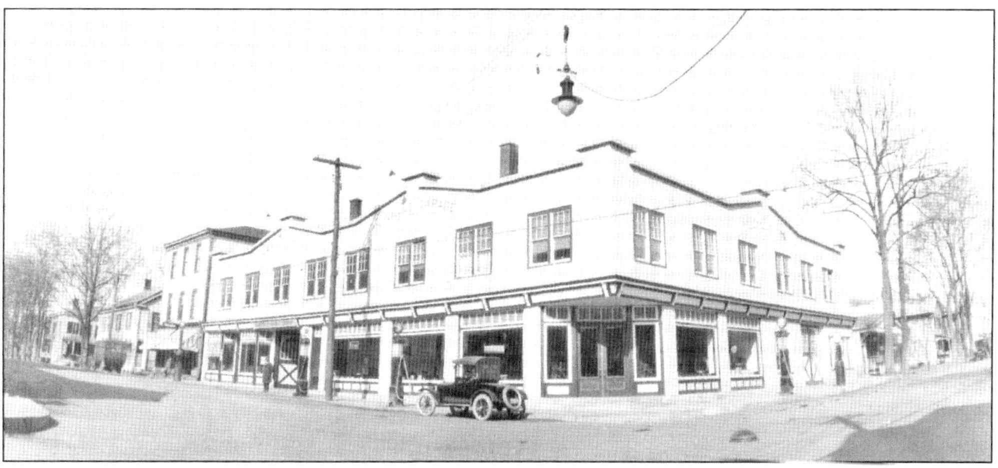

In 1916, Edgar M. Marshall and E. Gordon Jansen (of Marshall-Jansen Company) opened Innavalle Garage on Main Street. Featuring modern electric gas pumps, it was open 24/7, except for "gasless Sundays" during World War I. In 1923, Marshall and Jansen extended the building after purchasing the corner lot from David Watkins, who ran a millinery shop there (formerly Clyne's store). Henry Ford visited Marshall-Jansen Company in the early 1920s. This was later the site of Art Aaron Auto Accessories.

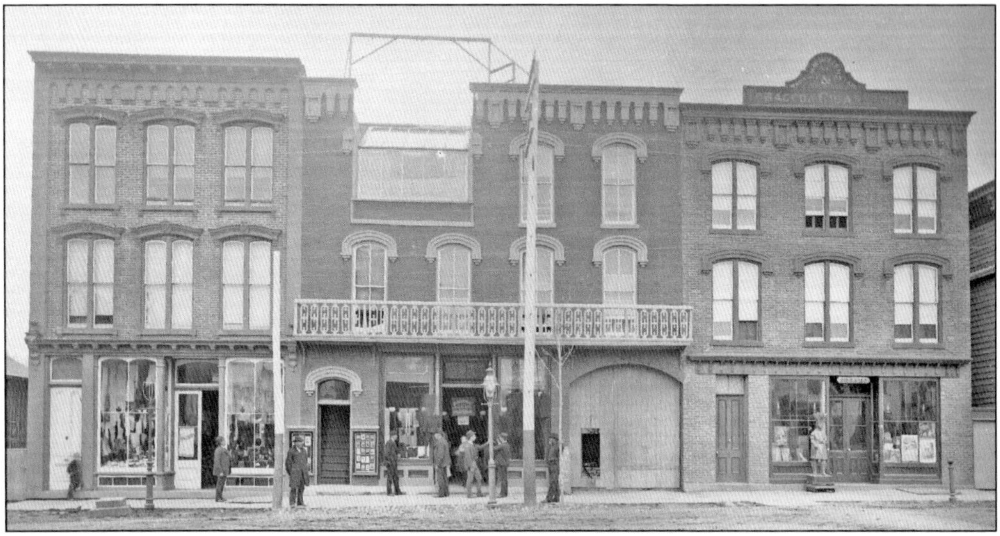

Born in Scotland, Michael McMullen came to Ellenville in 1837. His father was a glassblower, a trade his brothers followed. Because of a childhood spinal injury, McMullen learned the cigar maker's trade instead. He constructed the building on the right; his business was on the ground floor and he lived upstairs. On the left are milliner, photographer, and haberdasher shops. This building is the current location of the Shadowland Theatre.

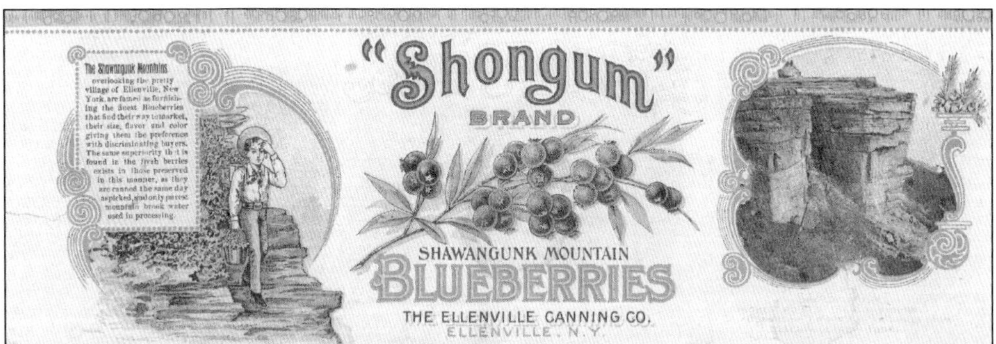

Farmers brought produce and cider to the Ellenville Canning Company, formed in 1900. An *Ellenville Journal* article mentions 20,000 cans of corn and over 1,000 cans of tomatoes being "put up" in one week. Silas VanWagener and First National Bank president M. Eugene Clark bought the company in 1902, naming it the Shawangunk Canning Factory; it closed a year later. The building, near the Hunt & Donaldson warehouse, burned in 1983.

Ellenville boasted several photography studios. Photographers were often engaged to take commemorative pictures of events, groups, and individuals, and postcards were reproduced from glass-plate and film negatives. Wurts Tice had an early studio during the Civil War era. The image at right is from the Albert V. Porter Studio at 157 Canal Street, which offered "the highest grade of work." This was formerly the location of W.S. Davis's studio, which promised an "instantaneous process used exclusively." The Shadowland Studio followed, with Casper S. Cosenza, proprietor. V.T. Wright's studio at 153–5 Canal Street was one of the finest. Wright worked as a newspaper photographer in New York City and came to Ellenville with his family in 1900. The image below with crop lines is of Wright as a young man. In addition to photography, Wright organized a drum and bugle corps in the village.

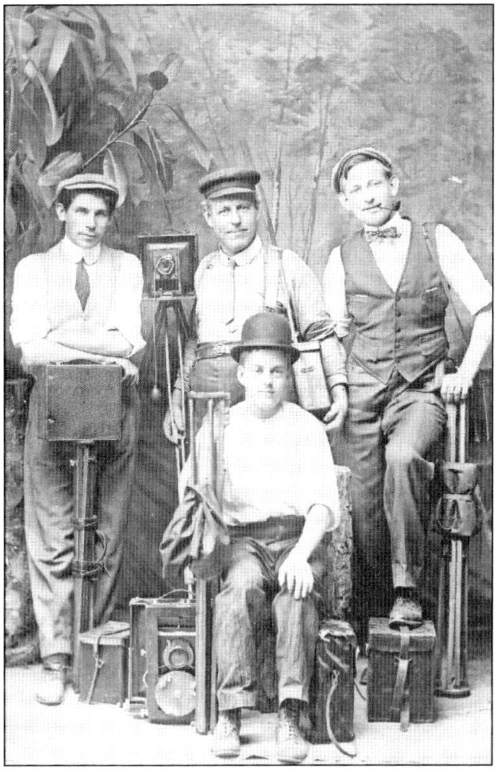

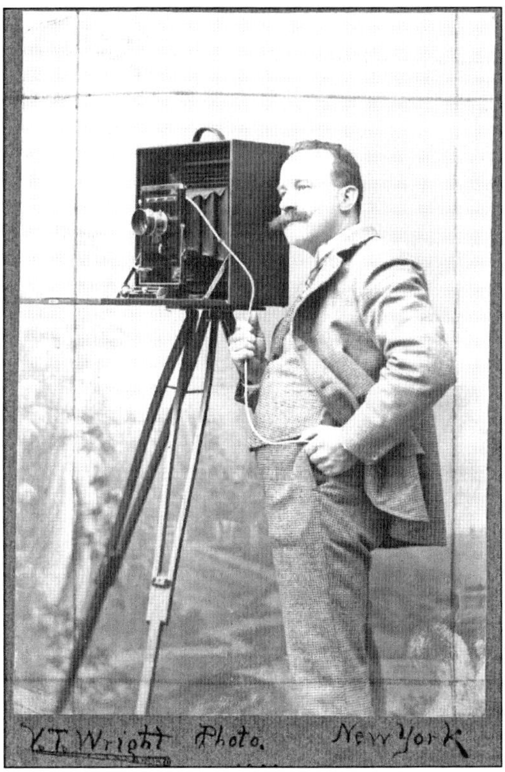

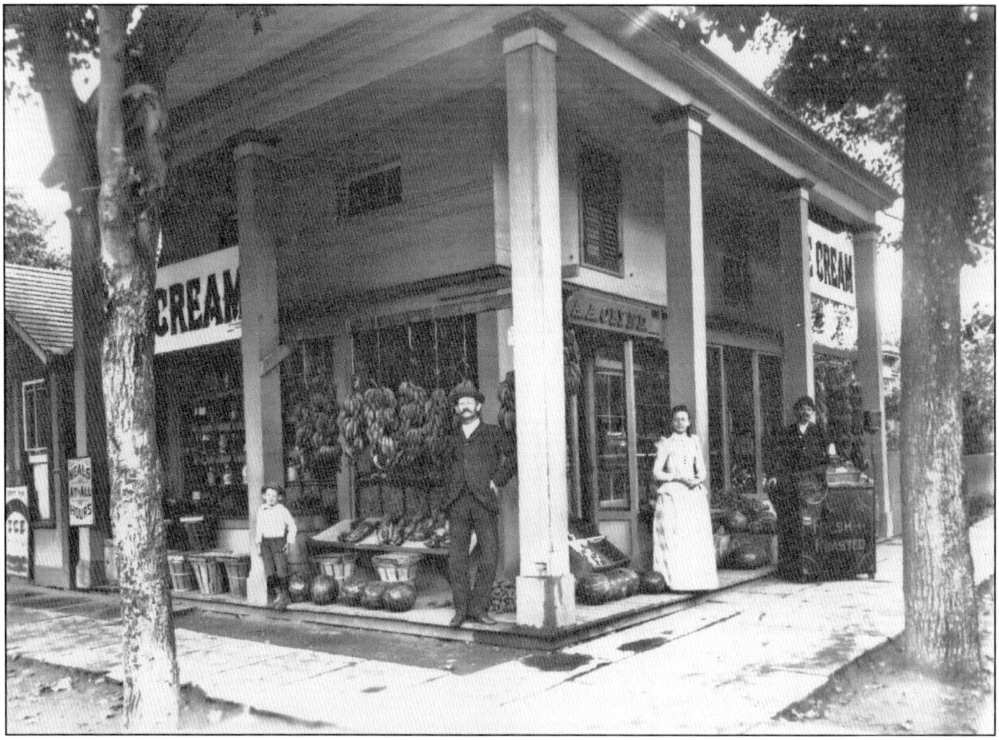

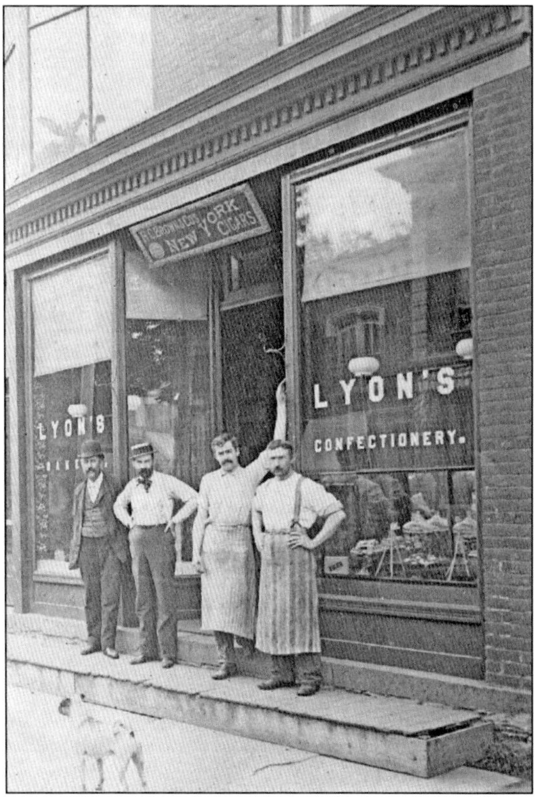

Abram A. Clyne operated an ice cream parlor, confectionery, and restaurant on the southwest corner of Canal and Main Streets, where Stewart's Shop is located today. His business included a dealership in raw furs, skins, and more. The 1880 census lists Clyne and his father, John, as lock tenders, presumably on the D&H Canal. Clyne later sold the store to his brother and Civil War veteran, Asa S. Clyne.

Previously belonging to C.J. Webb, Lyon's Confectionery and Bakery stood at 167 Canal Street. Born in Ellenville in 1861, proprietor Deyo B. Lyon was the son of John Lyon and Sarah E. Bevier. John Lyon, a lawyer and Ulster County district attorney, was the local provost marshal during the Civil War. Deyo B. Lyon, who married Olivia S. Bloomer, was a member of the consistory of the Dutch Reformed church.

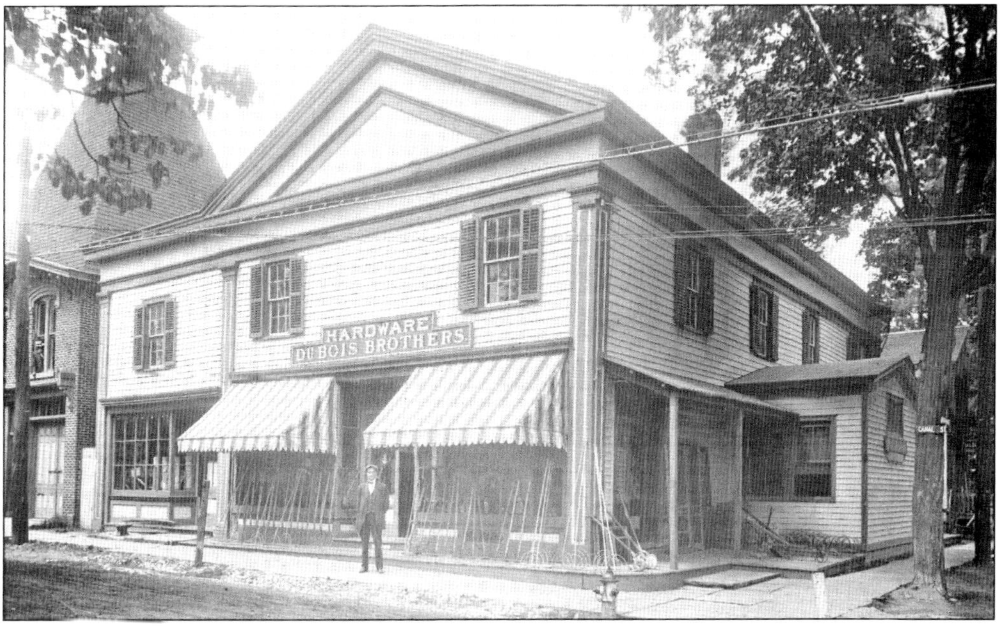

In 1875, Orlando and John Gosman DuBois formed DuBois Brothers Hardware on the northwest corner of Canal and Main Streets in a building originally operated by E.G. Fuller & Co. After Orlando's death, DuBois kept the name DuBois Brothers. His sons, Lemuel and William, continued the business after his death in 1895. Lemuel ran the store as L. DuBois & Co. after William retired. On the far left is the original Scoresby Hose Company.

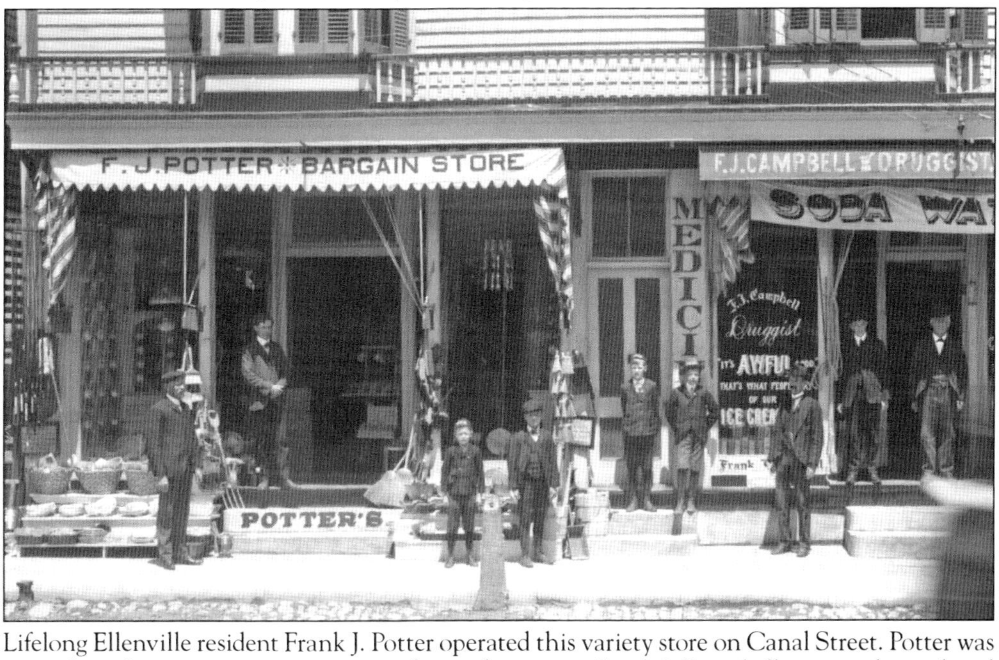

Lifelong Ellenville resident Frank J. Potter operated this variety store on Canal Street. Potter was a member of numerous organizations and served as mayor. Frank J. Campbell, previously employed at the Corbin drugstore, opened his pharmacy in 1902. Campbell, also active in the community, was an accomplished organist and taught music lessons. The *Ellenville Journal* occupied the second floor until relocating to the corner of Main and Center Streets.

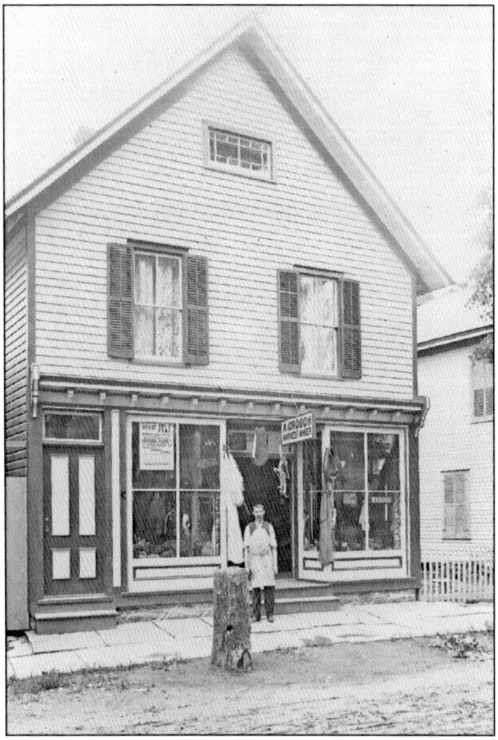

August Grosch stands in front of his harness-making shop in this 1897 photograph; he was a harness maker in Ellenville for more than 30 years. Initially, he operated from his home on Church Street, moving the business to 10 Market Street and then, in 1920, to 102 Center Street, diagonally across from where Cohen's bakery is today. Making their son a first-generation American, August's parents, Oswald and Josephine Grosch, came to this country from Bavaria and ran a farm in Fallsburgh, New York. Their neighbor John Butterfuss, also from Bavaria, taught him the harness-making trade.

When Benjamin Schweinfest closed his shop in 1947 after 58 years in business, he was the last active harness maker in Ulster County. This is the interior of Schweinfest's harness shop at 94 Canal Street. Schweinfest came to Ellenville in 1889 at age 17. He learned the harness-making trade from Charles Butterfuss (John's son), whose business was at this location; at that time, there were six harness makers in the village.

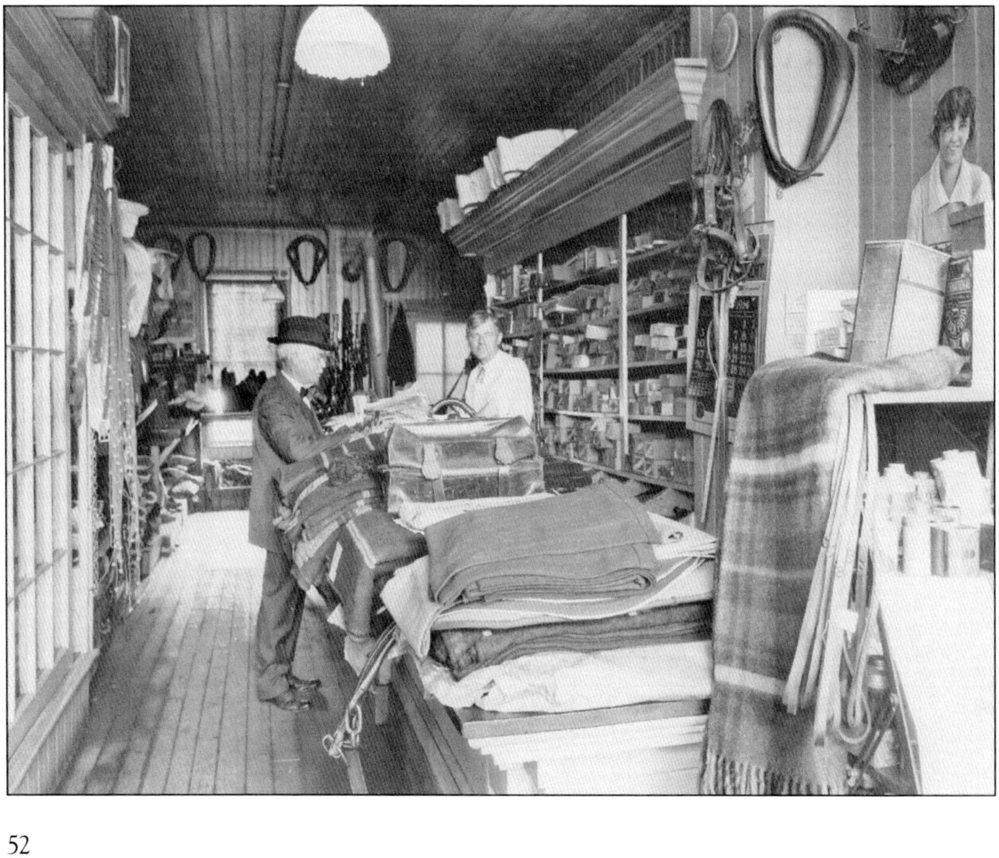

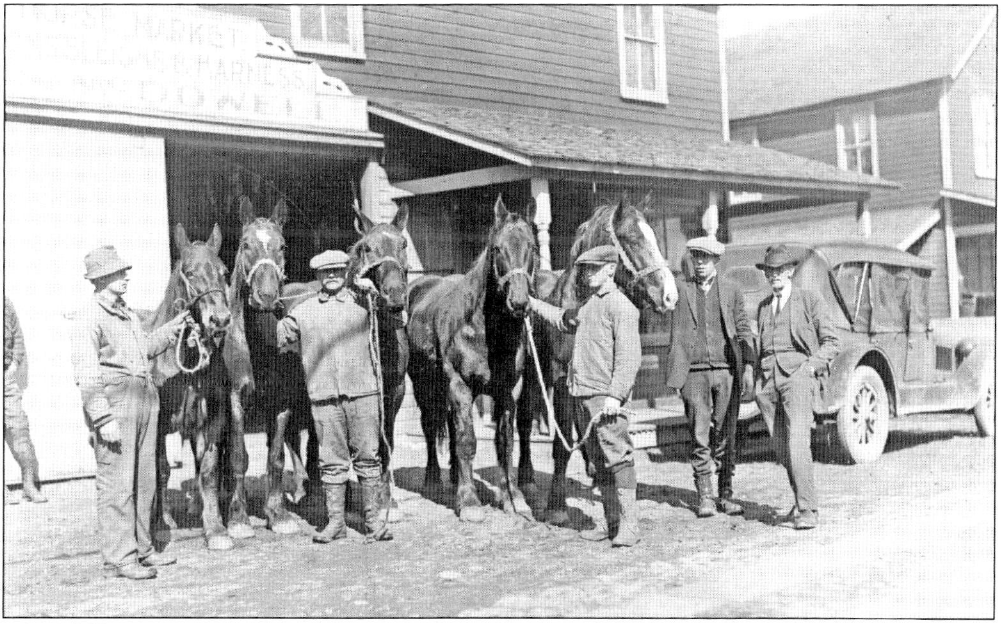

John McDowell operated a livery at 41–43 North Main Street after moving here in 1906. A member of St. John's Memorial Episcopal Church, McDowell lived at 53 Warren Street. Secretary of the Ulster County Agricultural Society, he was involved with the Ulster County Fair. McDowell's son, Tuthill, served as the Ellenville postmaster and wrote to FDR recommending that the new post office be constructed out of native fieldstone instead of brick. President Roosevelt responded affirmatively.

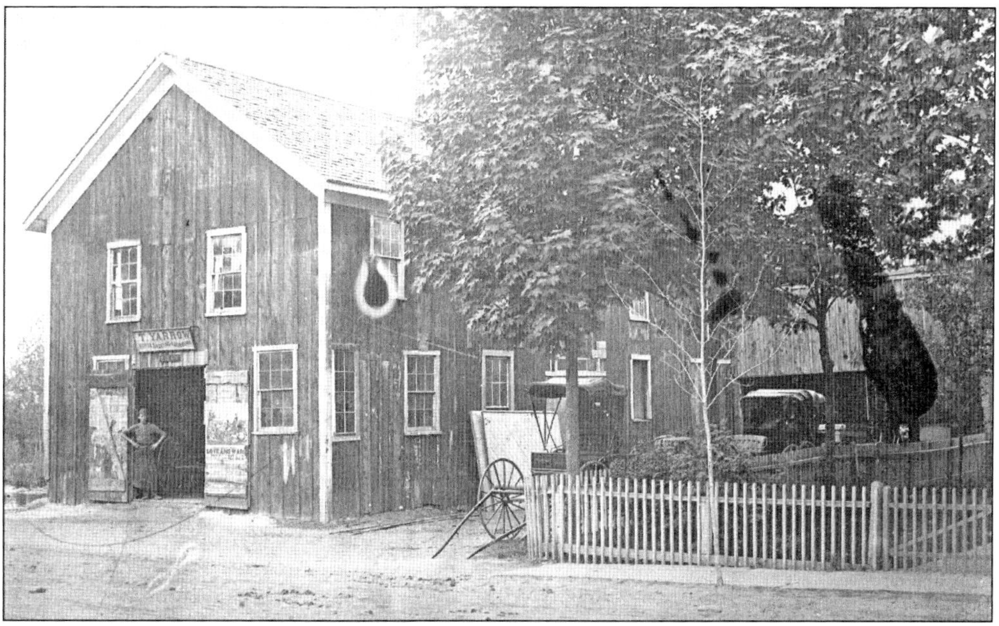

Thomas Yarrow Jr. was born in Ellenville in 1860 to Thomas and Elizabeth Yarrow, who had emigrated from England in 1856. Yarrow Sr. was a manufacturer of extracts, particularly wintergreen, which was used for medicinal purposes. He also made horse brushes. Yarrow Jr. ran this blacksmith shop on North Main Street at the Beerkill bridge. His sign and advertisement reads "Horse Shoeing and Jobbing."

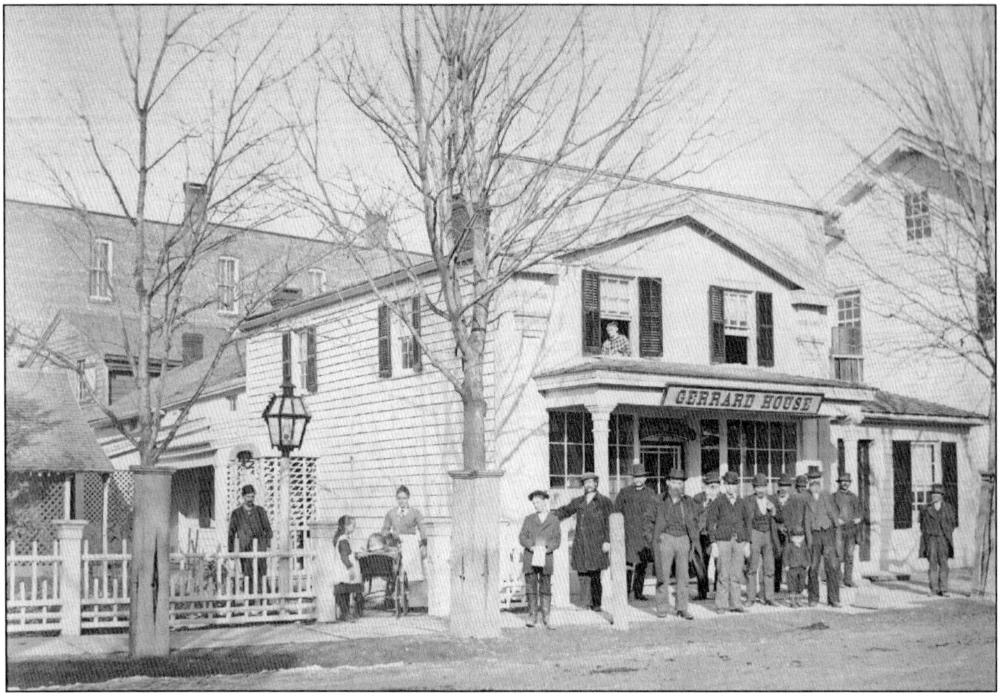

The Gerrard House at 4 Market Street was opened in 1849 by John Gerrard and his wife. Mary Gerrard ran an ice cream and candy store and a taxidermy museum inside. The saloon "conducted business upon Temperance principles." In 1880, the business was sold to John Wagner, whose family continued the tavern for 70 years. The photograph below shows an adjacent icehouse with a block of ice suspended from a pulley; it is possible that the ice came from Burlison's Ice Farm located up the road. Young Abie Wagner is in the baby carriage in the photograph above.

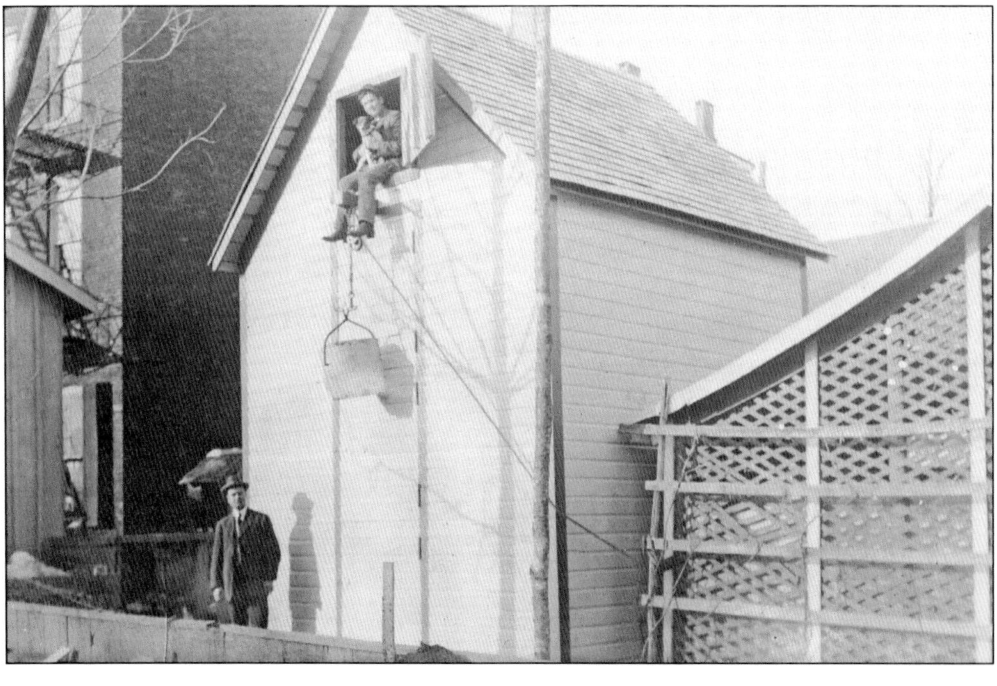

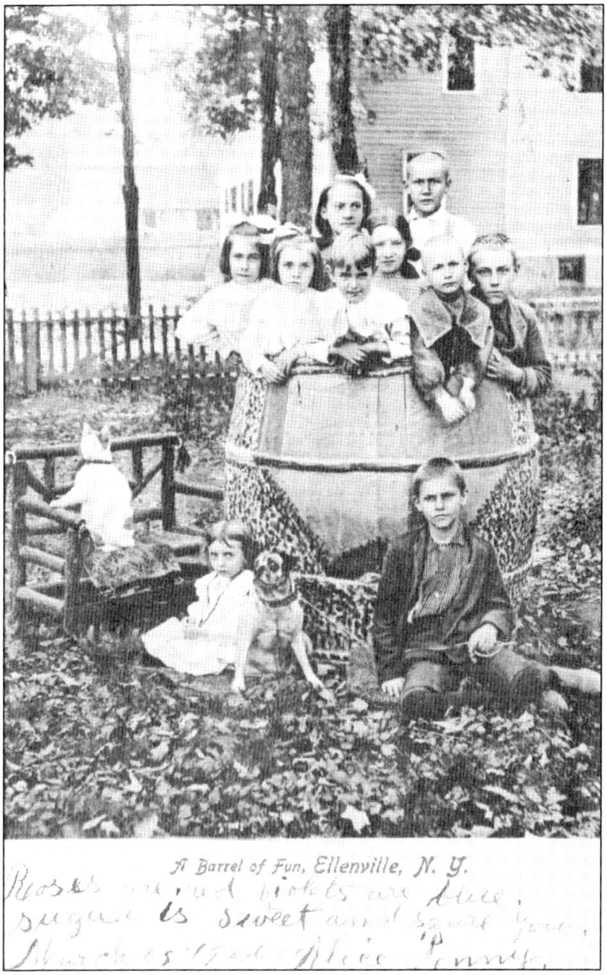

This whimsical image displays a typical barrel with wooden hoops used to bind barrels for flour and other goods. Hoop making was a major 19th-century industry that provided livelihood for a large number of local families, second only to agriculture. Theodore Wilklow was a hoop dealer in Ellenville from the late 1800s until 1907. For a time, Wilklow was the largest wooden hoop dealer in America; according to a 1914 newspaper article, he bought and sold over one billion hoops during his career. Other Ellenville hoop dealers were P.H. Hanley, Edmund Dutcher, and Thomas Yarrow.

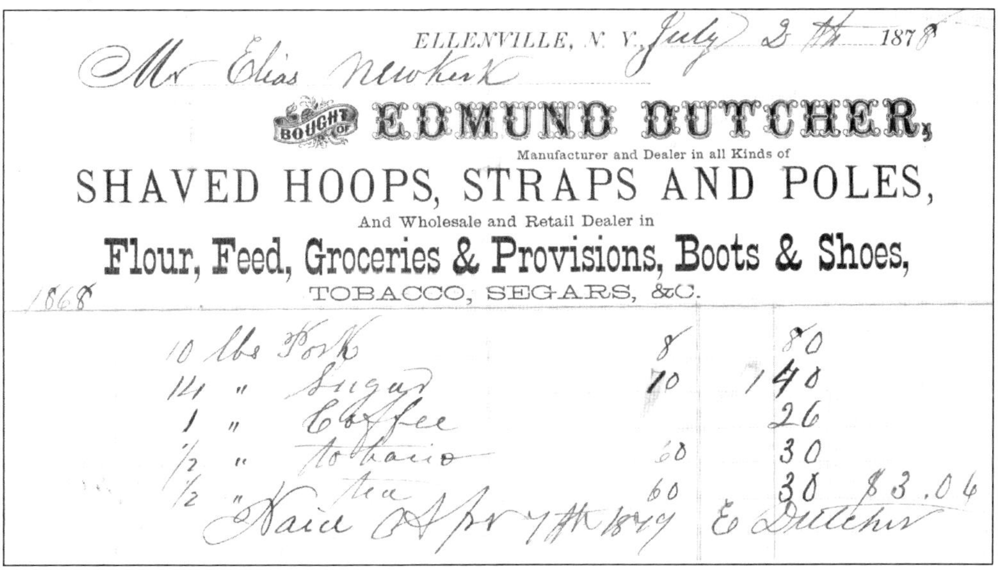
ELLENVILLE, N. Y., July 2th 1878

Mr Elias Newkerk

BOUGHT OF EDMUND DUTCHER,

Manufacturer and Dealer in all Kinds of

SHAVED HOOPS, STRAPS AND POLES,

And Wholesale and Retail Dealer in

Flour, Feed, Groceries & Provisions, Boots & Shoes,

TOBACCO, SEGARS, &C.

10 lbs Pork	8	80	
14 " Sugar	10	1 40	
1 " Coffee		26	
½ " Tobacco	60	30	
½ " Tea	60	30	$3.06

Paid Apr 7th 1879 E Dutcher

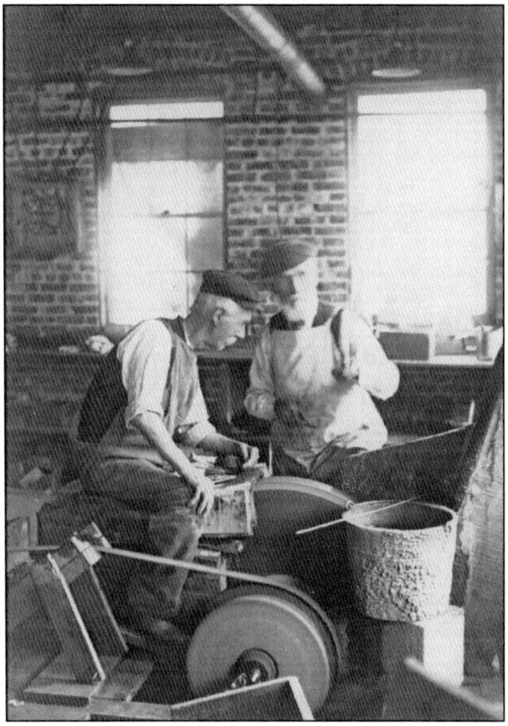

Master grinder Charles Joby, at his grinding station, confers with Ulster Knife Company superintendent William Booth. Both gentlemen were trained in knife making in Sheffield, England. In 1864, at the age of 21, Booth immigrated to Naugatuck, Connecticut, after completing an apprenticeship with a Sheffield cutler. Joby and his wife, Ann Elizabeth, came to Ellenville in 1880.

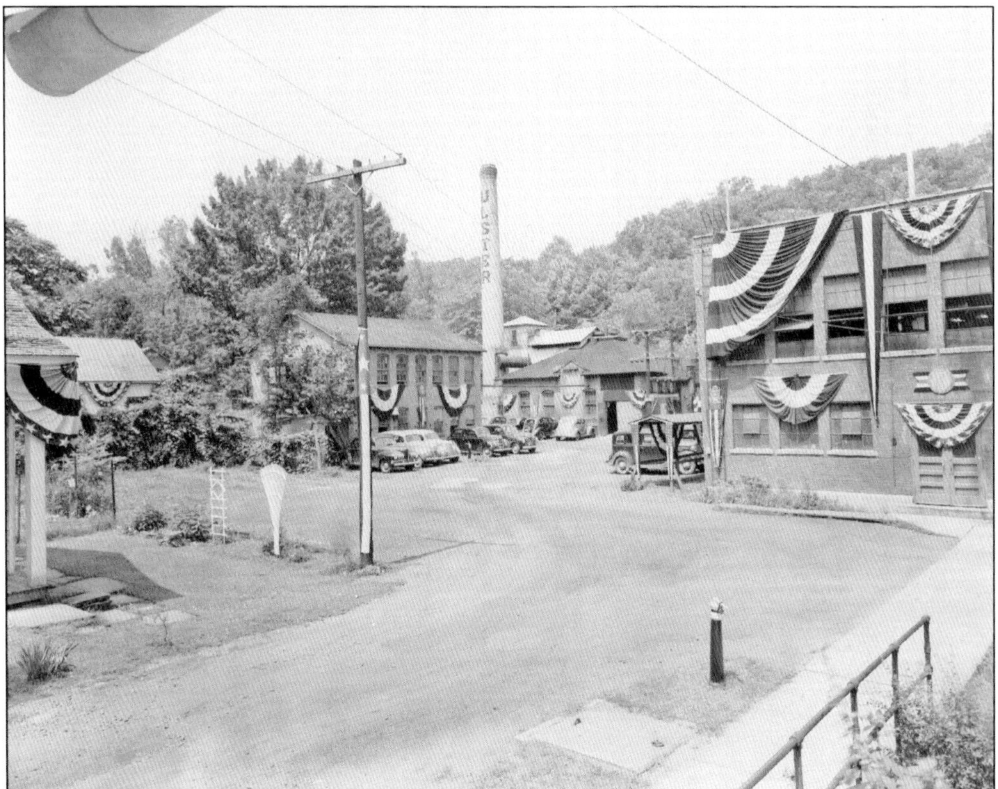

The Ulster Knife Company received the Army-Navy Production Award in July 1945 for "great accomplishment in the production of materials needed by our Armed Forces." A letter from Under Secretary of War Robert P. Patterson thanks employees of the company "for their contribution to the World War II war effort." They each got a lapel pin to wear as a sign of distinguished service. Canal Street Cutlery is located here now.

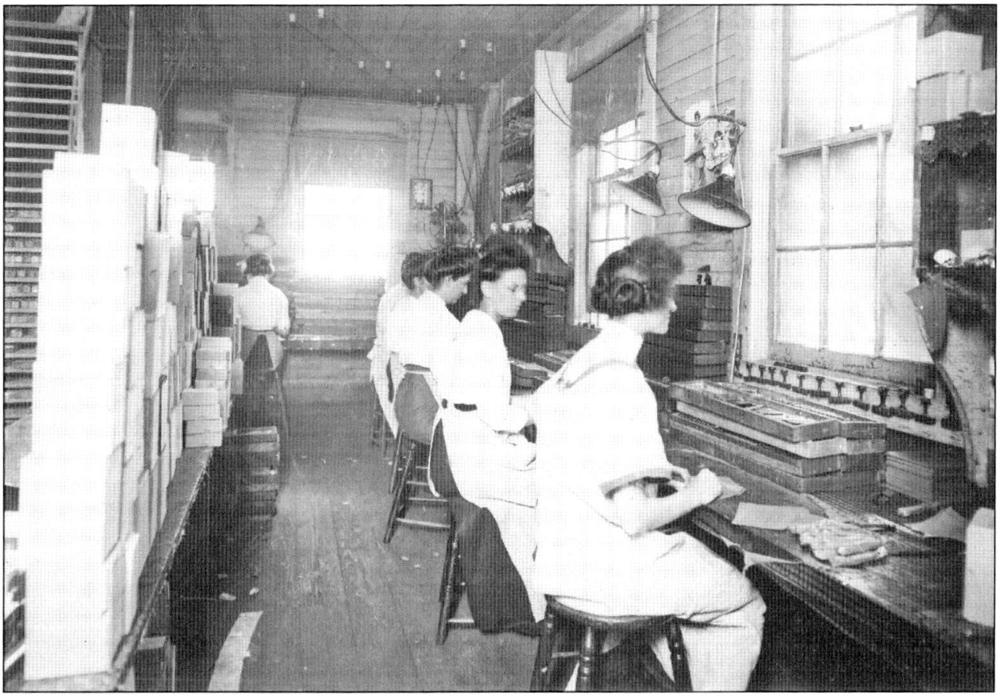

The photograph above is an early 1900s image of women working in the packing room at Ulster Knife Company on Canal Street. Women often worked in knife manufacturing factories in the packing department. This building is the current location of Canal Street Cutlery. The 1940s brought many changes to Ellenville knife manufacturing. In 1942, Imperial Knife Company of Providence, Rhode Island, united with Ulster Knife Company to become Imperial Knife Associated Companies. In 1946, Imperial Knife bought the Schrade Cutlery Company of Walden, New York. Pictured below are employees at the newly formed Imperial Schrade Cutlery Corporation owned by Albert and Henry Baer. Local managers were Herbert Hess, William Winchell, and William Smith. Among the employees are shipping clerk Virginia Bollin and office staff members Elvira Hess, Henriette Evans, Lillian Richards, and Freeda VanKeuren. The knife factory was located on the former site of Bloomer's Foundry, one of Ellenville's earliest businesses.

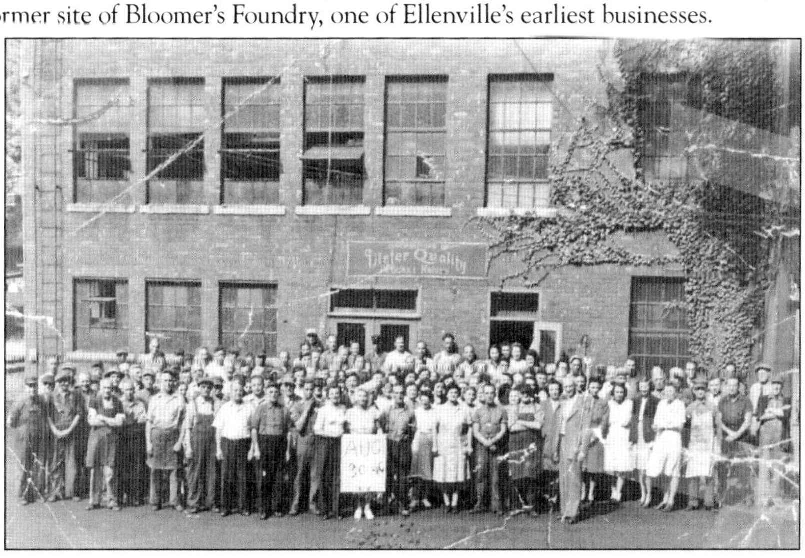

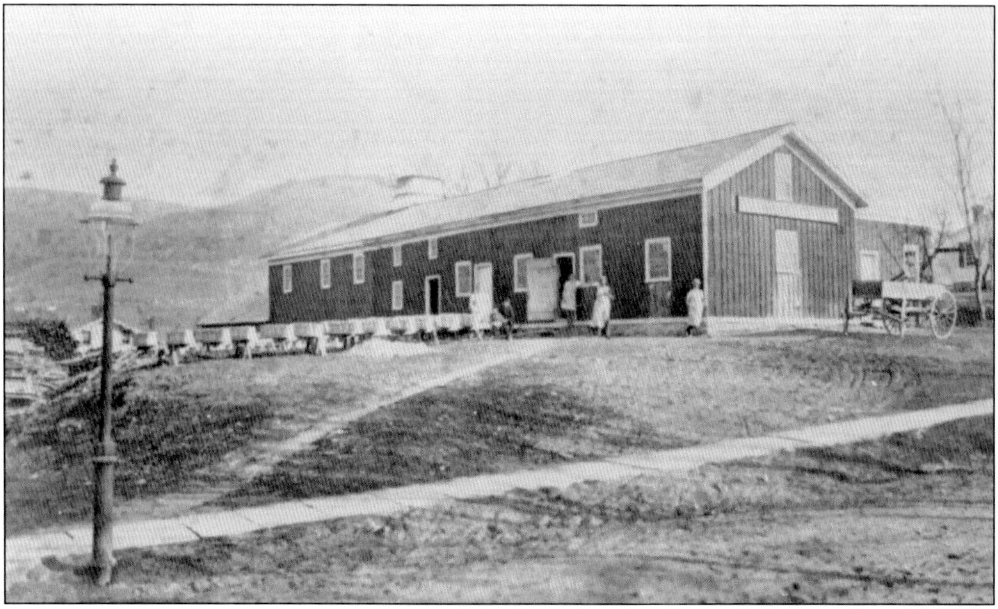

Pottery manufacturing was a major industry in Ellenville for nearly 80 years. Horace Weston, the regional Methodist circuit minister, began producing pottery in 1809 at a small shop on the corner of Market and Warren Streets. Weston, along with his new wife, Libby Briggs of Ellenville, started Weston & Co., and they were later joined in business by their sons William and Daniel. After the death of their father in 1848, the brothers operated as W.W. & D. Weston. The identifying mark on the pottery changed over the years, along with proprietors (W.W. & D. Weston, James A. Gregg, John and James Ryan). Storage crocks, preserve jars, butter pots, churns, and jugs were among the items produced. A salt glaze was used; artisans, often itinerant, painted designs on the stoneware. Hemlock and later coal were used to fire the kiln. The pottery industry in Ellenville ended in the early 1900s.

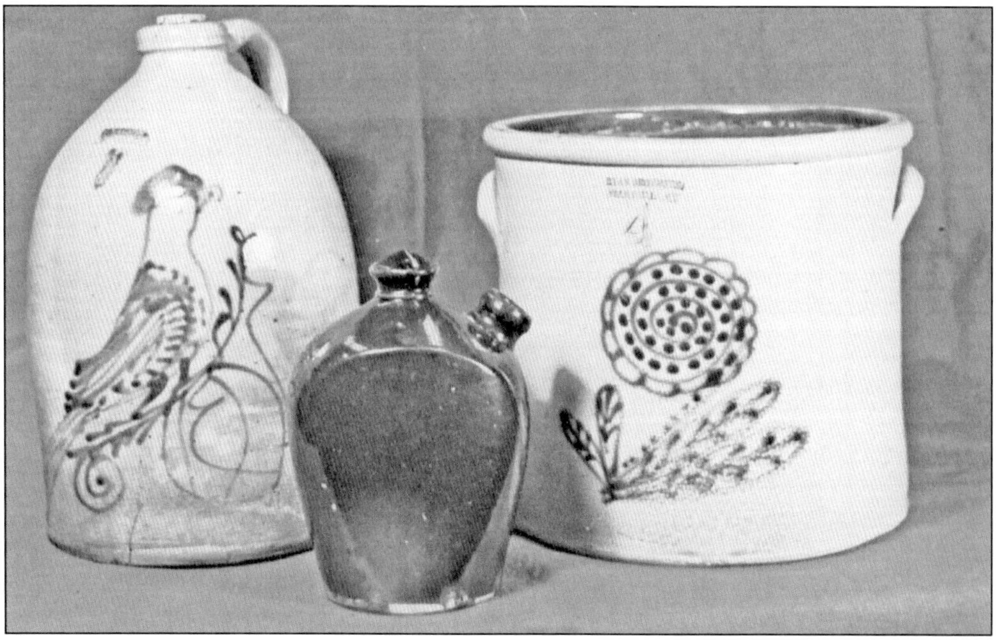

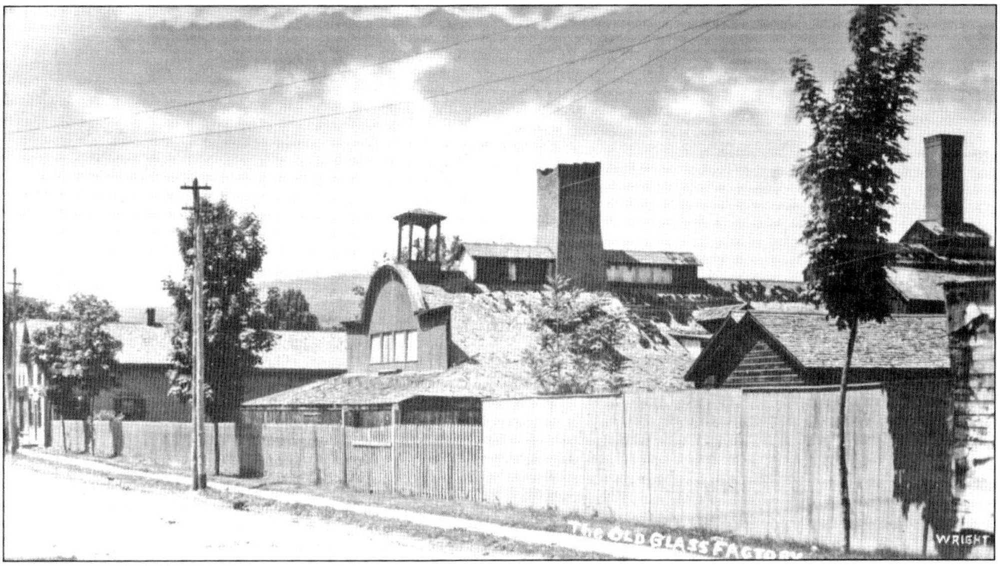

Glassmaking was a major industry here from 1839 until 1896. The Ellenville Glass Company was a large employer, operating under different corporations over the years. Located on Canal Street near Edwards, the company had its own canal slip and fleet of canalboats. The factory produced demijohns, bottles holding approximately five gallons; carboys, about twice that size; and a variety of other items. Ellenville was an ideal site for glassmaking because of the availability of wood for fuel and its proximity to the canal.

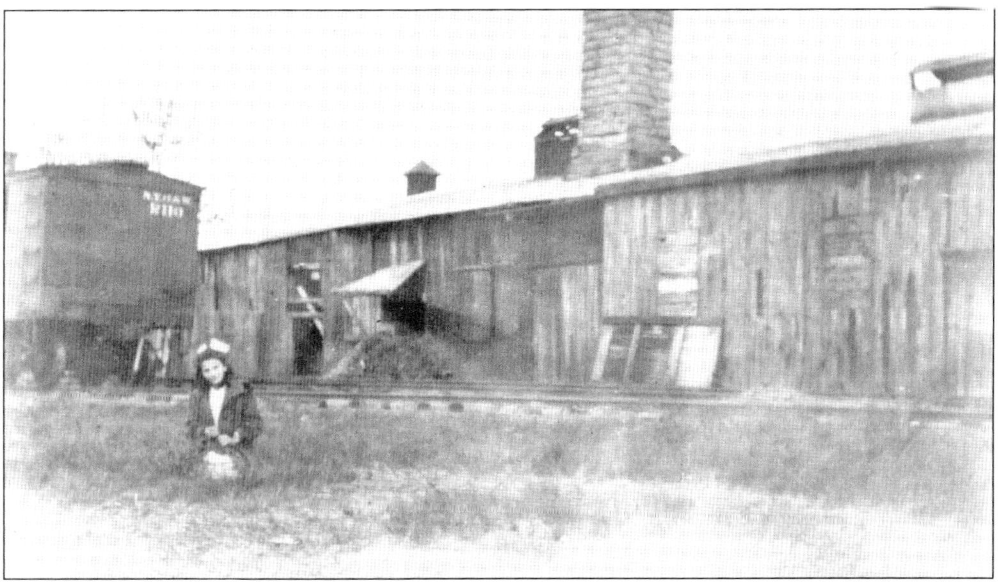

Jacob G. Bahr, a manufacturer from New York City, started the Bahr Demijohn Factory on Clinton Avenue in 1905. A demijohn was a narrow-necked bottle, typically covered with wicker. In the early years, willow from a swamp near Wawarsing was used for the wicker. Demijohns were sold in New York, New Jersey, and as far away as Cuba. The Bahr family ran the business until 1920.

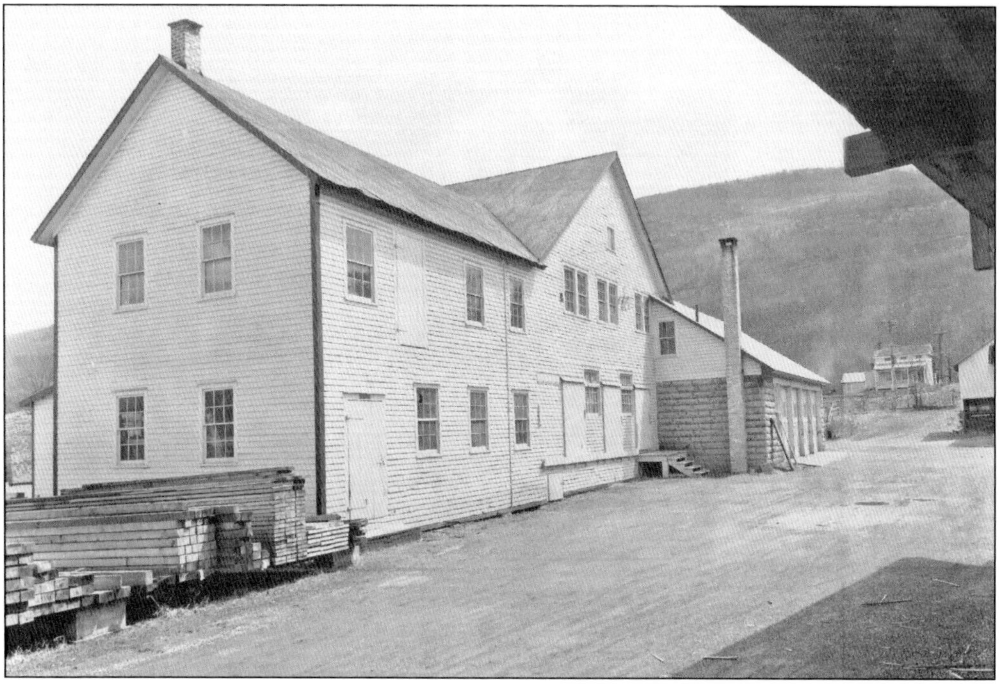

In 1869, William H. Deyo and Capt. Edwin J. Bailey, a Civil War veteran, established Bailey & Deyo Lumber Company on the corner of Canal Street and Towpath Road. Built directly on the D&H Canal, the business dealt primarily in lumber and coal and sold building materials, paints, oils, and more. Deyo and Bailey erected a mill to produce finished wood products from native lumber. When the railway was built, an extension ran between buildings for transfer of freight. The business later became William H. Deyo & Co. when Deyo bought out his partner's interest. The company was in business for over 125 years. It is the current location of Thornton Hardware, Inc.

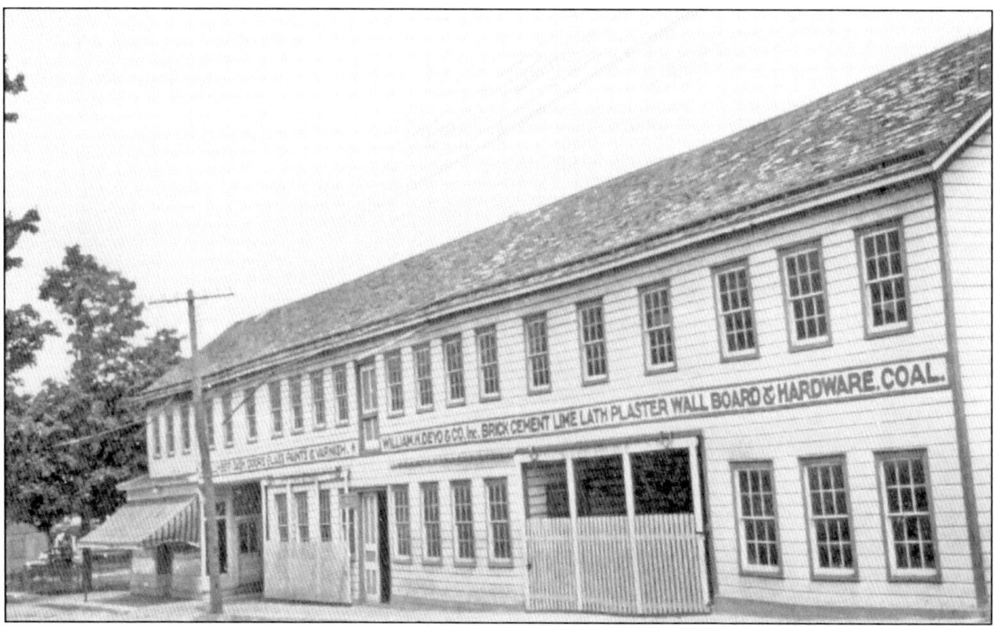

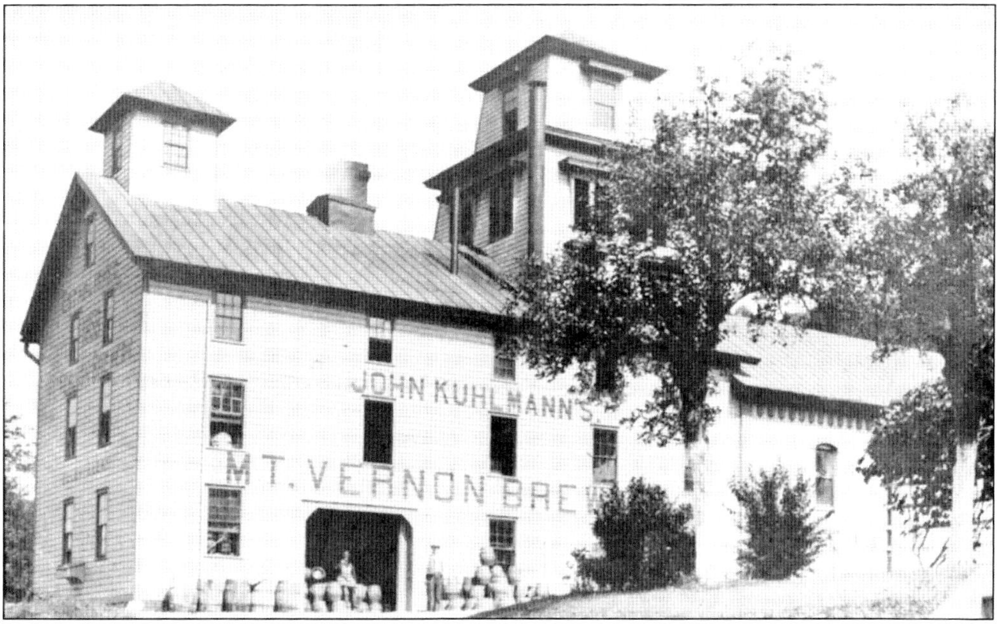

In 1858, John Kuhlmann and Jacob Kopf founded John Kuhlmann's Mount Vernon Brewery. Located at the base of the Shawangunk Mountains near the D&H Canal, the brewery made ale, lager, and soda for over 60 years. The official grand opening of the brewery was on December 21, 1859; the beer was said to be "capital." Kuhlmann soon became the sole proprietor of the business. The two-story building was set on solid rock with two cellars (one for ale and one for lager) hand-carved underneath. The first story contained the furnace room and malting and brewing equipment. The second stored barley, a mill to grind the barley, and a vat to cool the product before it was put into barrels. Two wings housed the office, stock, and horsepower machinery

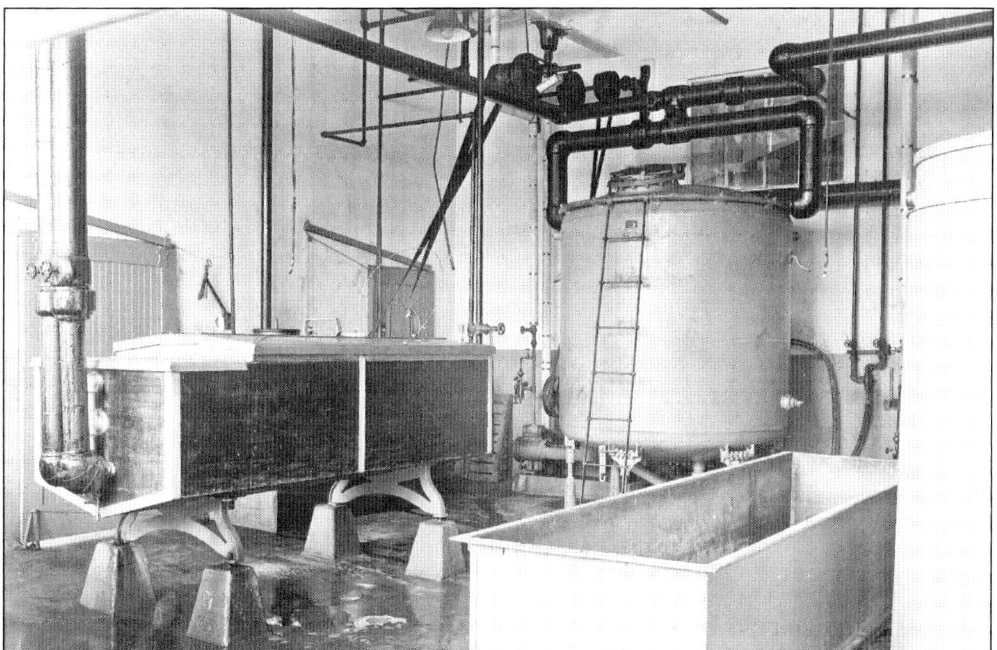

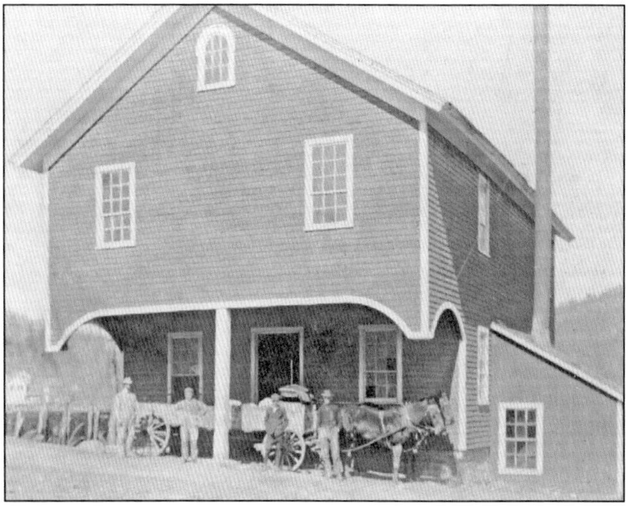

Located at Five Points on today's Cape Avenue next to Beerkill Creek, the Red Mill was built in the mid-1800s as a gristmill. Farmers brought grain for grinding and often paid with flour. The Beerkill was dammed to make the millpond, which was also used for winter skating. The property belonged to Alfred B. Terwilliger until his death in 1910, when Dwight Divine, who owned the neighboring knife factory, purchased it. Millers over the years included William Morse, John Morse, Sidney Decker, and James McKney.

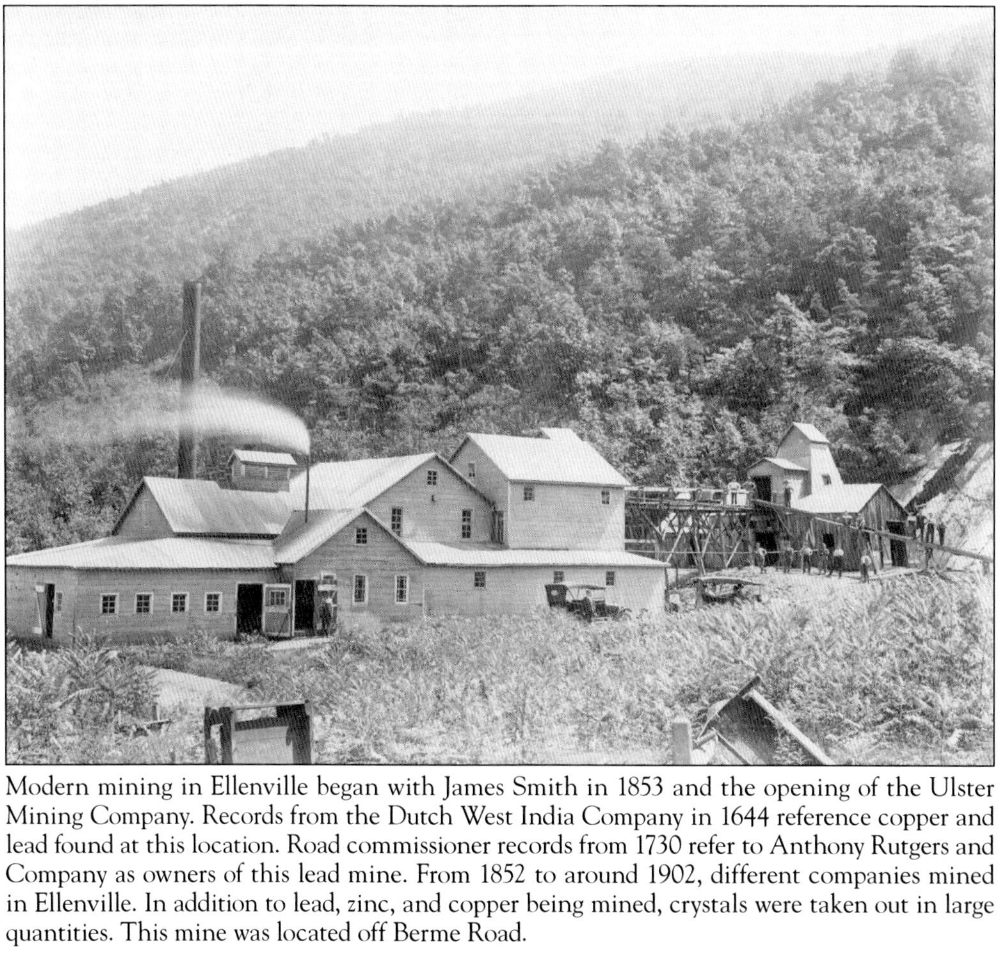

Modern mining in Ellenville began with James Smith in 1853 and the opening of the Ulster Mining Company. Records from the Dutch West India Company in 1644 reference copper and lead found at this location. Road commissioner records from 1730 refer to Anthony Rutgers and Company as owners of this lead mine. From 1852 to around 1902, different companies mined in Ellenville. In addition to lead, zinc, and copper being mined, crystals were taken out in large quantities. This mine was located off Berme Road.

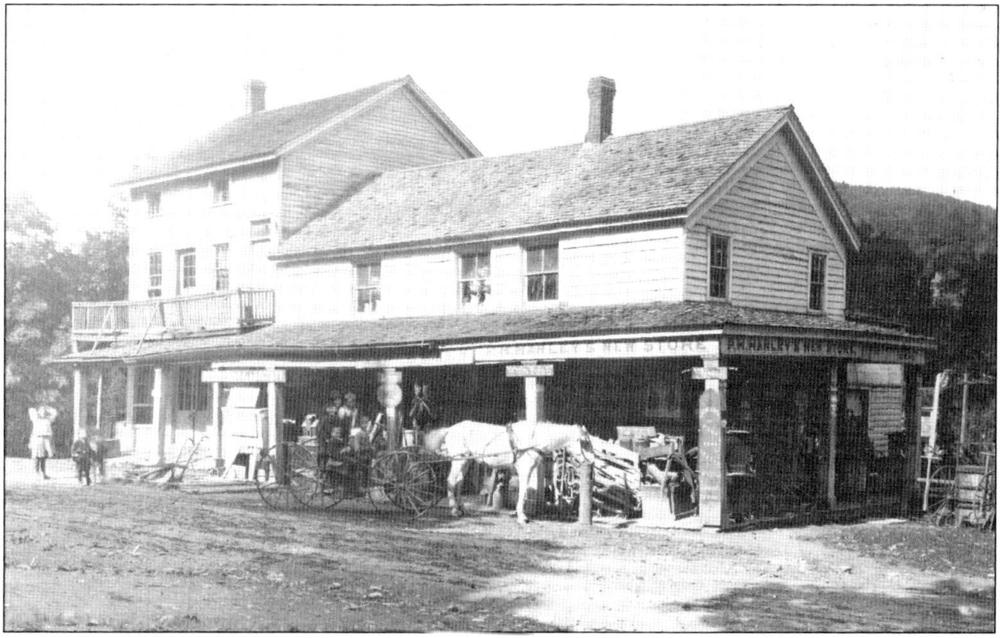

Patrick H. Hanley emigrated from Ireland as a child in 1846. Hanley ran a livery stable and dry goods business in Ellenville's west end; he also dealt in canalboats and related supplies. Brothers Thomas and Owen were blacksmiths. Hanley opened his new store at "the Points" on Canal Street around 1891. Wilson's Deli is located at the Points today, where one of Ellenville's oldest businesses, Bloomer's Store, once was. (Courtesy of Pam Kuhlmann.)

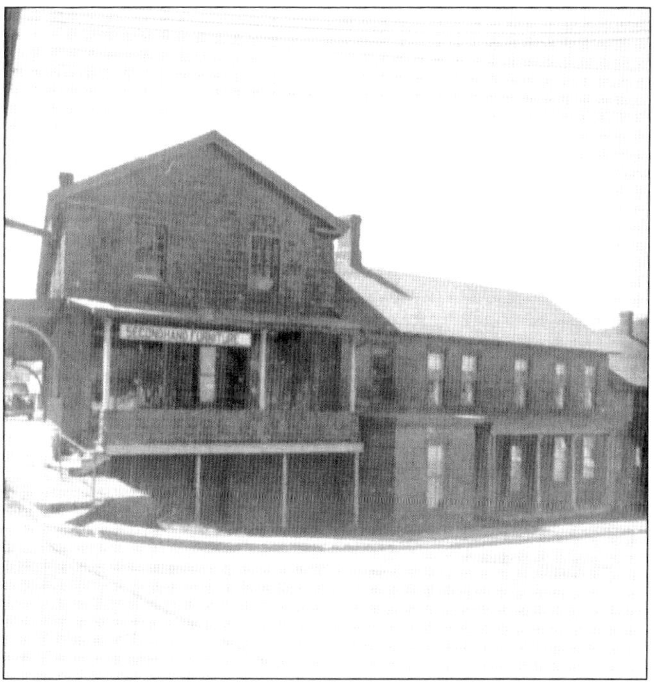

At the opposite end of Ellenville from Hanley's, VanWagener General Merchandise operated for 90 years at 223 Canal Street, facing the D&H Canal. An *Ellenville Journal* article written when the store closed in 1948 notes that "canalers considered the store their headquarters." J.J. VanWagener ran the store until his death in 1856. His son Silas continued the business until 1938, when longtime employee Edward Rippert took over. This is the current location of Family of Ellenville.

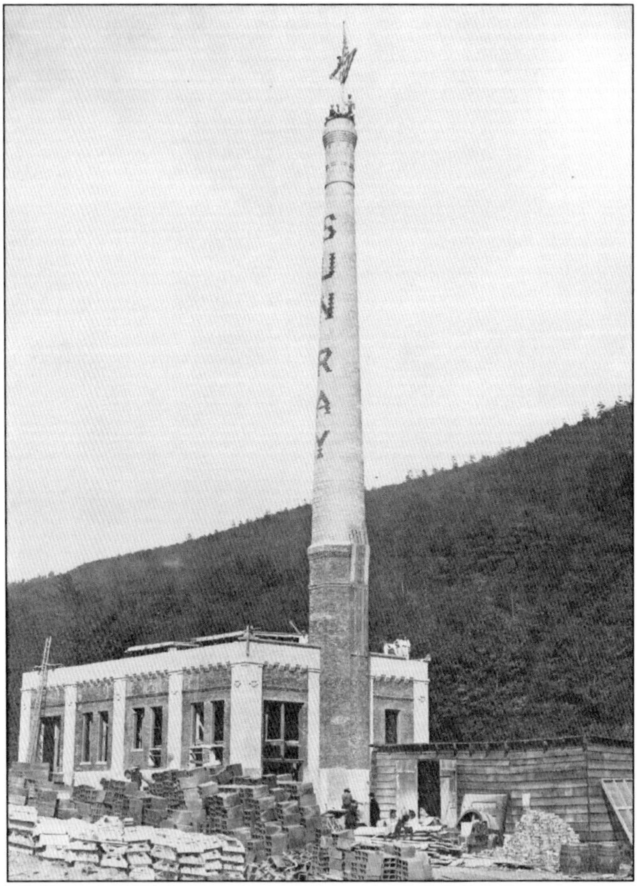

The first shovelful of earth for Sun Ray Bottling Plant was dug in February 1907. According to an *Ellenville Journal* article, "Sightseers flocked to watch its erection." Sun Ray was the largest bottling plant in the world at the time. Bottled water was first shipped on the O&W Railway in September of that year, and Clayton's Band played at celebratory ceremonies. The company was surrounded by a beautiful park for public enjoyment. Expectations were high for the amount of business and tourism that the plant and tunnel would bring to Ellenville; this influenced local growth, including the building of the Wayside Inn. When it opened, the plant produced approximately 30,000 bottles a day. Interior walls were lined with white glazed brick, and cleanliness was paramount. Employees at Sun Ray wore white. Alfred Gaskell from Wisconsin was hired as superintendent.

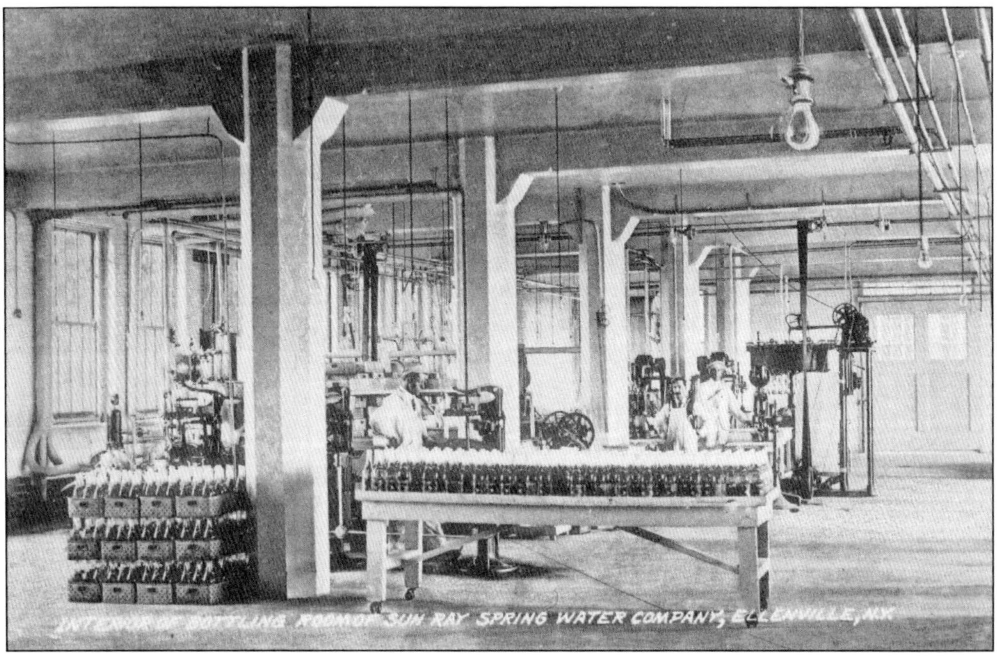

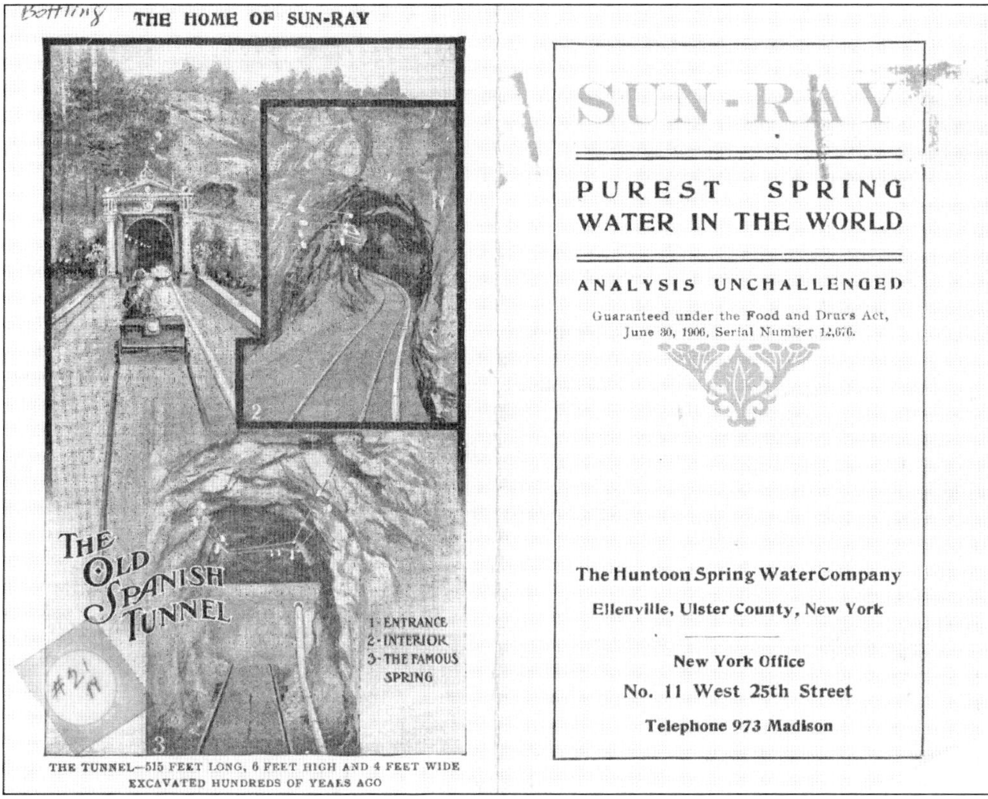

William R. Hinsdale, who worked for the Ellenville Zinc Company, believed in the local legend of an artisan spring and tunnel discovered and cleared centuries ago by early settlers. He purchased land where he thought the spring was, and after digging some 500 feet into the mountainside, the tunnel was cleared and the spring rediscovered. Tracks were laid so people could ride into the tunnel; the steady flow of water from the spring was estimated at 30 gallons per minute. A cement and stone trench now marks the entrance to the old tunnel, which may originally have been dug for mining. The spring still flows down the mountainside, and Sun Ray's water was publicized as the "purest spring water in the world." The company also produced ginger ale and sparkling water.

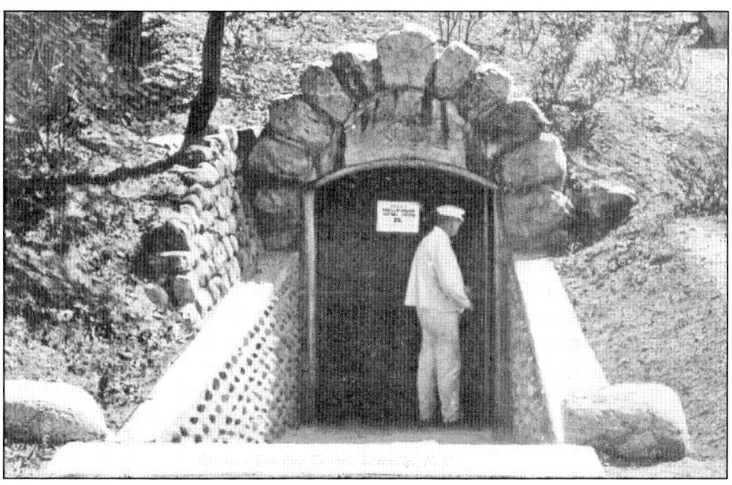

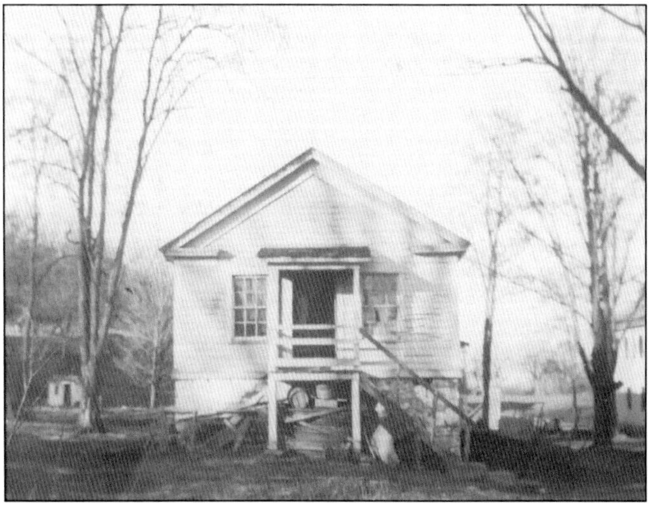

A successful tanner from Dutchess County, Abram Schultz moved to the area in 1839 and opened the Leurenkill Tannery. Schultz developed a tanning process using oak as well as hemlock in the leather baths. Called union leather, the product was more durable and attractive. Shultz's sons were active in the industry; one, Jackson, wrote a book on leather manufacturing. He was also appointed by President Grant to be chief commissioner to the Vienna Exposition of 1873.

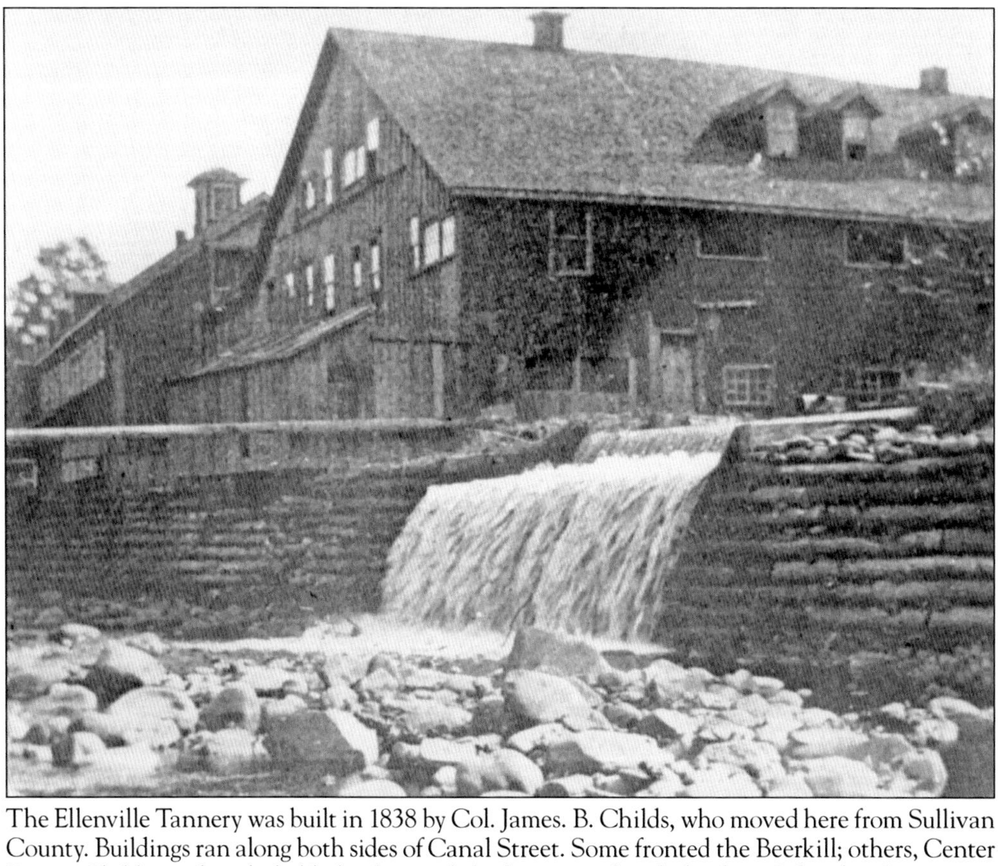

The Ellenville Tannery was built in 1838 by Col. James. B. Childs, who moved here from Sullivan County. Buildings ran along both sides of Canal Street. Some fronted the Beerkill; others, Center Street. Childs produced pliable leather and thicker, smooth sole leather. Other local tanneries included the Wawarsing Tannery, the Honk Hill Tannery, and smaller family-run operations. The loss of hemlock trees and the Industrial Revolution contributed to the demise of the tanning industry here.

Four

Where People Stayed and Played

Residents of Ellenville demonstrated a wide array of talents during the years depicted here, and they were known for their willingness to share them. Musicians and band concerts along with parades and holidays were a source of community pride. The Ellenville Driving Park, which later became the grounds of the Ulster County Fair, was the site of well-attended events such as horse and foot racing, public festivals, circuses, and other local competitions. With the onset of the hospitality industry that followed the arrival of the railroad, Ellenville became the home of several famous hotels and boardinghouses. These drew popular entertainers, artists, celebrities, and guests to the area. By the early 20th century, the new movie theaters became a great source of entertainment not only for weekend and summer guests but also for local residents. This chapter gives a taste of the vibrant public places and events that are characteristic of the Ellenville community.

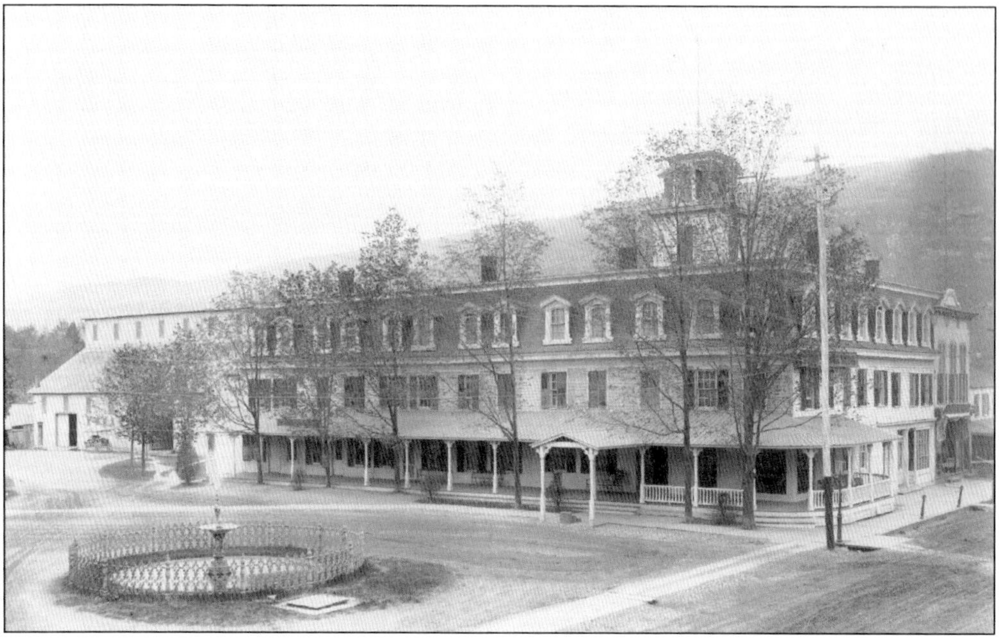

When fire destroyed his Cottage Hotel in 1847, Eli Terwilliger purchased a small hotel owned by George Bailey at the corner of Canal Street and Liberty Square. This photograph shows the Terwilliger House as it was expanded by 1869; the livery stable can be seen at the left. The hotel offered long-term residential as well as transient accommodations and provided areas for business and social functions for the community. In 1873, the hotel was sold to Abraham Constable, who operated Terwilliger House with a partner until 1880 and then as sole proprietor until fire consumed the structure in 1904. The image below shows guests playing cards in the parlor, one of the common rooms offered by the hotel. In addition, the dining room afforded fine cuisine and service, with quality wines and liquors available at the bar.

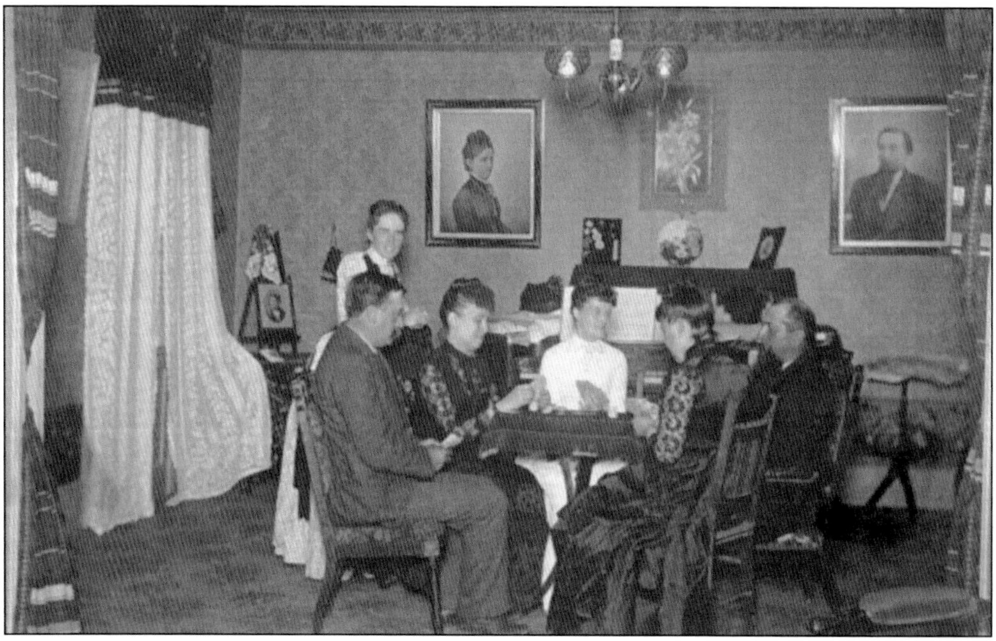

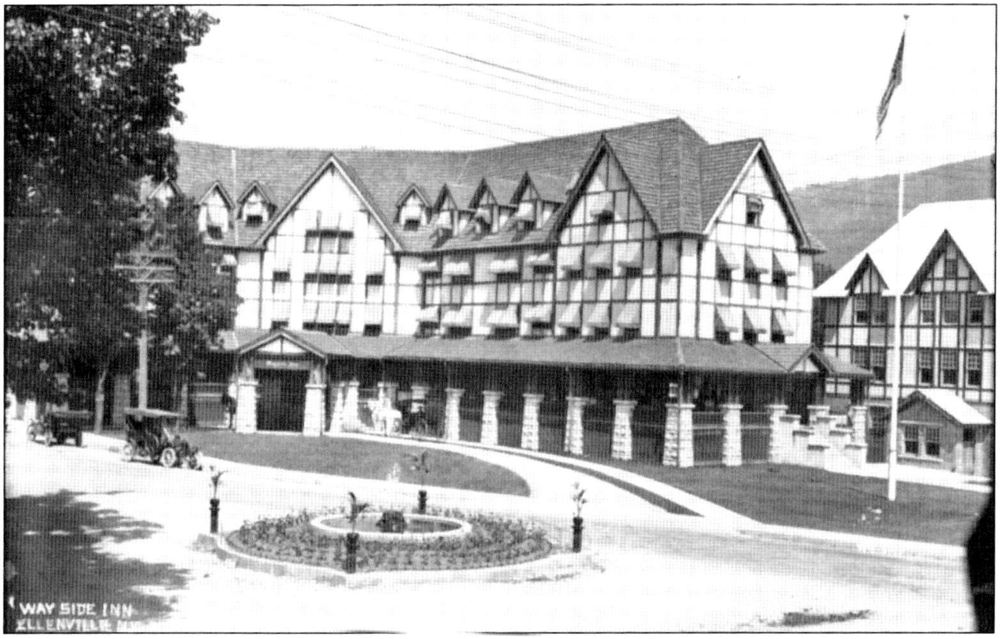

The Wayside Inn on Liberty Square opened in 1908. Built by Oscar and Laura Krause, it was owned by the Ellenville Hotel Company, with Krause as its first proprietor. A newspaper article highlights over 200 mahogany dressers, washstands, and chiffoniers with cut glass knobs made by Gregory & Barnes for the Wayside. In addition to accommodating guests and boarders, the hotel hosted numerous social clubs and organizations from throughout the region for meetings and events. The dining room could seat 400, and Sun Ray water was served. An electric bus shuttled guests to and from Ontario & Western trains. The Wayside was purchased and renovated by three New York City men after foreclosure in 1917; the inaugural banquet pictured below celebrated its reopening. The Wayside was destroyed by fire in 1967, but two of its 30 locally quarried stone pillars still stand on Bogardus Street. The Publik House restaurant is on this site today.

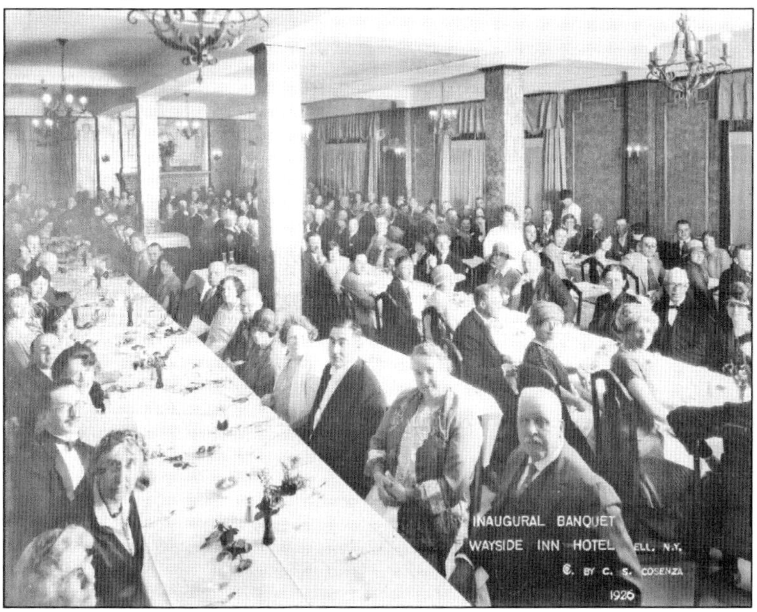

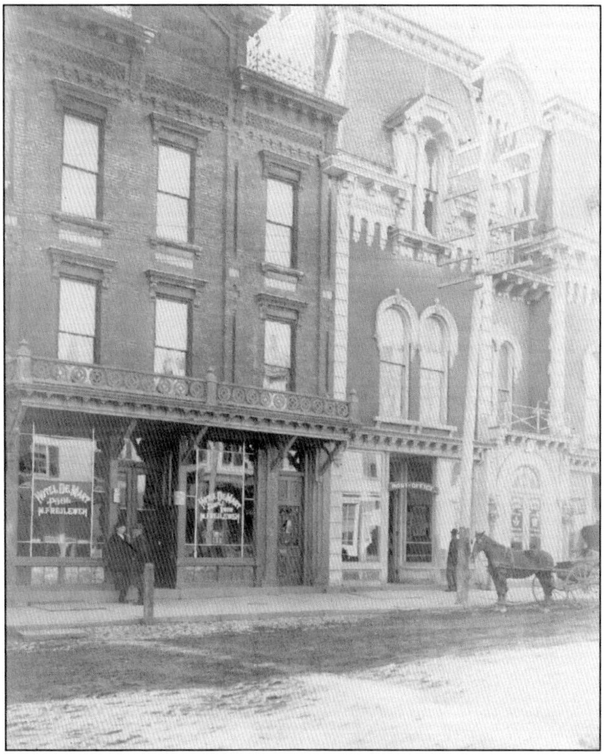

In 1890, Hotel DeMart boasted "the Best Building and Pleasantest Rooms in Ellenville" and served fine meals, superior wines, liquors, and cigars. Located at 139 Canal Street and operated by proprietor Martin Freileweh, Hotel DeMart later became Higgins Hotel, then Central House (Hotel), and finally, the Rendezvous, a bar. The building burned down in the 1960s.

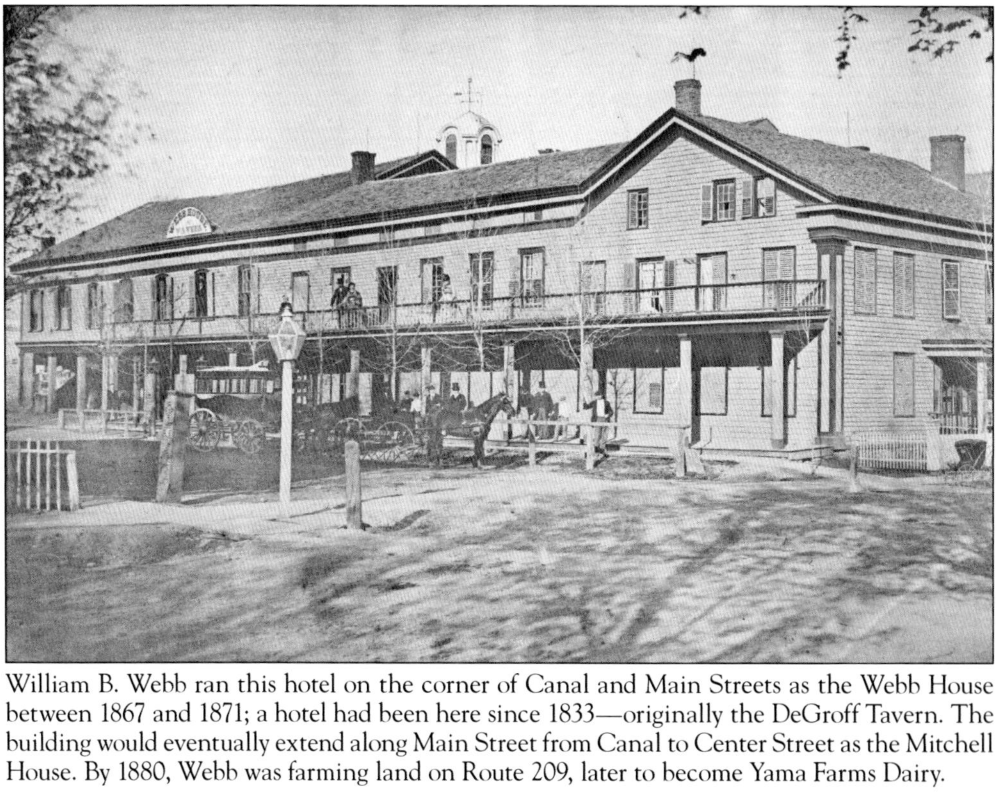

William B. Webb ran this hotel on the corner of Canal and Main Streets as the Webb House between 1867 and 1871; a hotel had been here since 1833—originally the DeGroff Tavern. The building would eventually extend along Main Street from Canal to Center Street as the Mitchell House. By 1880, Webb was farming land on Route 209, later to become Yama Farms Dairy.

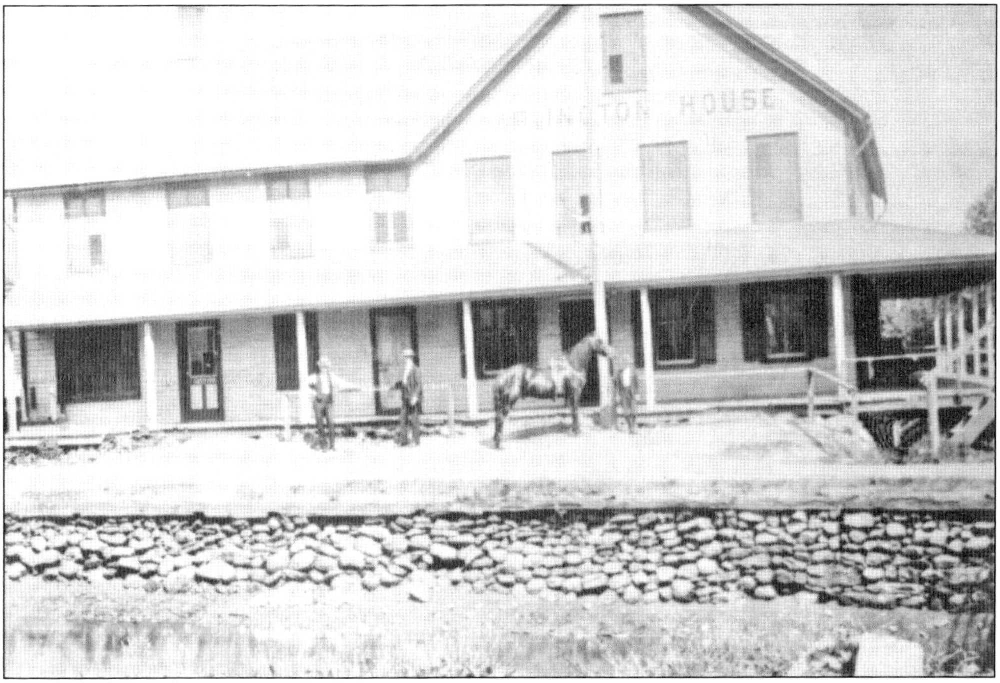

Formerly the Russell House, the Arlington House on the canal opened in 1899. As early as 1832, a hotel called the Boatman's House was here, operated by Zabina Lee. Arlington House offered accommodations for permanent or transient guests, dinner, a well-stocked bar with cigars, and a poolroom. In 1911, the building was converted into a handkerchief factory, and later became an apartment building. It was torn down in the 1970s.

Originally DeGroff Tavern, the corner of Main and Center Streets had been the site of a hotel since 1833, including the Webb House, Cushman House, and Elting House. It became known as the Mitchell House when it was purchased by Walter E. Mitchell in 1893. Future owners would keep this name until the building was demolished in 1956 for the construction of the First National Bank and Trust Company.

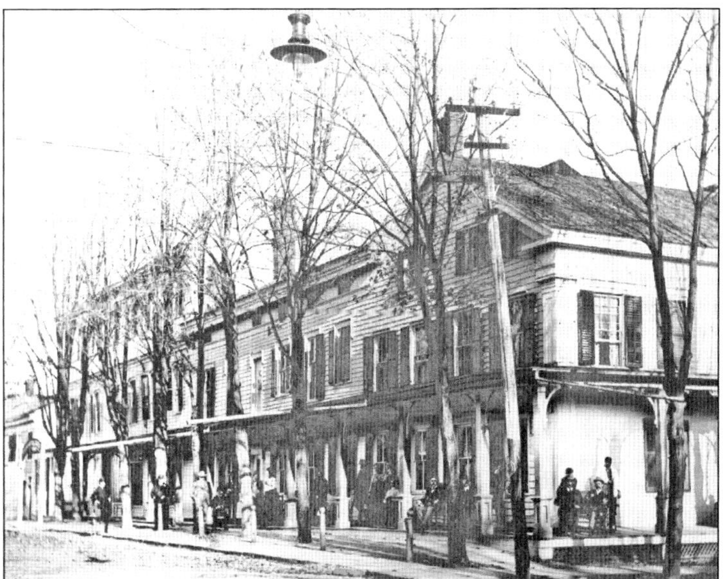

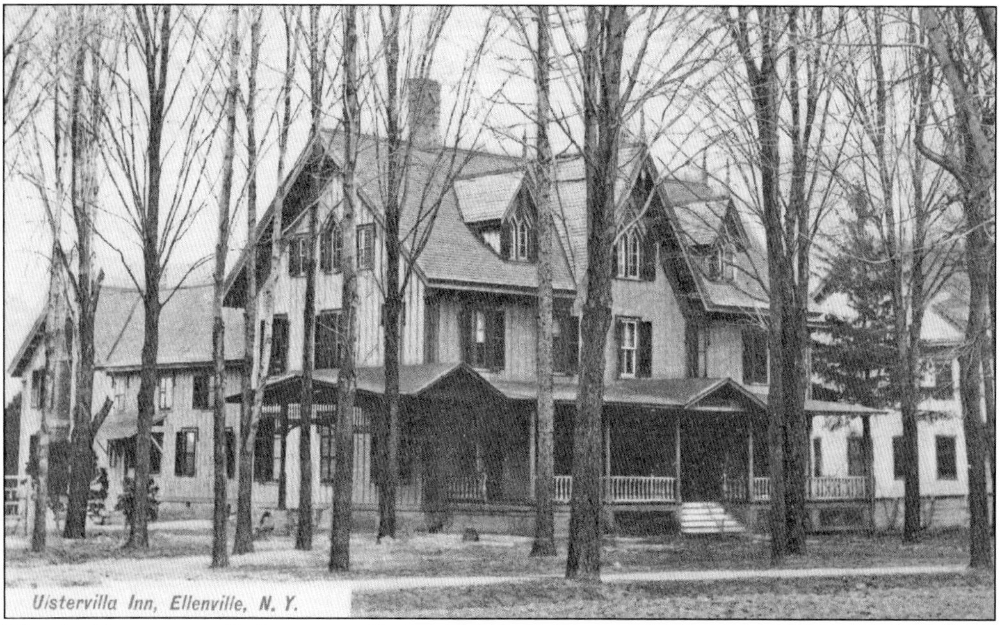

This building, originally known as Gothic Hall, had been used to house students attending Post Academy, the precursor to Ellenville High School. In 1871, Laura Post converted it into Maplewood Boardinghouse. It was run by Emma Hardenbergh (Mrs. Newton) LeFevre until purchased by Daniel E. Hoornbeek, who renamed it Ulster Villa Inn. The hotel accommodated 75 guests from May 1 through October.

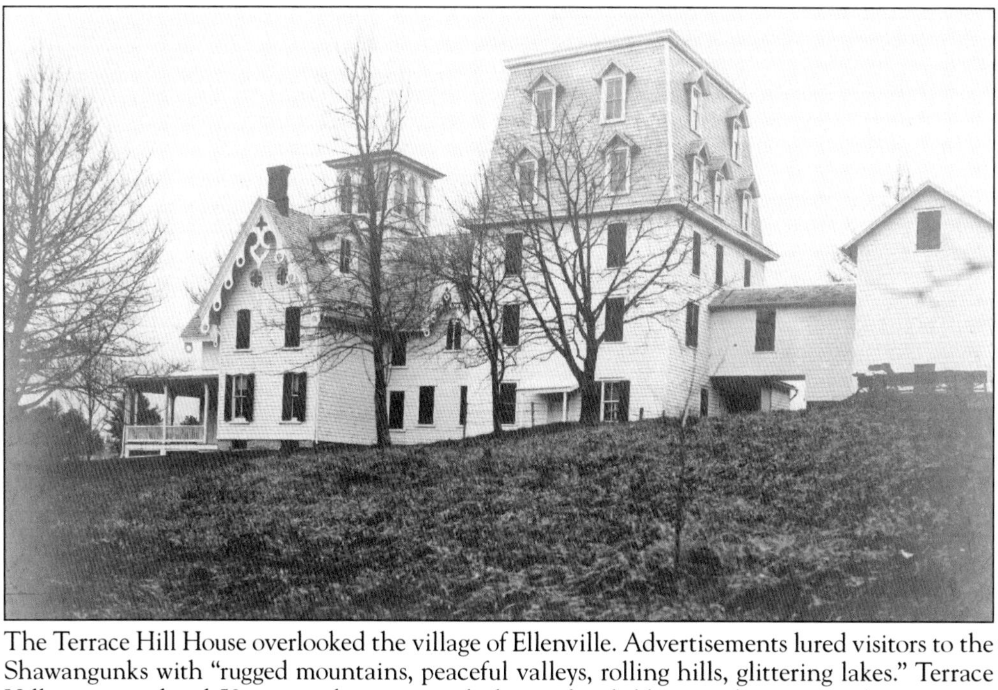

The Terrace Hill House overlooked the village of Ellenville. Advertisements lured visitors to the Shawangunks with "rugged mountains, peaceful valleys, rolling hills, glittering lakes." Terrace Hill accommodated 50 guests; there was a playhouse for children, with tennis and croquet. In 1917, weekly rates were $10 to $15 or $2 daily for transients. Fire destroyed much of the building in 1952. The central portion is part of the Terrace Hill Motel, operating there today.

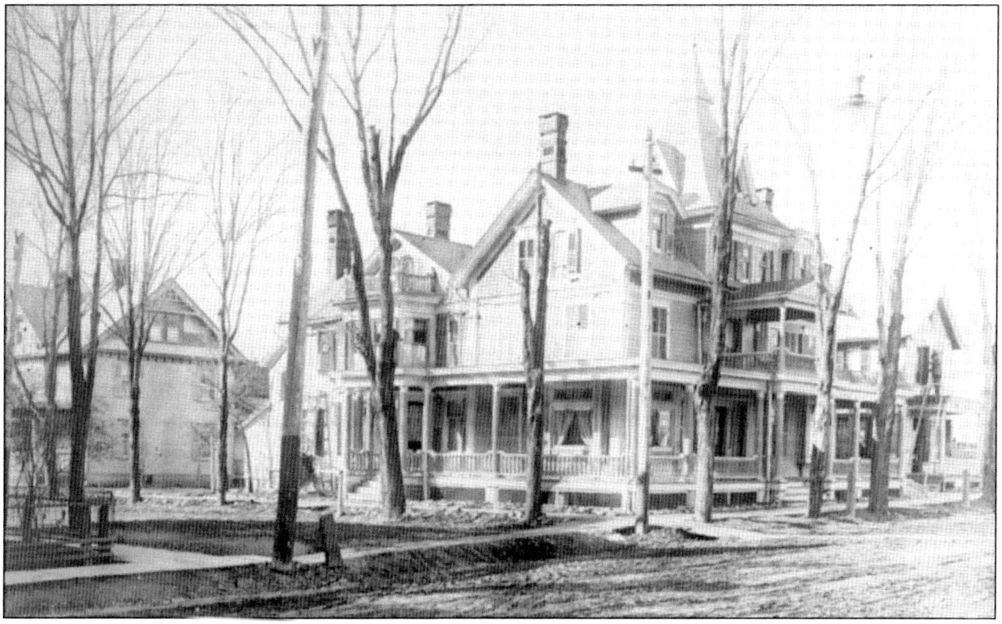

This ornate Victorian building was operated at the turn of the 20th century as Ulster Villa, a boardinghouse, by Daniel E. Hoornbeek. It was located on the corner of Canal and Church Streets, directly opposite the Reformed church. Hoornbeek owned a woodworking plant nearby. In 1905, he sold this property and purchased a boardinghouse on Maple Avenue known as Maplewood, changing its name to Ulster Villa Inn.

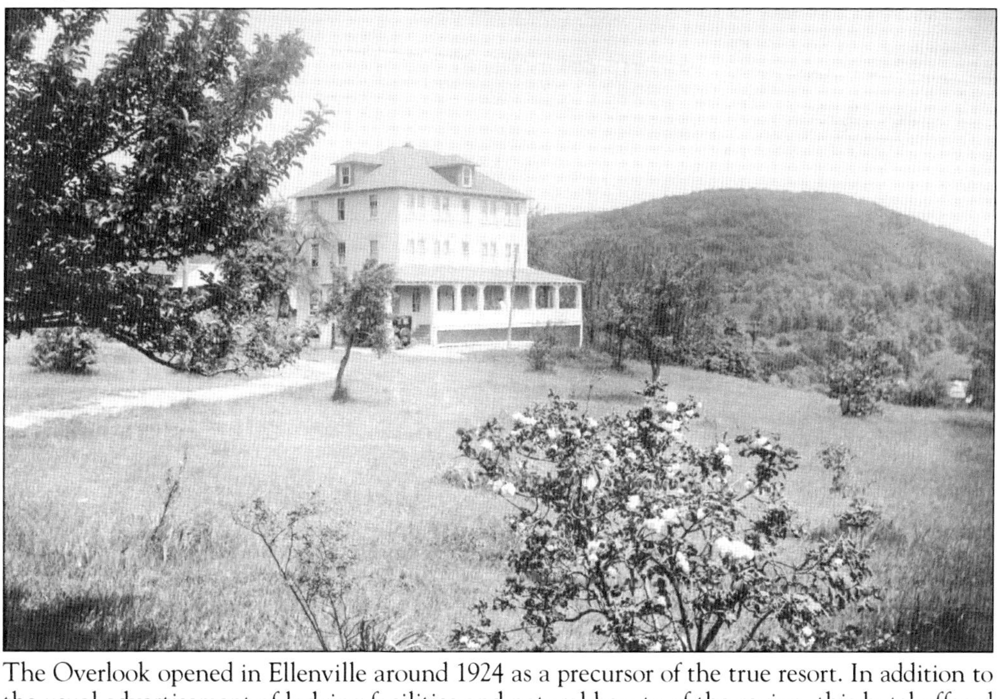

The Overlook opened in Ellenville around 1924 as a precursor of the true resort. In addition to the usual advertisement of lodging facilities and natural beauty of the region, this hotel offered a private pool and lake with swimming, rowing, and fishing. A common living room boasted a radio, and an orchestra furnished music for the dining room and casino.

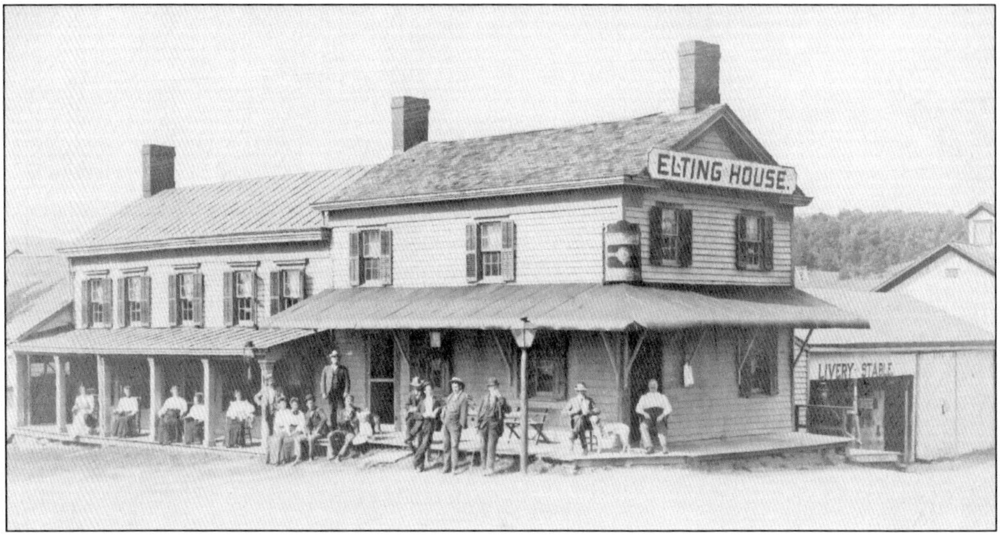

The Elting House included a hotel and summer residence for transient and permanent guests. An 1890s advertisement promises a well-stocked bar with fine wines, liquors, and ales, as well as choice foreign and domestic cigars. Also at the Elting House was a barbershop and hairdressing salon. A livery stable, operated by Richard Elting, dealt in fine road horses, wagons, and carriages: "Fine Teams and Matching up a Specialty."

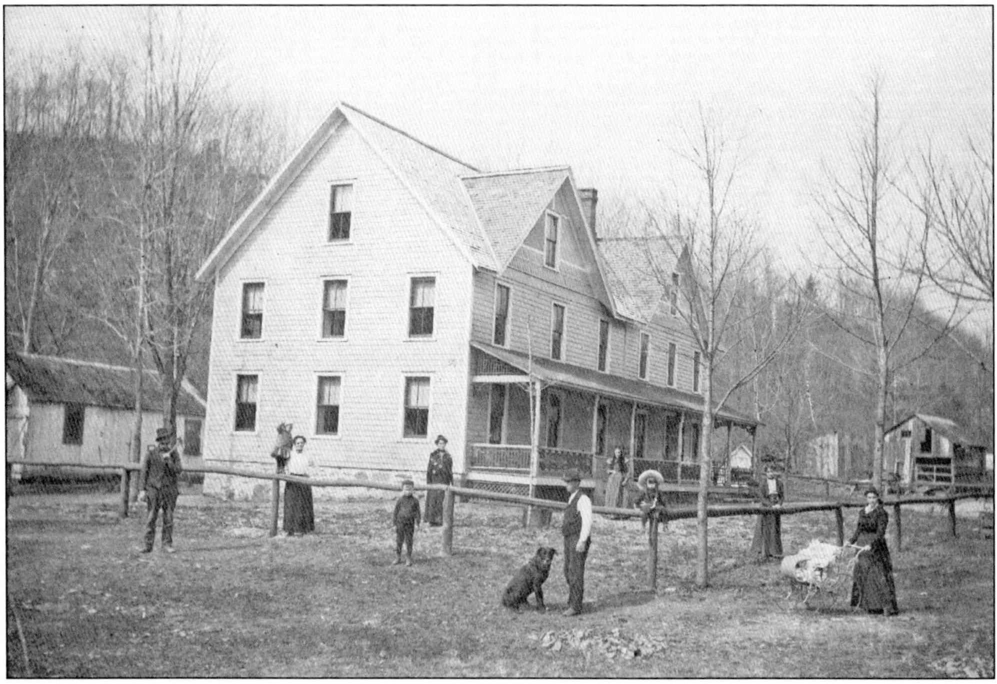

The Hasbrouck House was a summer boardinghouse between Ellenville and Greenfield. Owned and operated by generations of the William Hasbrouck family, it was open from the mid-1800s until 1945. The Hasbrouck House accommodated 40 guests and offered tennis, croquet, swings, hammocks, and many wooded paths. Guests were encouraged to swim in the "swimming pool" of Beerkill Creek. In the late 1950s, the house, which still stands, was made into apartments. (Courtesy of Pam Kuhlmann.)

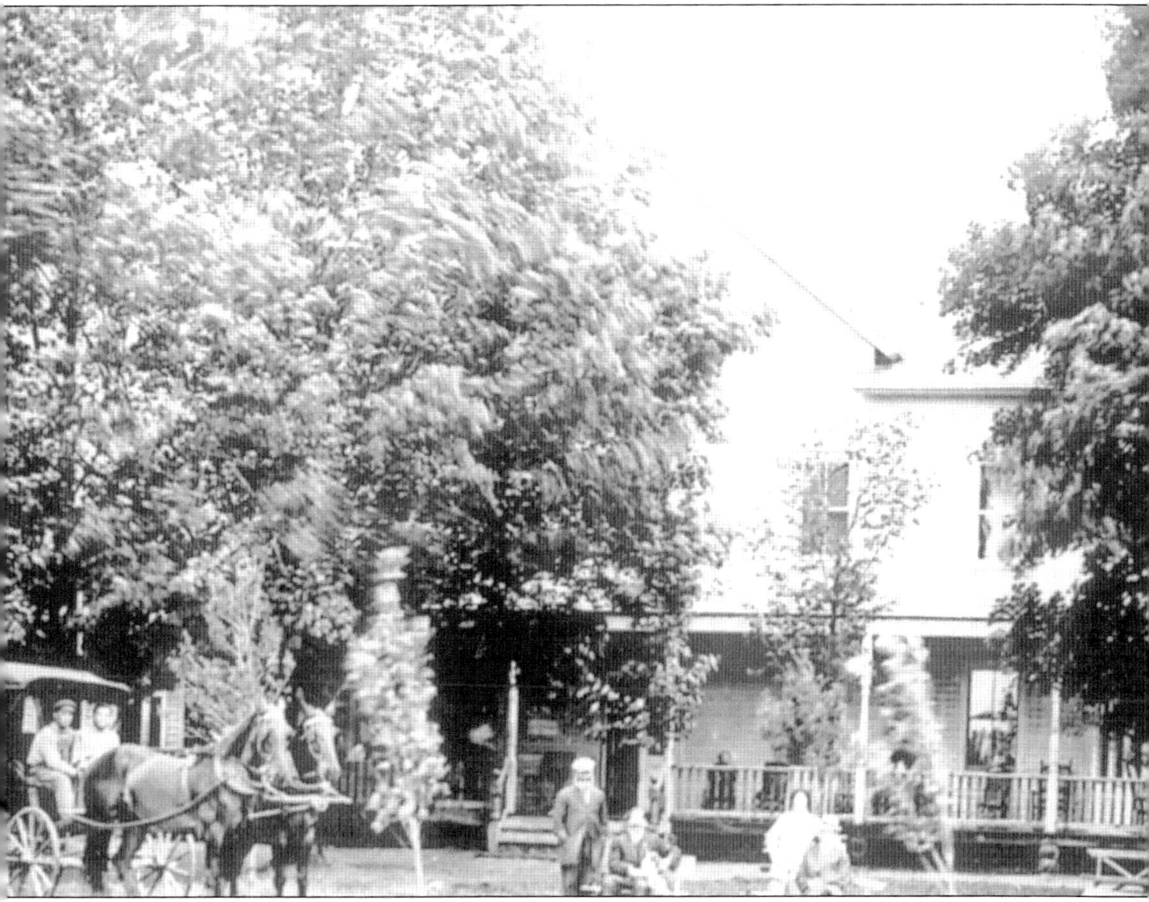

Charles Slutsky (center) emigrated from Russia around 1902 with three of his children; his wife, Rebecca, and remaining five children followed. Slutsky purchased a small farm, where he ran a boardinghouse named the Nevele, after nearby Nevele Falls. The story is told that the name Nevele originated when a group of young ladies visited the falls for a picnic in 1898. They decided to reverse the spelling of their number—there were 11 in the party—hence, the name Nevele was born. By 1932, the Nevele had grown into the Nevele Mansion hotel. Slutsky's sons Benjamin and Joseph split the business, creating the Fallsview Hotel (now Honors Haven) and the Nevele Country Club. The Nevele would become one of the most renowned resorts in the area, owned by the Slutsky family for several generations. (Courtesy of J. Bernard Slutsky.)

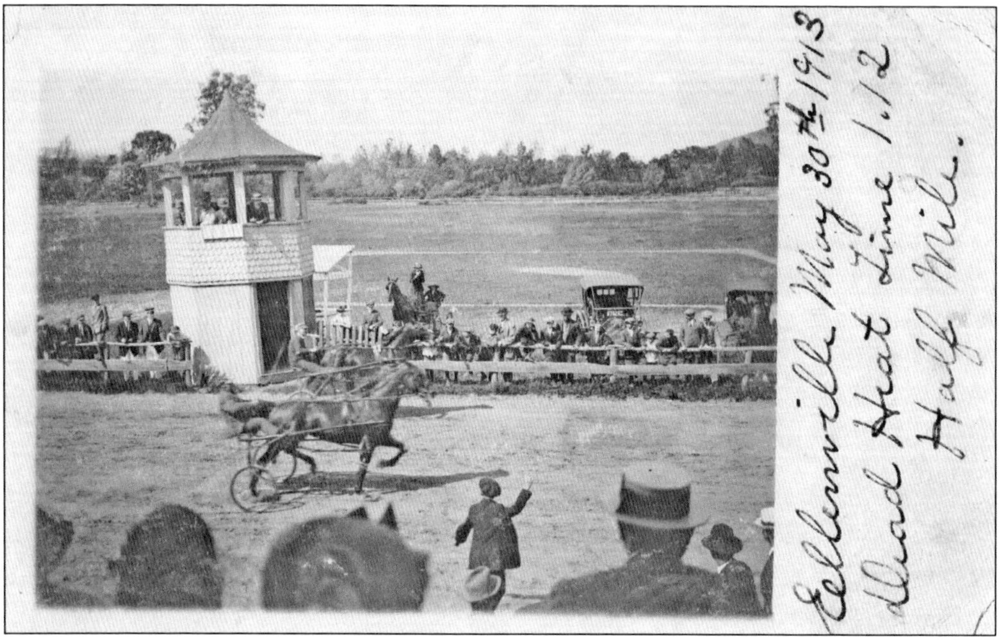

A number of prominent citizens of Ellenville, including Eli Terwilliger and John William Rode, were instrumental in the construction of a half-mile race track in 1869 called the Ellenville Driving Park. The track was located at the site of the present Ellenville Central School. Reputed to be one of the finest racetracks in the state, it featured horse racing—both trotting and pacing—at various times during the year.

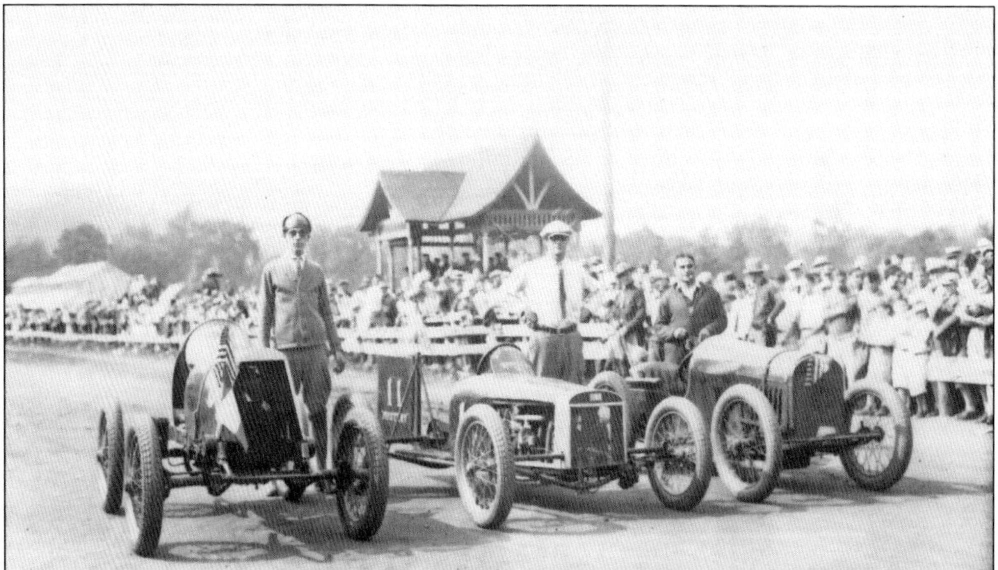

By 1920, automobile racing was one of the events at the Ellenville Driving Park, exclusive to Ford cars here. The first motorcycle race was held that year during the Ulster County Fair. Early races consisted of 10 laps around the half-mile track, with exciting turns since the track was originally designed for horse racing. The bandstand in the background was moved here from Liberty Avenue in 1911.

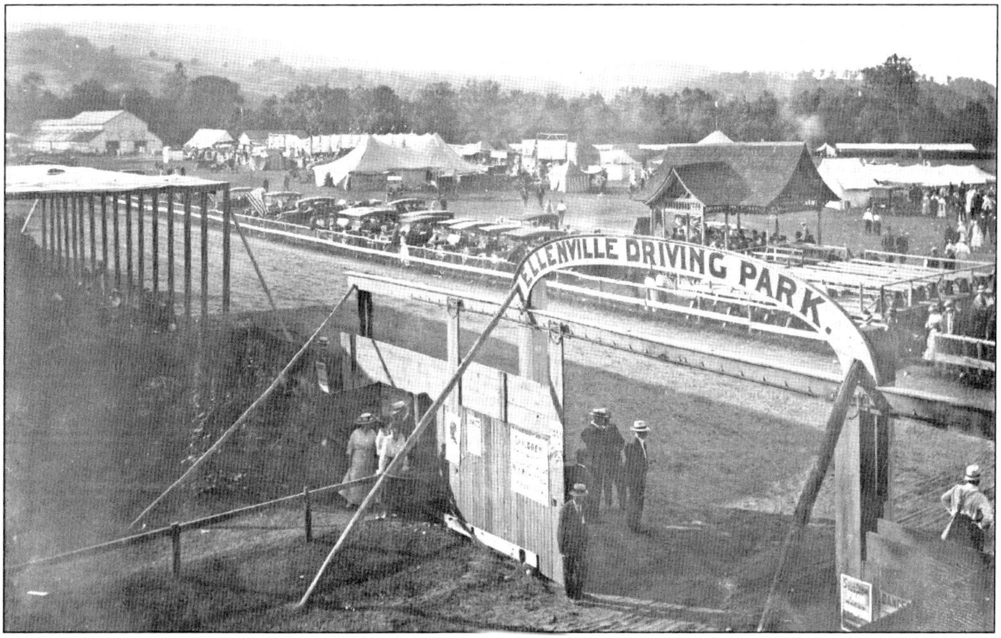

When the Ellenville Driving Park was built, a small fair with agricultural exhibits was held there during the summer; this later became the annual Ulster County Fair. The fair was a boon to the community, bringing visitors from around the county and beyond, particularly after the railroad connected Ellenville to Kingston and Port Jervis. A notice on the fence denies entry to children under age of 15 due to the 1916 polio epidemic.

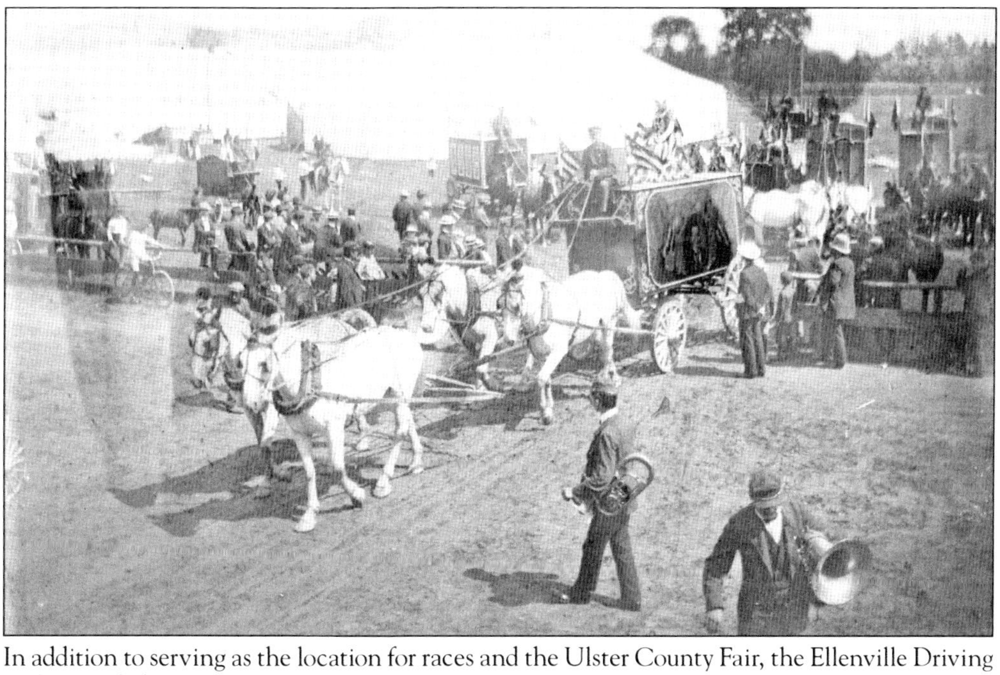

In addition to serving as the location for races and the Ulster County Fair, the Ellenville Driving Park provided a venue for traveling circuses. Several circus companies visited Ellenville during the late 1800s and early 1900s, including the Walter L. Main Circus, Downie Bros. Circus, and Ringling Bros. Here, a horse-drawn circus caravan leaves the Driving Park.

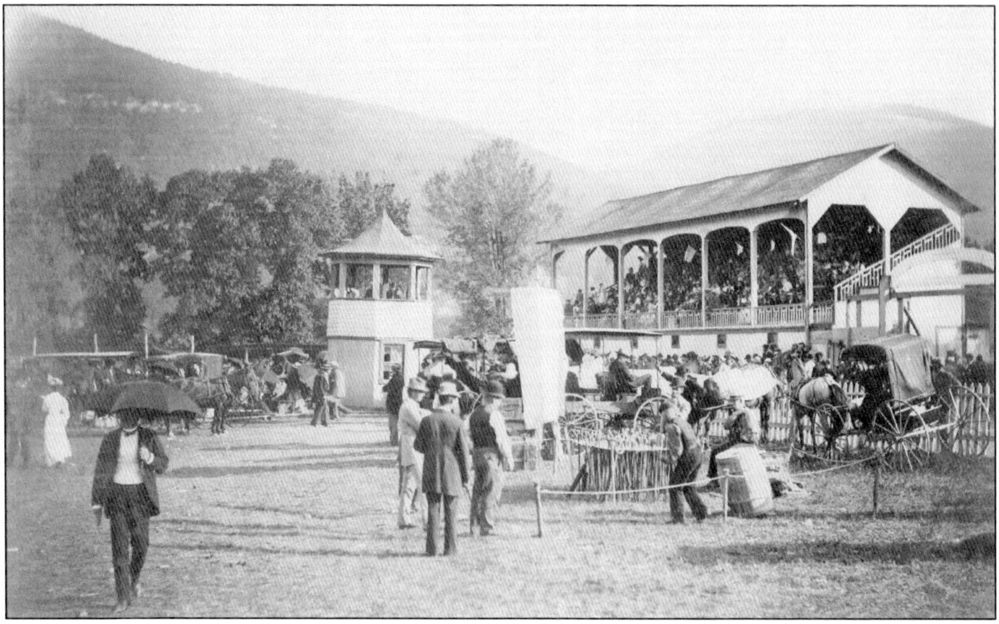

The Ulster County Fair began in Ellenville in 1886, organized by the Southern Ulster Agricultural Society. Held at the Ellenville Driving Park, it continued there until the grounds were sold to the Ellenville School in the early 1930s. The fair moved to Kingston the following year. This grandstand with a view of the entire track seated 500 people. The fair attracted 18,000 visitors in 1908. It was considered one of the finest in the state.

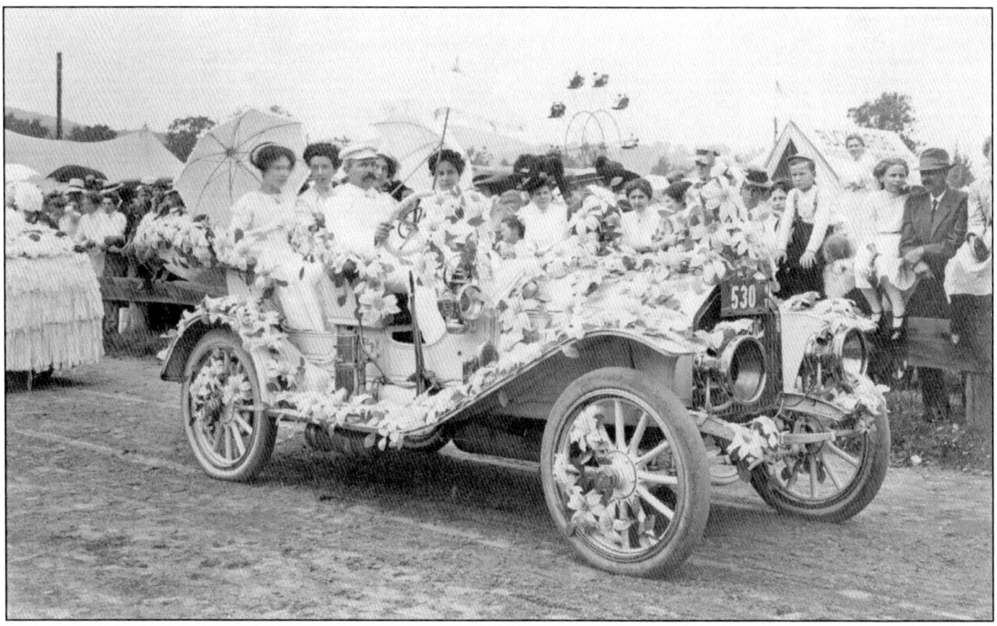

The floral parade was a huge attraction at the Ulster County Fair. Of the many prize categories in the early 1900s, several were for automobiles. Ellenville dentist Dr. L.E. Vernon won first prize for his automobiles several times. This photograph is of Vernon's decorated Buick, possibly taken at the 1908 floral parade, in which he won first prize for Automobile Seating Five. Notice the Ferris wheel in the background.

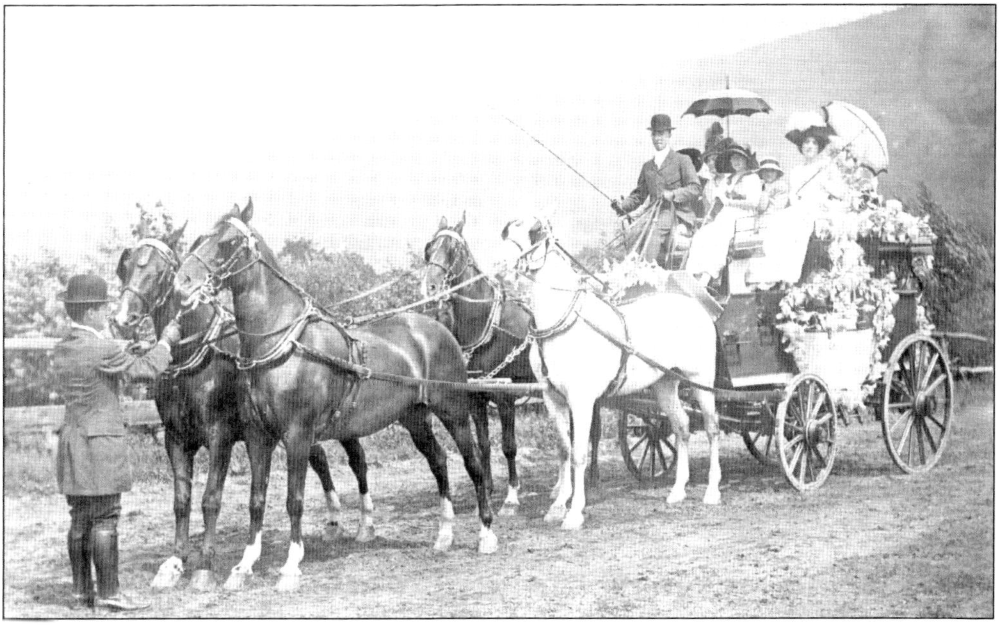

The popular Coaching Day Parade at the Ulster County Fair included horse-and-pony-drawn wagons and, later, decorated automobiles. Pictured is a tallyho (a type of four-in-hand carriage) owned by Dr. Woodend of Ellenville. The horses are handled by Woodend's coachman and footman, and the women are members of the Woodend family. This coach won a blue ribbon at the parade in 1912.

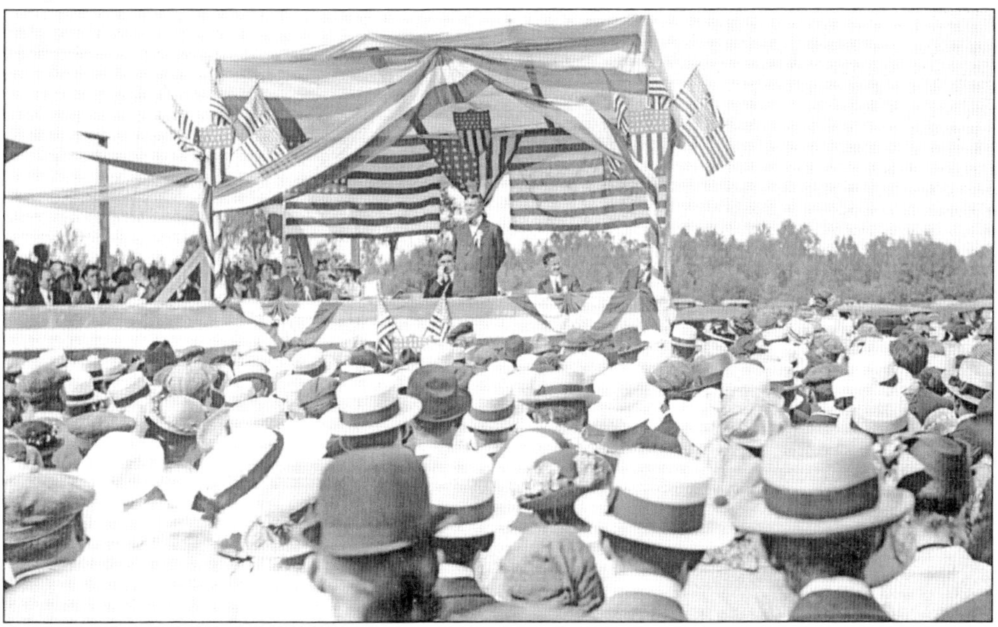

A high point for the village of Ellenville occurred when New York governor Charles S. Whitman visited the Ulster County Fair in 1915. His party included the state commissioners of agriculture and highways and Ulster County officials. The group was entertained by Frank Seaman at a Yama Farms luncheon. In his speech, Whitman referred to the war currently raging in Europe. He spent time shaking hands with the crowd of spectators.

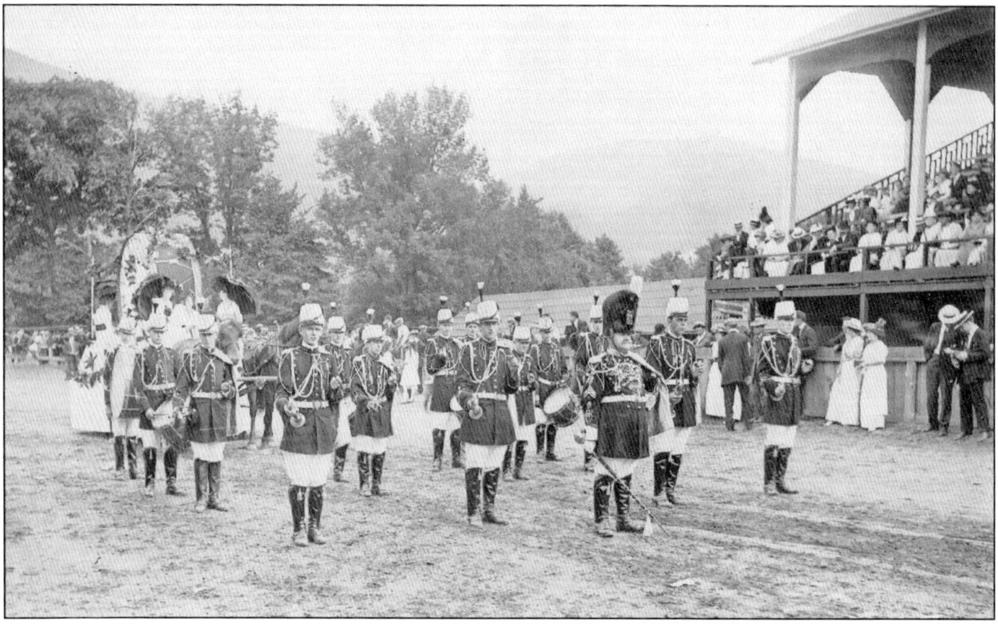

A well-known photographer, V.T. Wright, was the founder and band leader of the fife and drum corps, pictured here in front of the grandstand at the Ulster County Fair. Wright had formerly been a drum major in charge of bands at West Point Military Academy and Cornwall Military Academy before coming to Ellenville. One of Wright's photographs, shown below, shows Liberty Square around 1906. The bandstand, on the right, was built in 1886 on Terwilliger House property for open-air concerts to be performed by Clayton's Band. When the Wayside Inn was built, the bandstand was moved to the corner of Liberty and Main Streets; when the Scoresby Clubhouse was built, it was moved again to the Ellenville Driving Park.

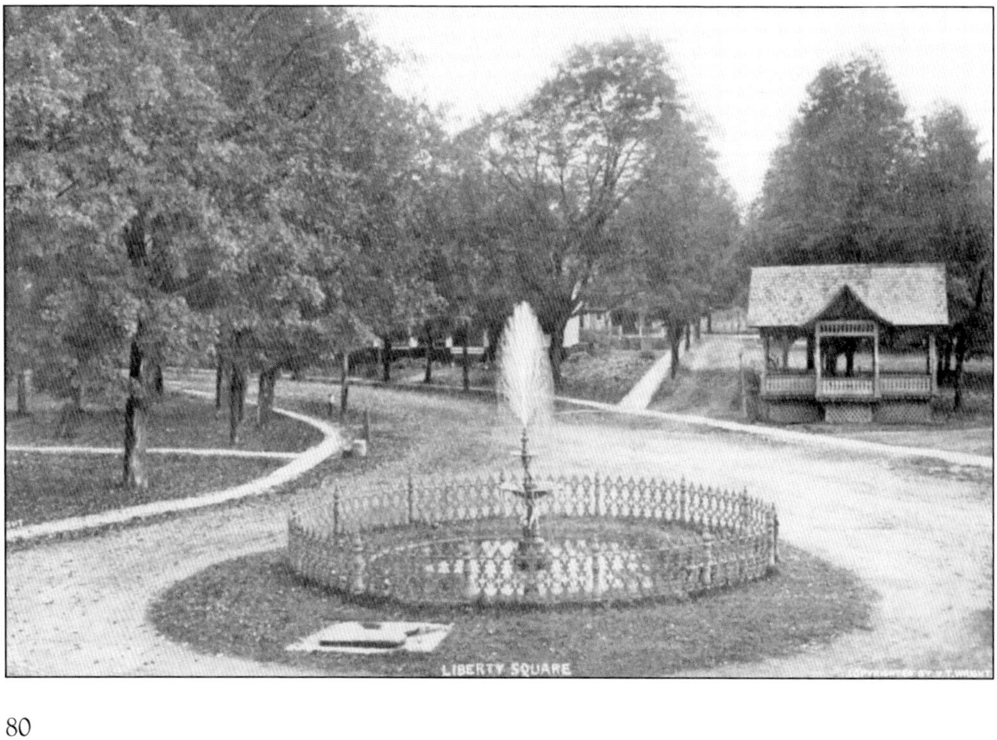

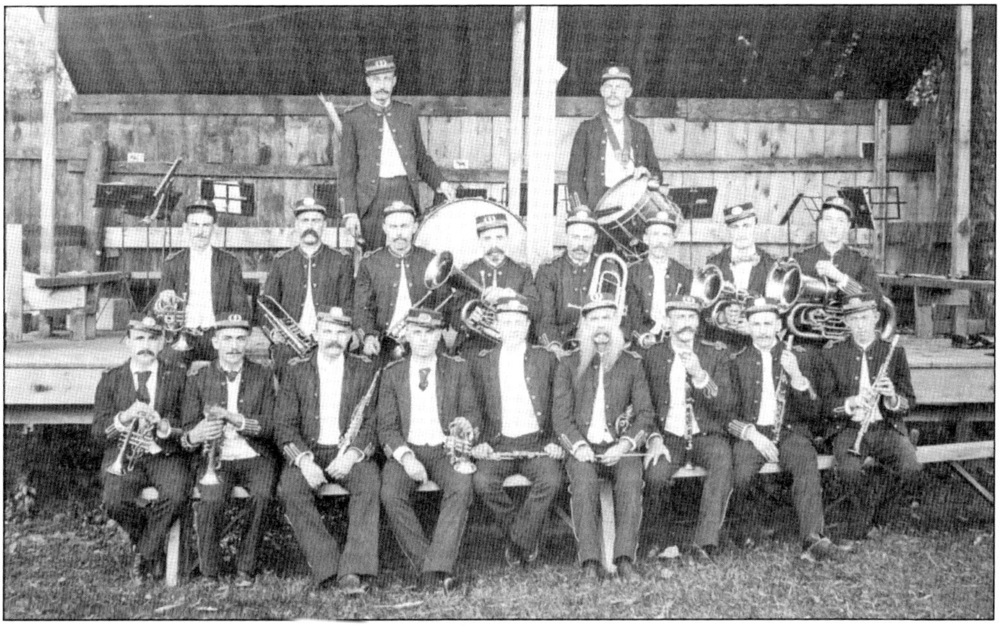

Clayton's Band was established by Tom Clayton, an immigrant from England who came to Ellenville in 1878. He was one of many employees of Ulster Knife Company who had learned the trade in Sheffield, England. Clayton had played in the band of the 14th Infantry during the Civil War and began his band here with 12 instruments. The photograph above was taken in 1891 at the Ulster County Fair, where the band played annually. They also played summer concerts at a bandstand constructed by the village near the Terwilliger House. By 1916, the band was known as Clayton's Military Band. The band marched in parades locally and as far away as Boston until the early 1960s. The photograph below depicts the band in 1939.

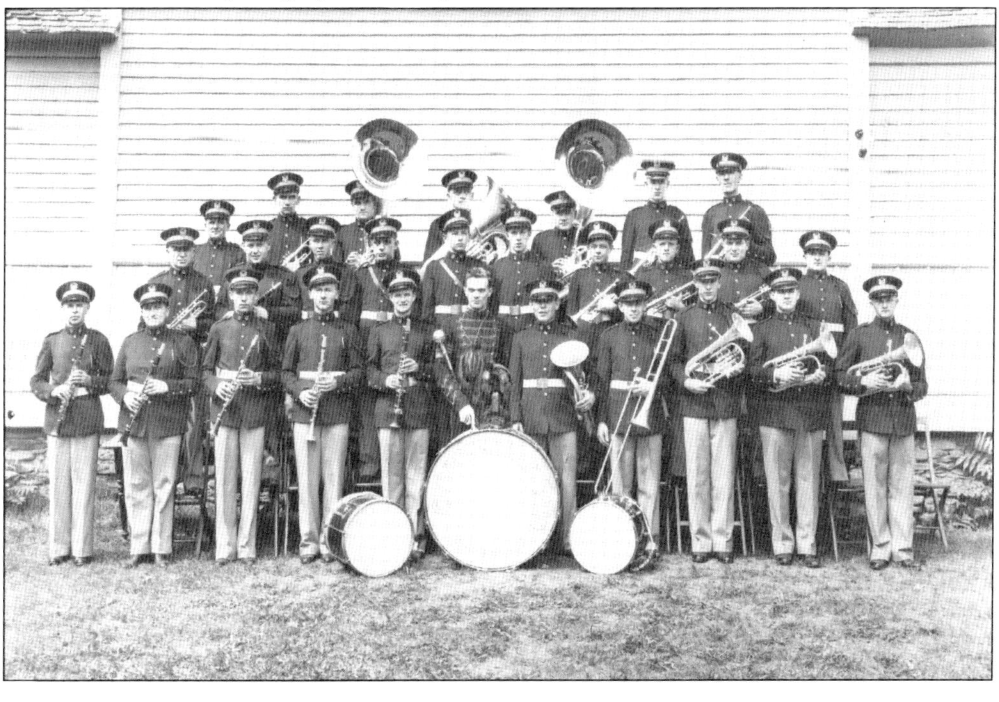

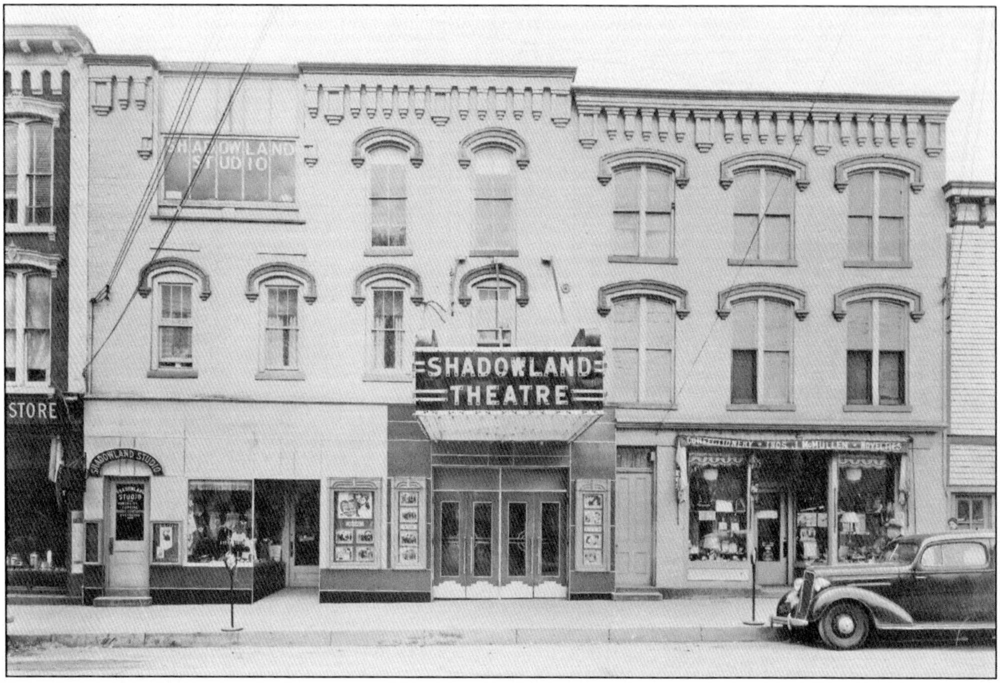

A group of local businessmen purchased a portion of the McMullen Building on Canal Street for a theater, and a contest was held to decide on a name. Grocer George Hoornbeek and 10-year-old Francis Lathrop both came up with Shadowland, which won. Movies and live performances entertained the community here. *Don't Ever Marry* was the first feature film shown at the 1920 opening. A classic Art Deco theater (see below image of interior), the Shadowland Theatre retains its original character to this day; it is the only nonprofit Equity theater in the area. In the exterior photograph, the shop on the right was owned by Thomas McMullen, son of the original builder. The Shadowland Studio upstairs was a photography studio run by Casper S. Cosenza.

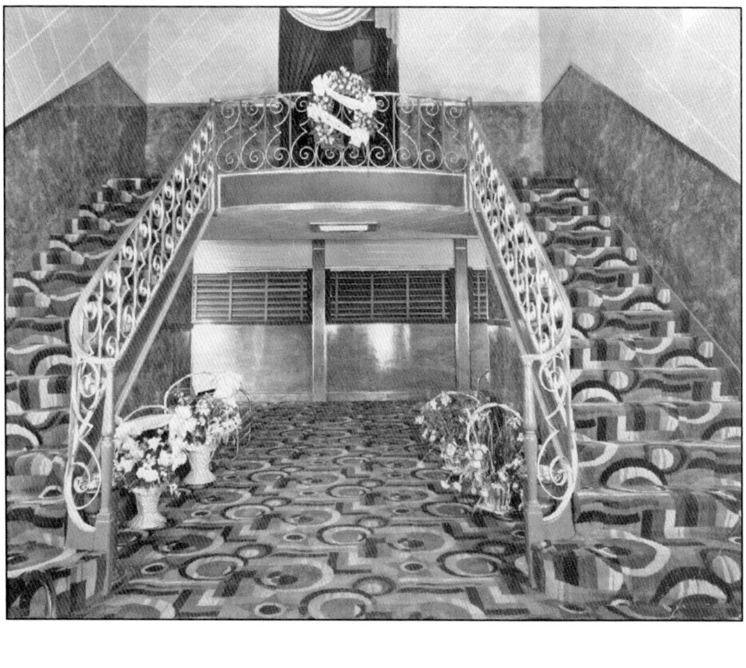

Five

Community Organizations

From the beginning, the people of Ellenville were committed to the care of the village, striving to improve living conditions and services to citizens through public organizations. To achieve this vision, fire companies, business associations, and charitable groups and organizations were formed. These included the Ellenville Board of Trade, the Law & Order Society, the Ellenville Women's Club, and Boy and Girl Scouts of America. Some—the Shawangunk Garden Club and the Noonday Club, for example—remain active as thriving organizations to this day. Schools and education were a primary concern of village citizenry and leadership. Related improvements to buildings and public services were given high priority. This commitment to progress remains vital; more recent years have witnessed the establishment and growth of community-based organizations such as the Ellenville Branch of the NAACP, the Wawarsing Council of Agencies, the Elks Lodge, and many others that provide services to improve the lives of the people Ellenville.

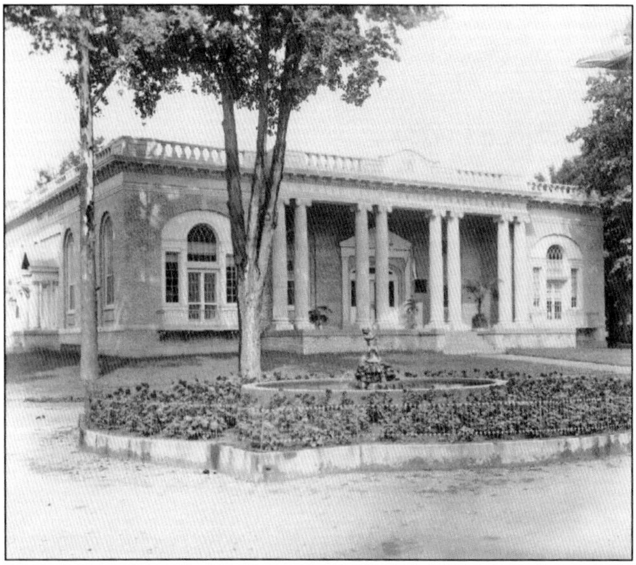

In the National Register of Historic Places, the George and John R. Hunt Memorial Building at 2 Liberty Street stands on the site of the former Hartshorn home. Hunt (of Hunt & Donaldson) bequeathed a major portion of his estate to the Women's Christian Temperance Union (WCTU) of Ulster County for the local union's use. Dedicated in 1918, the building has housed a variety of professional offices, including Ellenville Public Library for almost 50 years and, currently, the Ellenville-Wawarsing Chamber of Commerce.

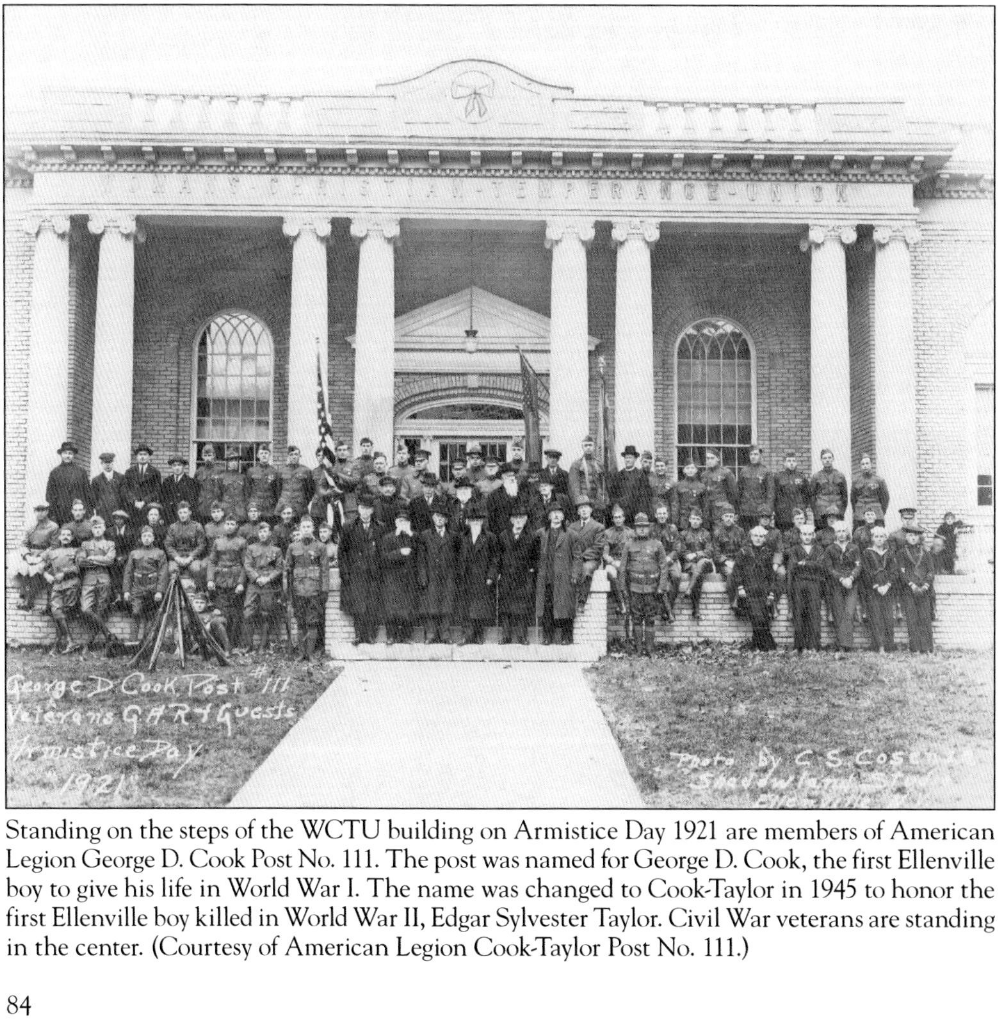

Standing on the steps of the WCTU building on Armistice Day 1921 are members of American Legion George D. Cook Post No. 111. The post was named for George D. Cook, the first Ellenville boy to give his life in World War I. The name was changed to Cook-Taylor in 1945 to honor the first Ellenville boy killed in World War II, Edgar Sylvester Taylor. Civil War veterans are standing in the center. (Courtesy of American Legion Cook-Taylor Post No. 111.)

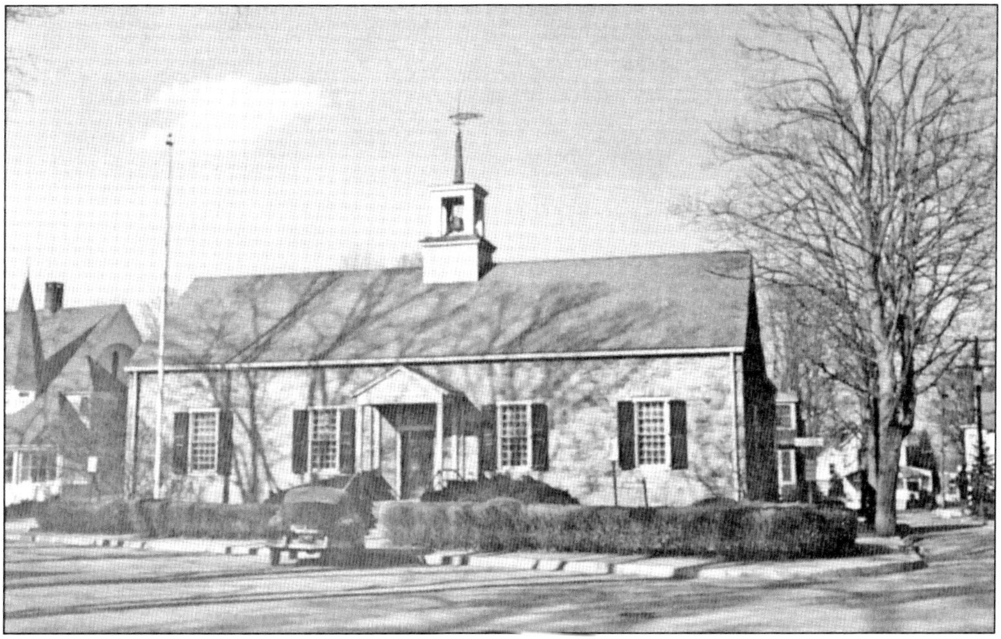

Located on the site of the former Eaton home in Liberty Square, the Ellenville Post Office is one of six New Deal post offices built in the mid-Hudson valley during the Great Depression. Pres. Franklin D. Roosevelt was personally involved in the design and style of these buildings. Roosevelt had hoped to be present at the dedication in Ellenville on October 15, 1940, but was called to Washington by pressing events in Europe. Made of stones quarried in Accord, the Ellenville Post Office reflects the architecture of 18th-century stone houses in Ulster County and the Dutch Colonial style seen throughout the mid-Hudson. Guggenheim Fellow Louis Bouché painted a mural on an interior wall that depicts the early history of the Ellenville Post Office. The distinctive copper bell (made by the McShane Bell Foundry of Baltimore) on top of the building was last rung on America's bicentennial in 1976.

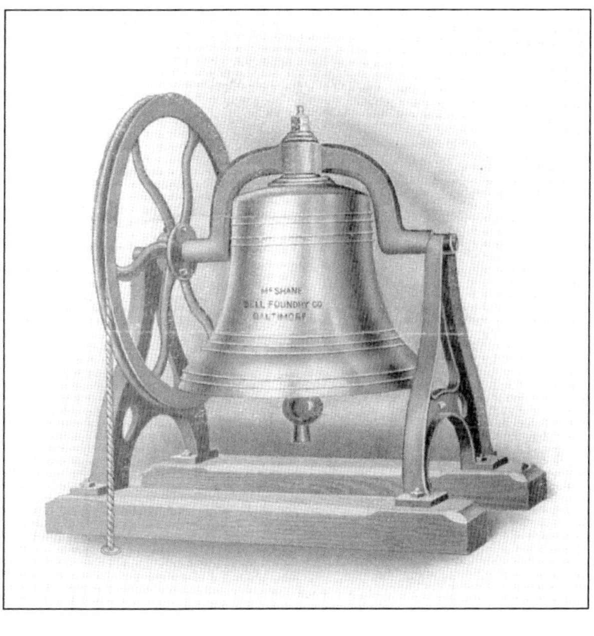

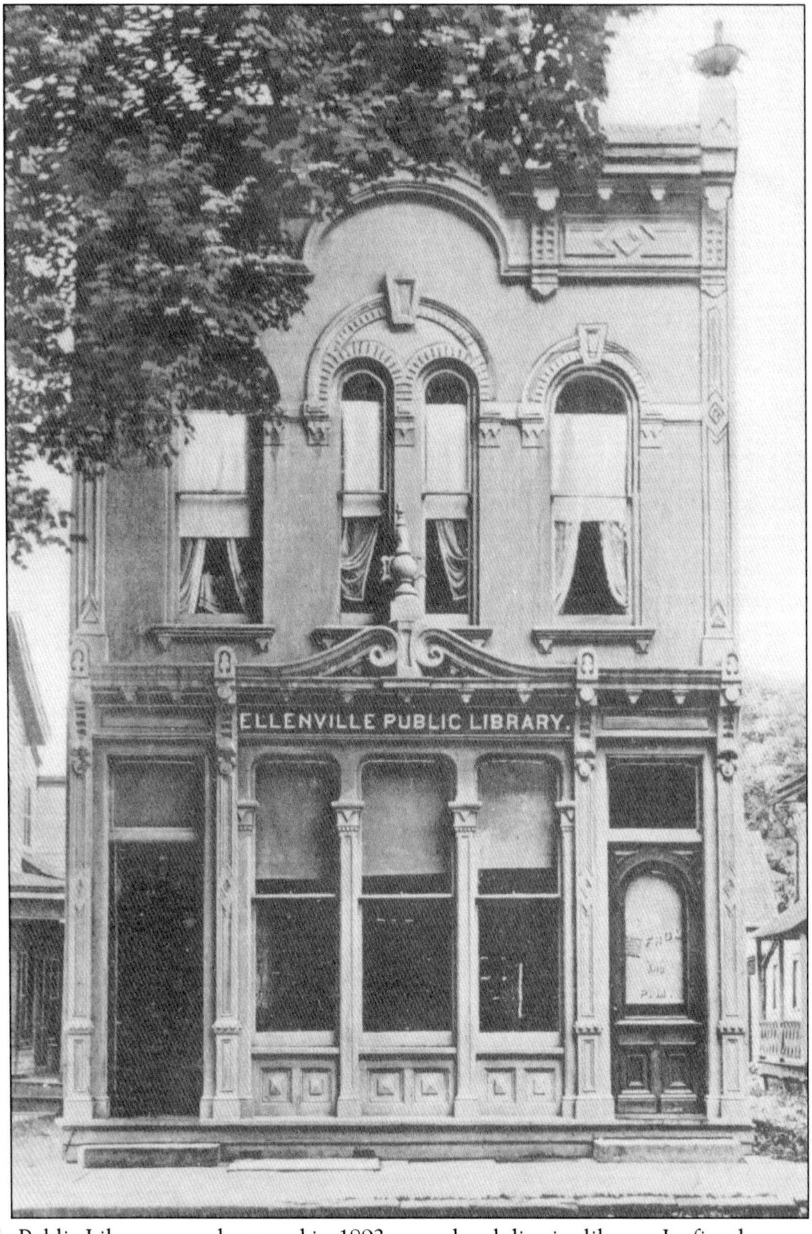

Ellenville Public Library was chartered in 1893 as a school district library. Its first home was in the First National Bank Building (currently Sprague and Killeen) on Canal Street; it boasted some 1,000 titles. In 1897, it moved to the former Weinberger home at 107 Canal Street, near today's Aroma Thyme Bistro, and then, in 1912, to the second floor of the Ellenville Savings Bank building (currently the Town of Wawarsing offices). In 1928, it relocated to the Hunt Memorial Building, where many people today will remember it. In 1966, the charter was changed to Ellenville Public Library & Museum and its historic collections formally organized. The library moved to its present location on Center Street in 1975. One of the first libraries to implement an online catalog, it now holds nearly 50,000 print titles and offers thousands of electronic resources. EPL&M is a member of the Ramapo Catskill Library System, the Ulster County Library Association, and the Greater Hudson Heritage Network.

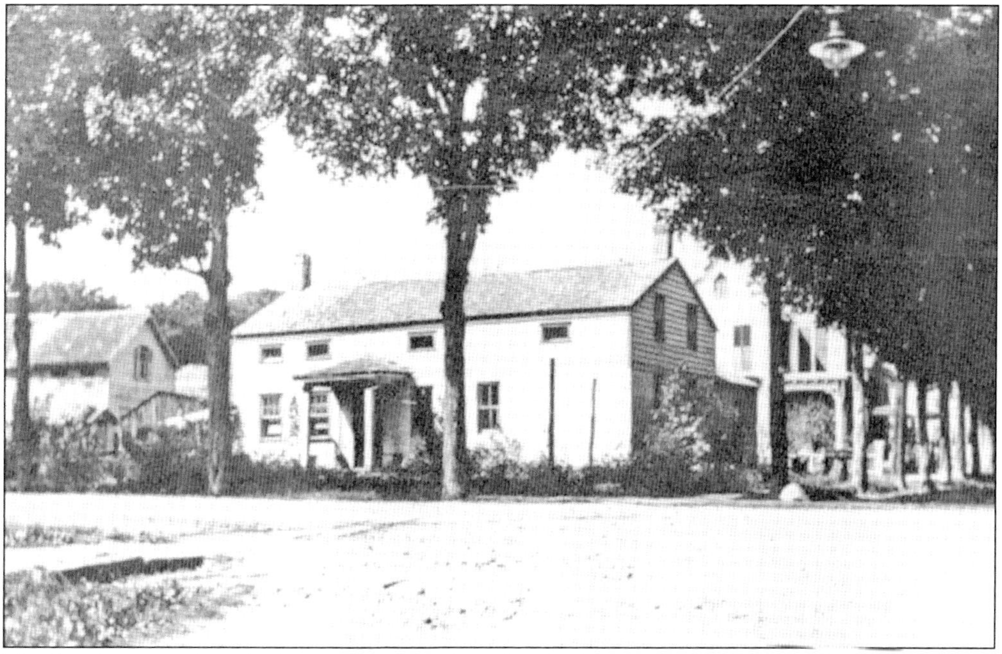

The first known school building was erected in 1830 at the corner of Market and Warren Streets. It was constructed of Leurenkill brick by minister and potter Horace Weston. Weston, who started Ellenville Pottery, had a brickyard at Leurenkill as well. School was taught here until 1848, and the building remained until 1960.

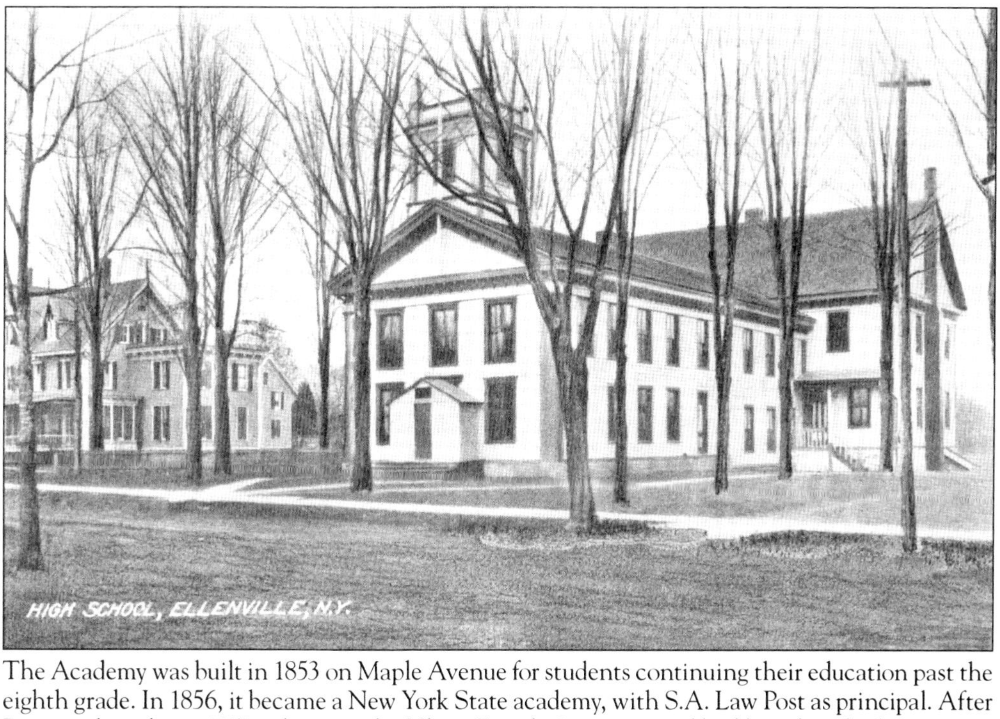

The Academy was built in 1853 on Maple Avenue for students continuing their education past the eighth grade. In 1856, it became a New York State academy, with S.A. Law Post as principal. After Post purchased it in 1859, it became the Ulster Female Seminary and had boarding facilities. It was popularly known as Post Academy. From 1876 until 1914, it served as Ellenville's high school.

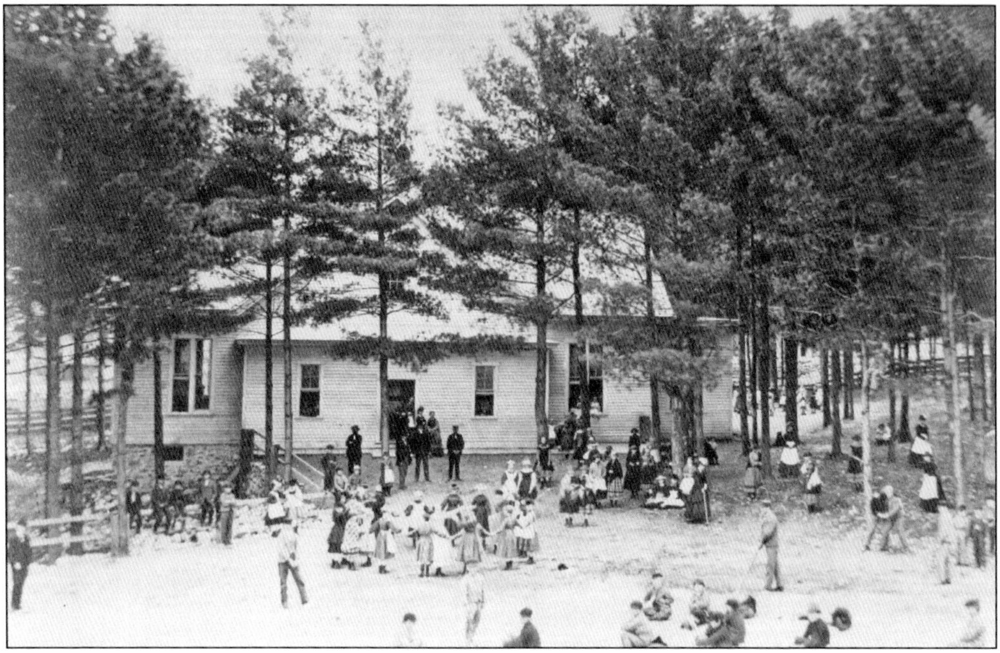

Officially School No. 2, the Pine Grove School was built in 1867 for 200 students. Located at the east end of the village near the end of Center Street, it closed in 1975 after 108 years as a school. In 1976, it was sold to the village for $1. Today, the building houses Ellenville's Head Start program.

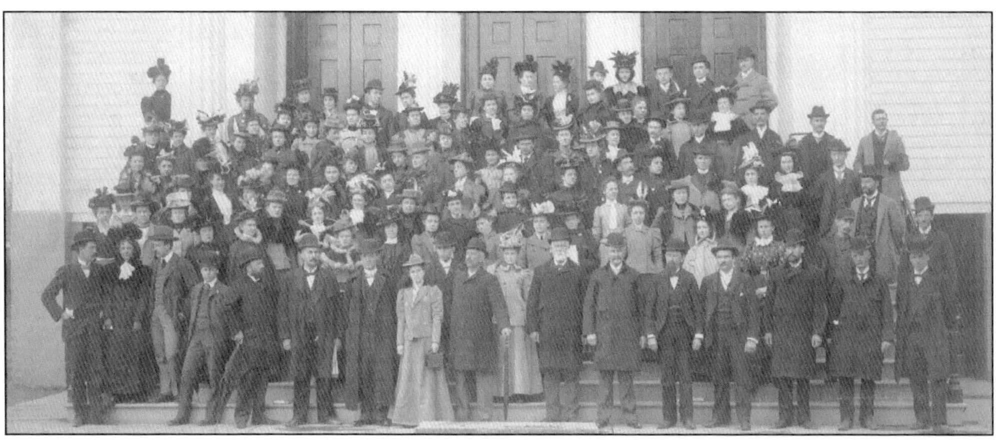

"What can we do to encourage self-reliance and independent effort on the part of our pupils?" was a question raised at the 1908 Ulster County Third District Teachers' Association. Ellenville had its own training class for teachers from 1984 through 1914, headed by Elsie J. Roat. Roat later became the first woman district superintendent of schools in the region. The image above taken on the steps of the Reformed church on Canal Street is identified only as "Teachers, 1898."

School No. 1, or the Brick School, as it was called, was erected in 1873 on the corner of Main and Warren Streets to accommodate a growing student population. First through eighth grades were taught here, and William E. Hull was principal. In the mid-1800s, education above an eighth-grade level was not the responsibility of public institutions; rather, it took place in private schools. In 1915, a new, more spacious school was built on Maple Avenue. The class photograph below was taken just outside the door on the left of the Brick School, right.

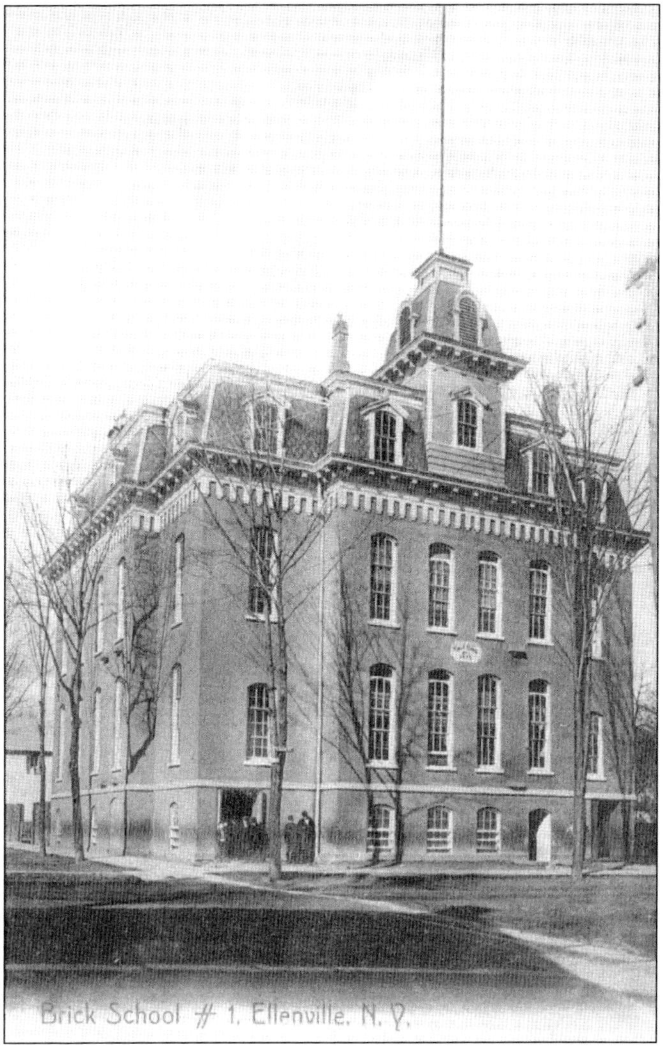

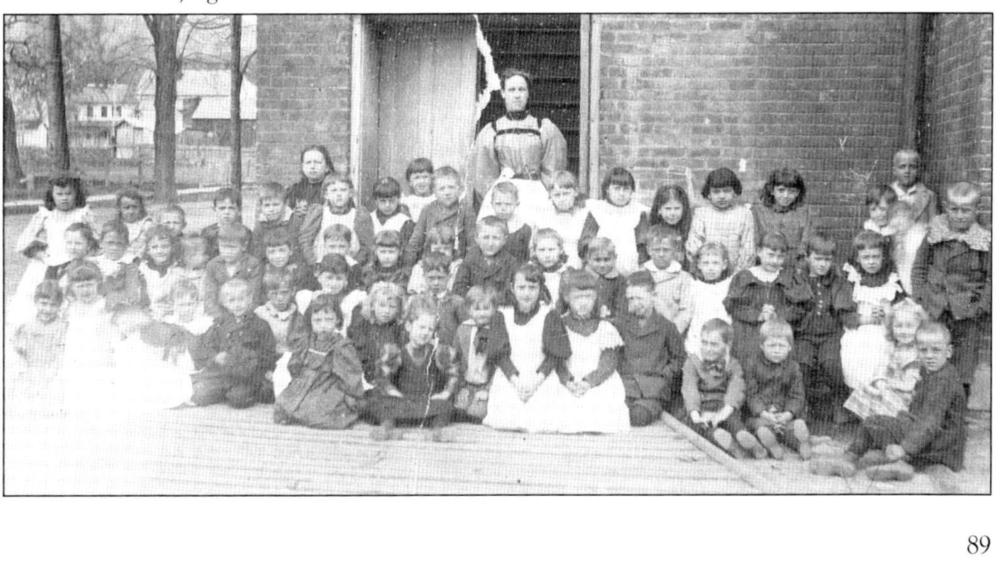

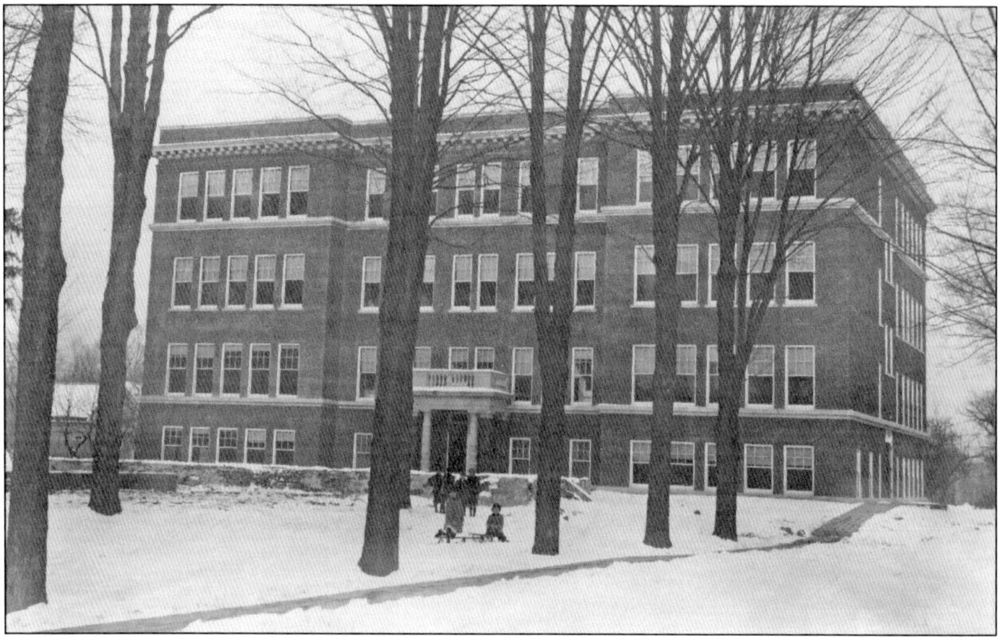

In 1915, this school was built on Maple Avenue to relieve overcrowding. Replacing the Old Academy High School, this four-story building housed first through 12th grades. The third floor of the new school featured an auditorium that could seat 500, and a stereopticon was available for presentations and classes. In 1935, an addition was built, followed by another in 1957. The original 1915 building was demolished in 1997, and the one that currently houses the Ellenville Central School District offices was erected. The high school was committed to serving the needs of four categories of students: those entering into "active life upon completion," those preparing for college, those preparing for professional or technical school, and those preparing to teach. Judging by hairstyles and hemlines, the class picture below was taken in the late 1920s.

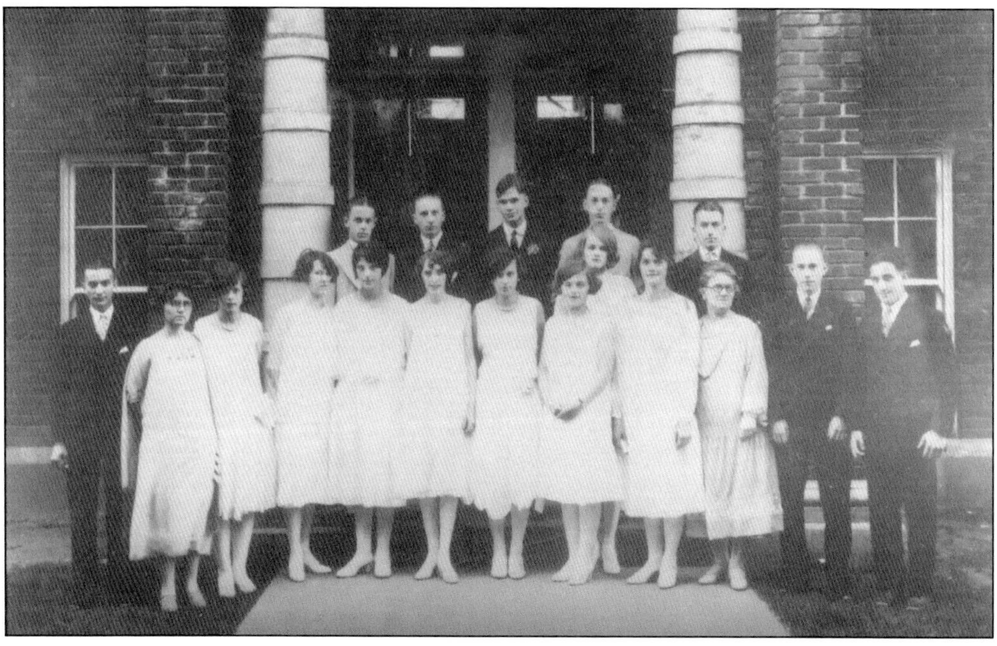

Founded in 1927 by Jennie Devine Young, the Shawangunk Garden Club has a mission to study gardening, promote conservation, and beautify the community. Special events over the years include garden tours, bridal pageants (young women wore heirloom gowns at the Hunt Memorial), flower shows, workshops, and a Victorian tea at Terwilliger House. Still active, the garden club also provides scholarship money to graduating students with horticultural interests.

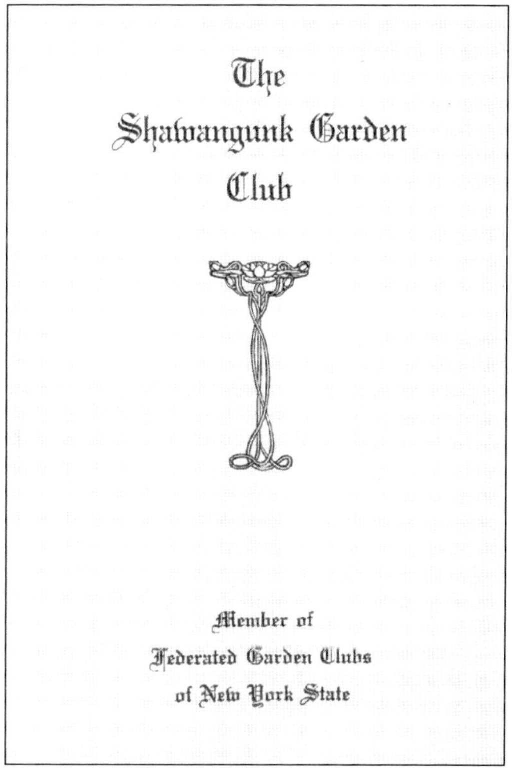

The
Shawangunk Garden
Club

Member of
Federated Garden Clubs
of New York State

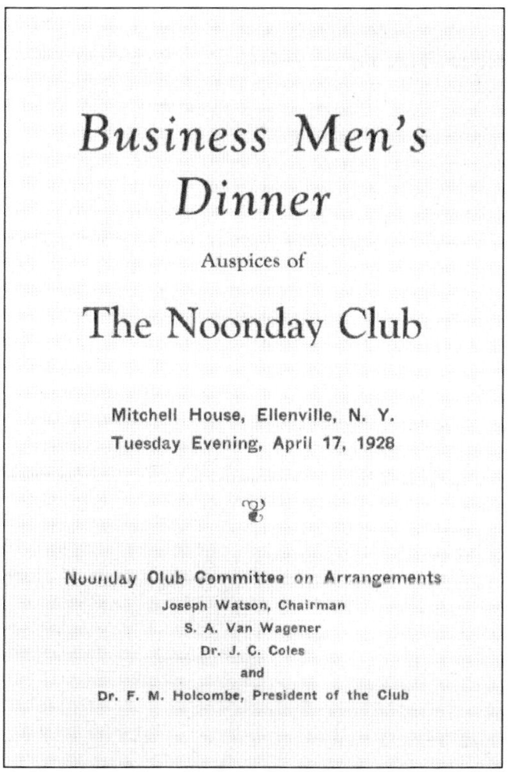

Business Men's
Dinner

Auspices of

The Noonday Club

Mitchell House, Ellenville, N. Y.
Tuesday Evening, April 17, 1928

Noonday Club Committee on Arrangements
Joseph Watson, Chairman
S. A. Van Wagener
Dr. J. C. Coles
and
Dr. F. M. Holcombe, President of the Club

The Noonday Club was formed by 25 businessmen in 1923 to "serve the community in any way possible toward upbuilding its business and social life." An article from the *Ellenville Press* promises that the Noonday Club would welcome membership applications from any "live business man." Present at the first meeting, held at Mitchell House, were Deyo Johnson, Frank Sprague, Burton Wood, Ward Wilklow, and William Douglas, among others. The Noonday Club is still active, hosting fundraisers, an annual senior holiday dinner, and a Citizen of the Year Award.

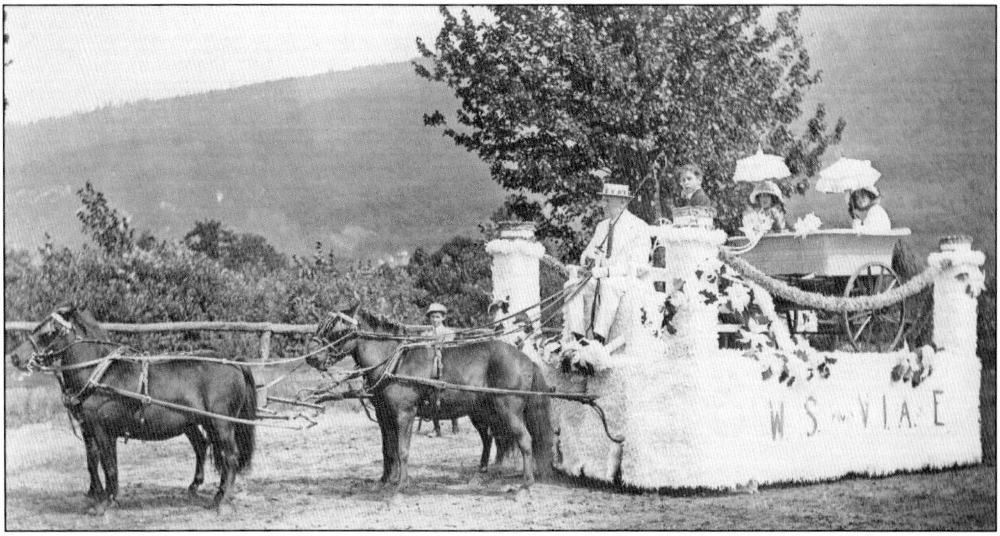

The Women's Sanitary and Village Improvement Association (WSVIA) of Ellenville won first prize with this float in the floral parade at the 1912 Ulster County Fair. Like other similar organizations, such as the Ellenville Women's Club and Ellenville Improvement Society, the WSVIA was committed to caring for the poor, improving village conditions, and hosting community events like an evening of games at the Wayside Inn. The float is driven by Dr. W.E. Woodend with four of his ponies.

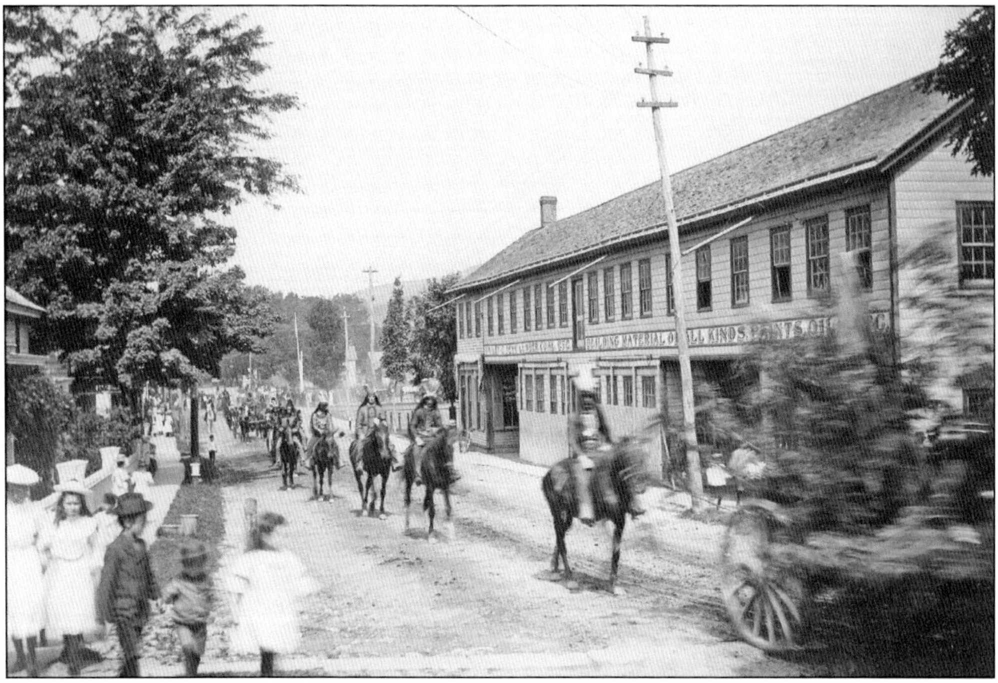

A fireman's parade passes by Bailey & Deyo Lumber on the east end of Canal; pictured here may be members of the Improved Order of Red Men. Napanog Tribe No. 204 met in Ellenville. The order, whose members were typically Caucasian, adopted Native American dress in solidarity with the Sons of Liberty at the Boston Tea Party. They sought to do good works, raising money for charitable causes.

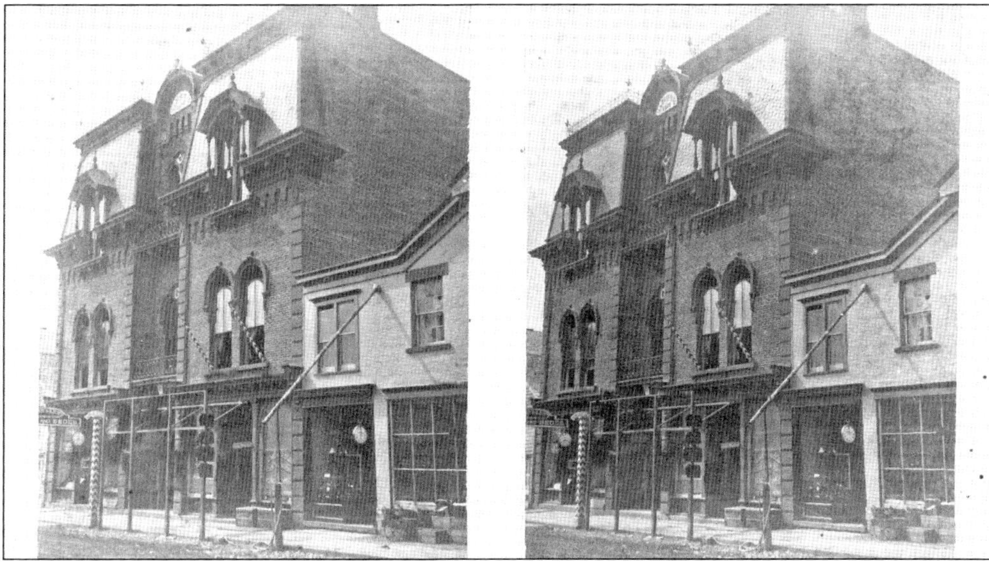

The Masonic Theatre (Masonic Hall), was a grand Canal Street building that housed the Wawarsing Masonic Lodge No. 583, Free and Accepted Masons, instituted in 1865, above, with shops below. In the early 1900s, high school graduations were held in the main hall here. The lodge hosted annual balls, featuring "music by Clayton's Orchestra," and other social events for the community. The above images were taken for a stereopticon. The Order of Eastern Star is a women's Freemason organization; Wawarsing Chapter 253, affiliated with Wawarsing Lodge 582, is shown below on a float for the Ulster County Fair floral parade, in the early 1900s. Both organizations are still active, and their lodge is now at 14 Center Street. The Masonic Theatre was taken down during urban renewal.

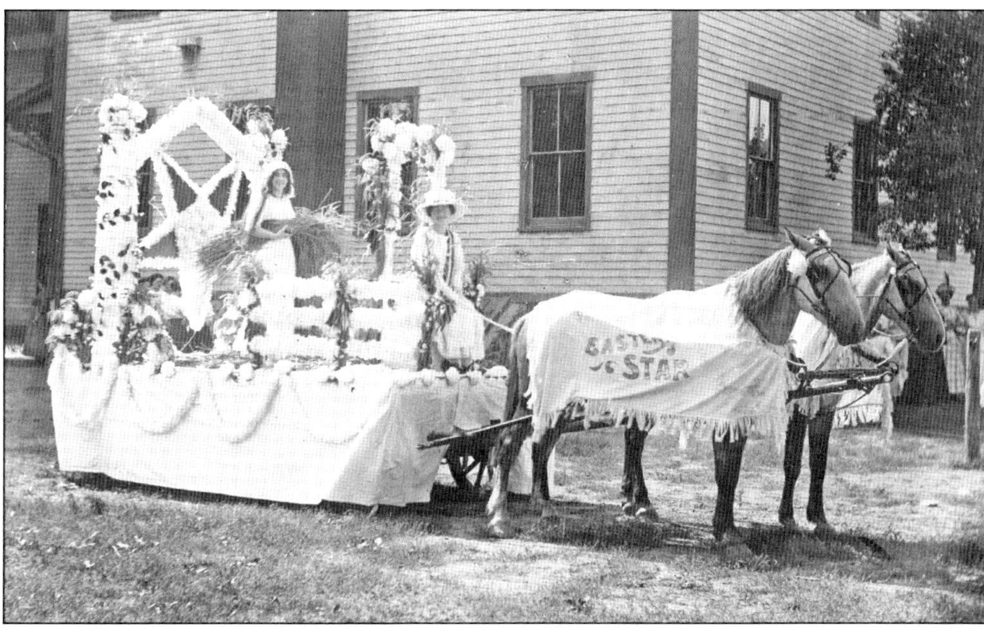

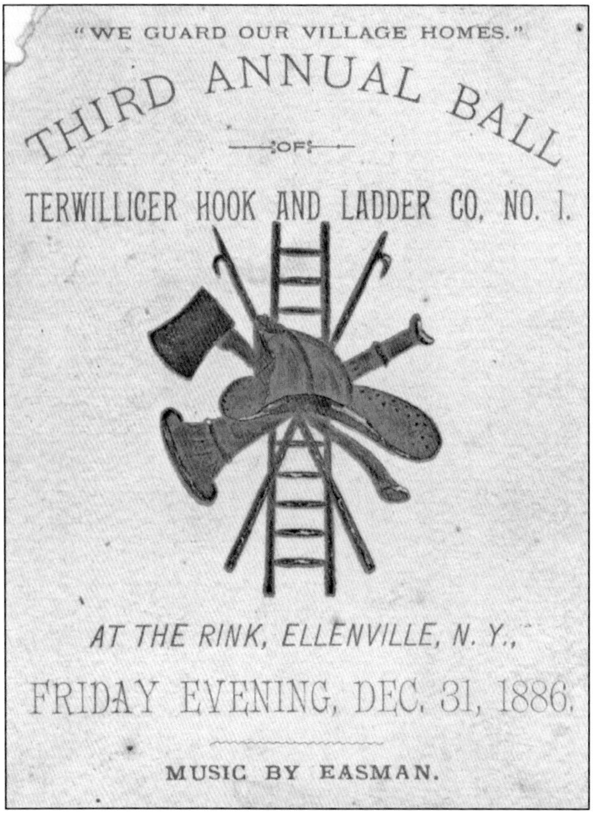

In 1884, the Terwilliger Hook & Ladder Company was organized. Disbanding in 1899 for lack of membership and resources, the company gave its equipment to the Scoresby Hose Company, which changed its name to Scoresby Hose and Hook and Ladder Company No. 1. Fire companies often hosted public events such as skating parties and annual balls to help raise money.

The Pioneer Engine Company clubhouse, although modified over the years, is still in use today. In 1904, when the decision to build was made and the Center Street location selected, fundraising began. Sarah Norbury learned of the project and immediately donated a large portion of the construction cost. The building was named in her honor. Social events, dances, and meetings were held here, as were basketball games.

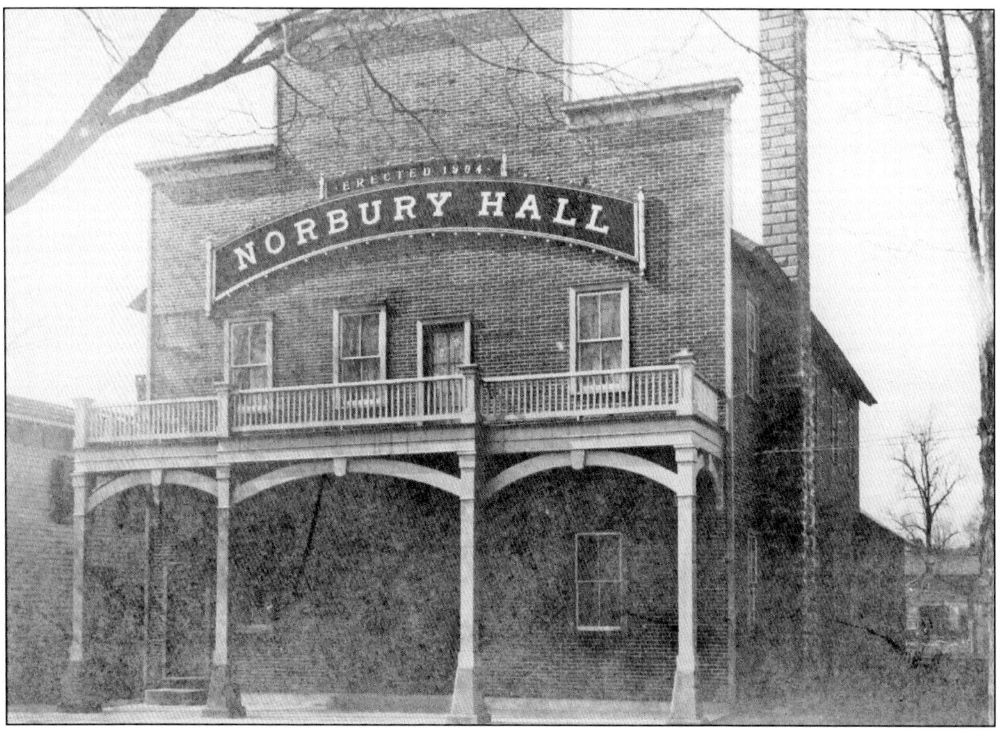

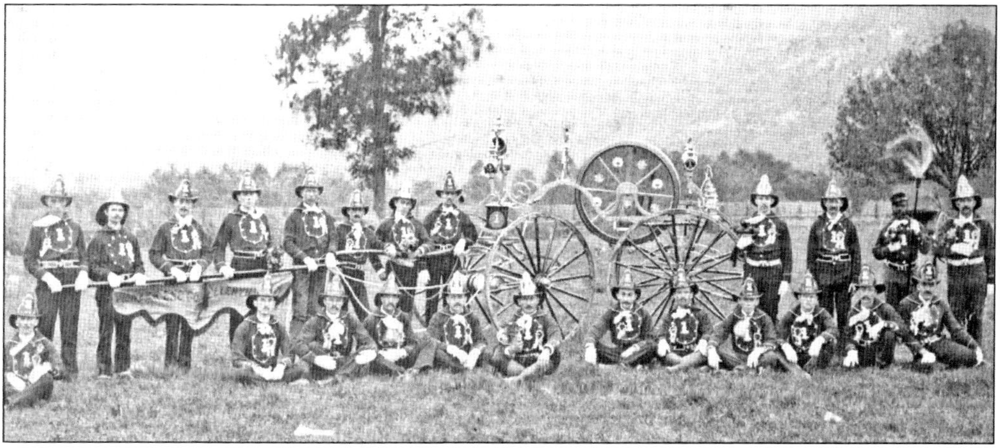

Ellenville's first fire response team, Pioneer Engine Co. No. 1, was formed in 1857, one year after the incorporation of the village. Village president Charles Hartshorn summoned his new board of trustees to a meeting at Terwilliger House in response to a local petition demanding the formation of a fire department. Within a matter of weeks, Pioneer was officially established and rapidly became the pride of the community. Because the fire company received no public funds for equipment or uniforms, its members contributed their own money. The Pioneers later built Norbury Hall on Center Street as their home. The photograph above shows the company in 1883. Pioneer had an amateur basketball team, seen below; players are, from left to right, (standing) Harry Wilklow, Baxter Taylor, Jack Mentnech, Julius Wolf, and Frank Wintish; (sitting) Albert Wolf, Ben Taylor, and Max Taylor.

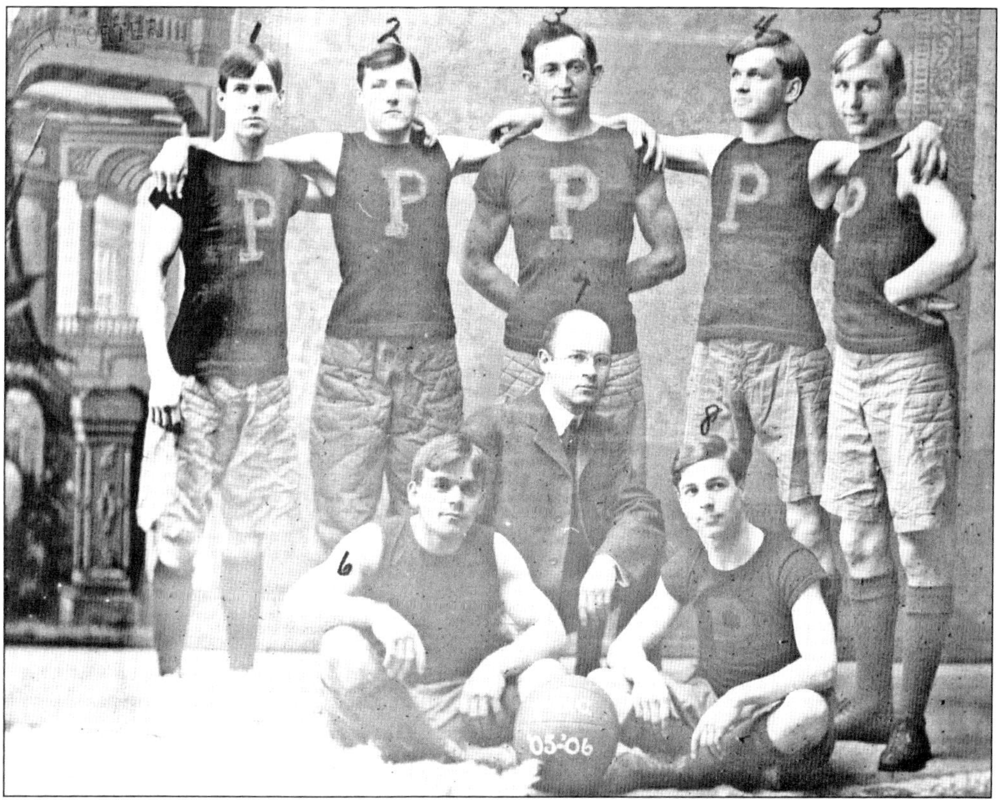

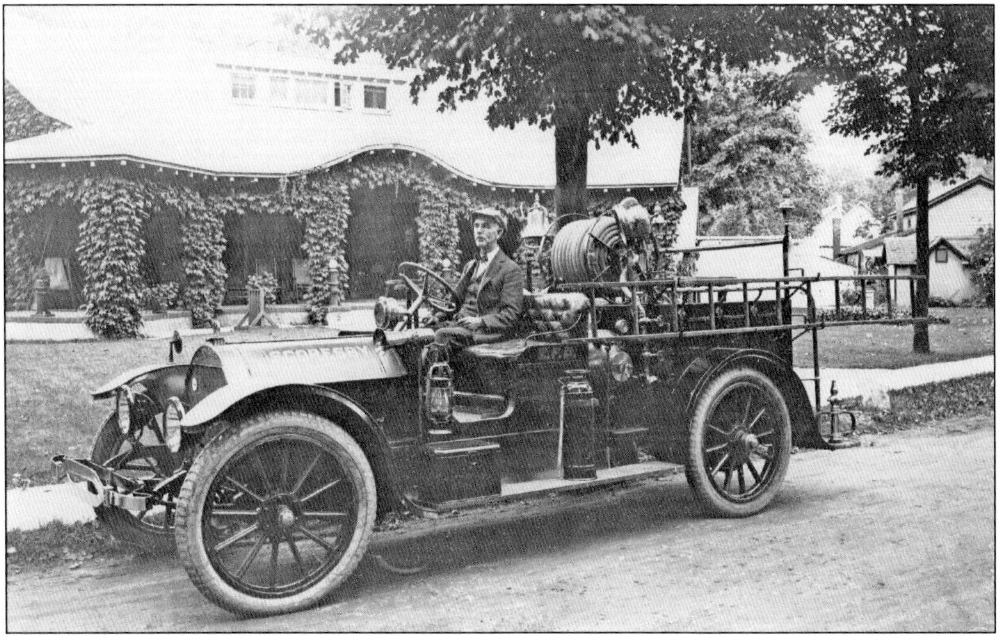

In 1872, village trustees established Scoresby Hose Company No. 1, partially in response to the completion of Ellenville's reservoir, Lake Maratanza, and a pipe system bringing water to the village. Using gravitational force, this system revolutionized firefighting. Local hydrants made it possible for firemen to work effectively with more powerful hoses, rather than relying on bucket brigades or hand pumps. Scoresby Hose proved its worth only a few days later, successfully fighting a fire in the Morse Mill at Five Points (aka "the Points"). In 1899, the company was renamed Scoresby Hose and Hook and Ladder Company No. 1. Chief Charles G.A. Fischer, who joined Scoresby in 1886 at age 19 and served more than 50 years, is pictured above in the fire truck. The Scoresby Club House, opened in 1912, is in the background. Below is the first Scoresby firehouse on Canal Street near Main; village offices were upstairs.

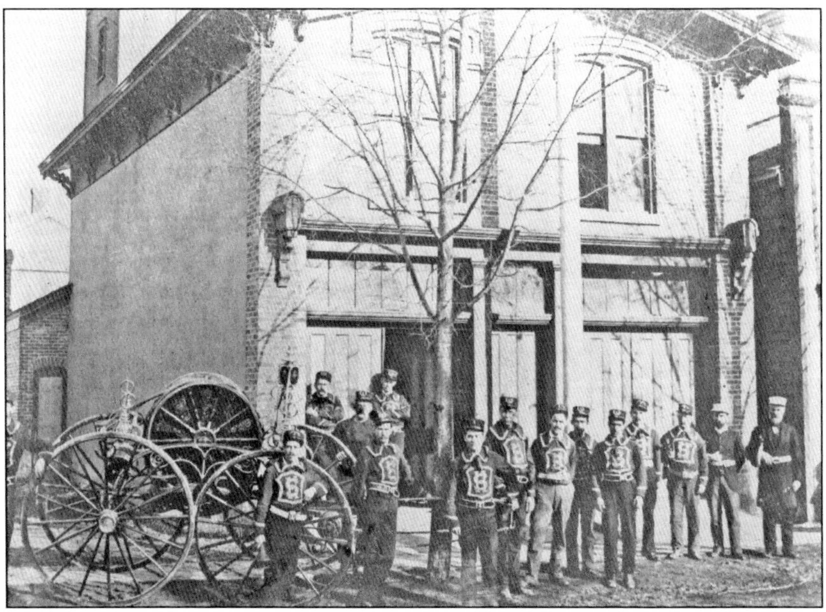

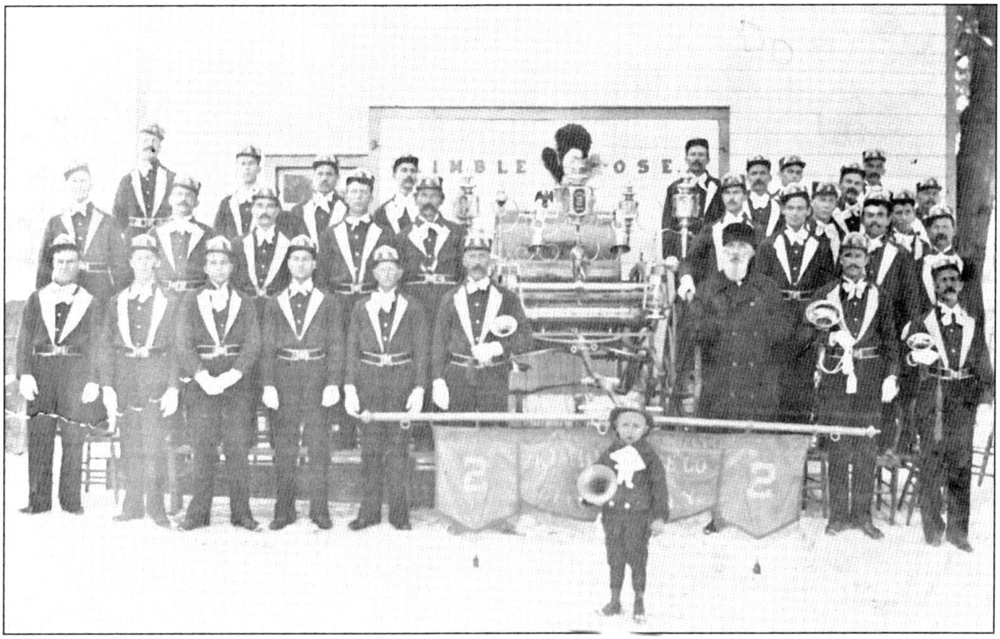

In response to concerns of people living in the eastern part of Ellenville, the village board formed the Kimble Hose Company No. 2 in 1889. Original charter members were all D&H Canal workers, and the company was named for George Kimble, superintendent of the Ellenville section of the canal. Kimble's first firehouse was on Clinton Avenue; the building later became an office for the Ellenville Wood Novelty Company and is now a two-family home. Before moving to its present location on Berme Road, Kimble Hose Company was located on Kimble Lane, between Canal and Center Streets. Kimble amateur basketball team players pictured below are, from left to right, (standing) Bill Schupp, John Odell, Edward Young, (?) Wintish, and George Frye; (kneeling) George Traphagen, Stanley Stickles, George Harrington, and John Traphagen.

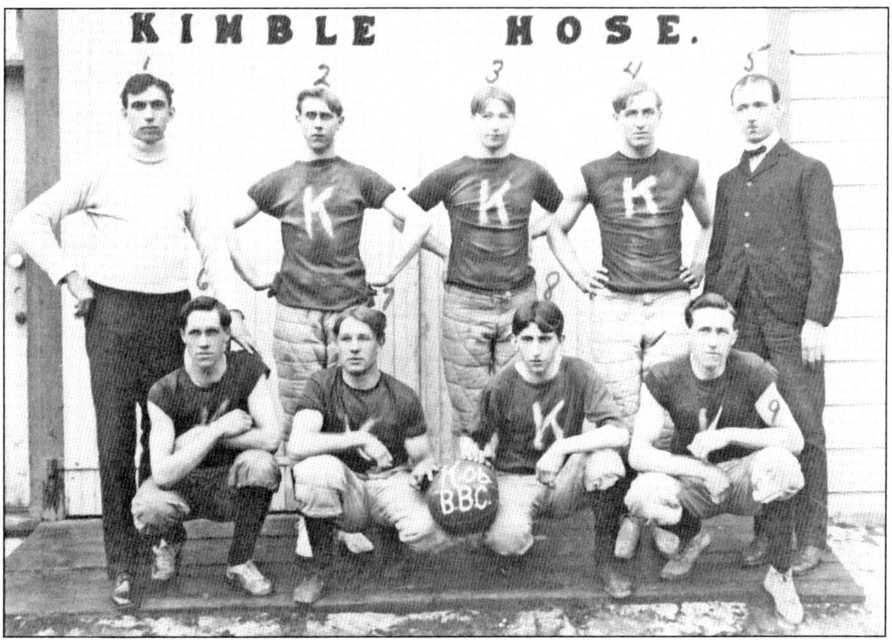

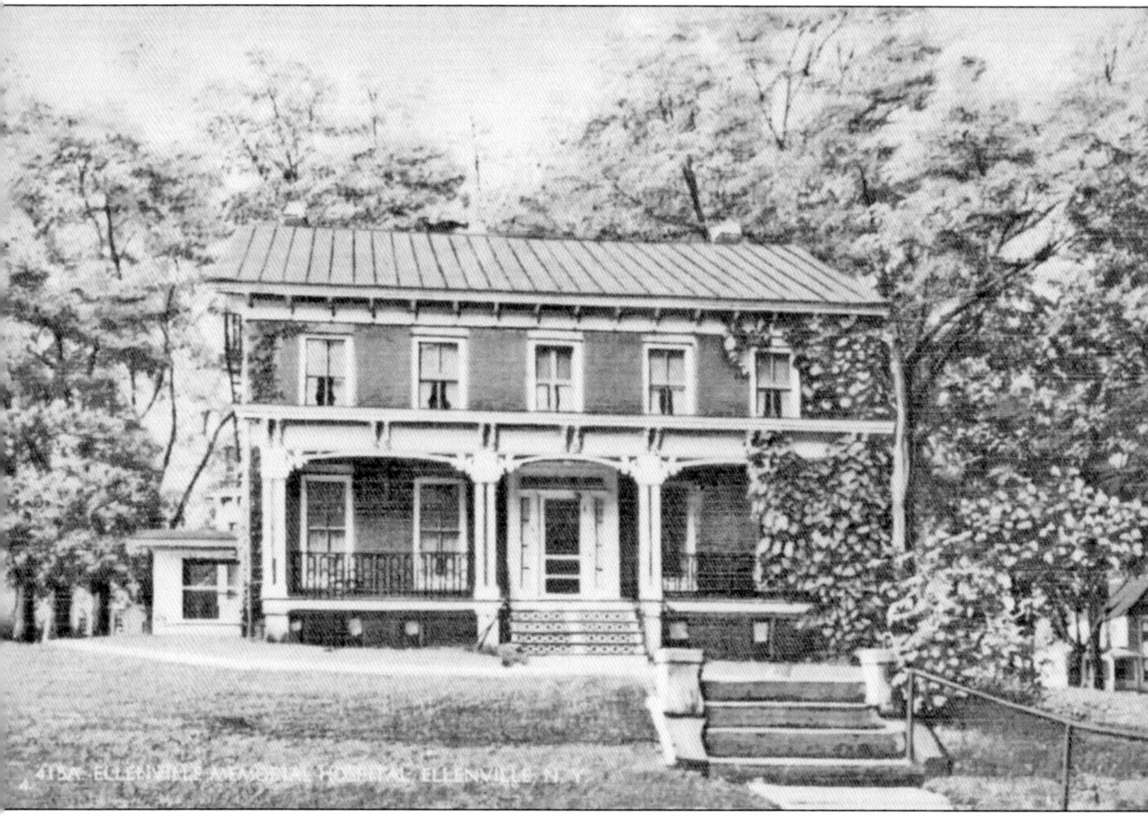

Dr. George F. Wilklow and members of American Legion George D. Cook Post No. 111 were instrumental in building the Veterans Memorial Hospital. Money was raised locally, and the former Scoresby estate on Center Street was purchased. Opening ceremonies took place on May 30, 1924, with a parade from Liberty Square to the site of the new hospital. Lieutenant Governor Lunn spoke, the American Legion raised the flag, and Clayton's Band played. Dr. George F. Wilklow was the first president of staff at the hospital. Within a few years, additions had been built; the hospital continued to grow until 1965, when it moved to its present location off Route 209 and became Ellenville Community Hospital. (Pres. Lyndon B. Johnson and Senator Robert Kennedy attended the ground breaking.) It is now the award-winning Ellenville Regional Hospital. The hospital's Ladies Auxiliary was formed in 1924; it continues to fundraise and advocate for the hospital to this day.

Six

Where People Worshipped

In the early years of Ellenville, most religious-minded residents attended the Old Dutch Church of Wawarsing. By 1826, the village's population had grown enough that residents asked the Wawarsing church to allow them to organize a branch church in Ellenville. In 1833, the Methodists built their first church in Ellenville. After the arrival of the D&H Canal and the subsequent manufacturing boom, people of many faiths started to arrive. In 1830, three hundred people lived in Ellenville; by 1850, that number increased to 1,500. Ellenville's first two churches experienced this growth and needed to build larger facilities. In 1852, the Dutch Reformed church erected its present building; the original was moved to Main Street, where the Roman Catholic Church of St. Mary's used it as worship space for the next 100 years. By 1858, the old Methodist church was moved to Canal and Maiden Lane, where it was used for retail and community space. The Lutherans built their church in 1862. Then, in 1850, Catholics of German descent built St. Mary's of the Assumption. An Episcopalian congregation, organized as St. Paul's in 1853, built their chapel on Market Street in 1866, erecting St. John's Memorial Church next door in 1874. Chapter six gives a modest look at these 19th-century places of worship, the congregations of which are active to this day. Over the years, many other houses of worship would be built, including the Church of Jesus Christ, the Shiloh Baptist Church, and Congregation Anshe Tzaydik.

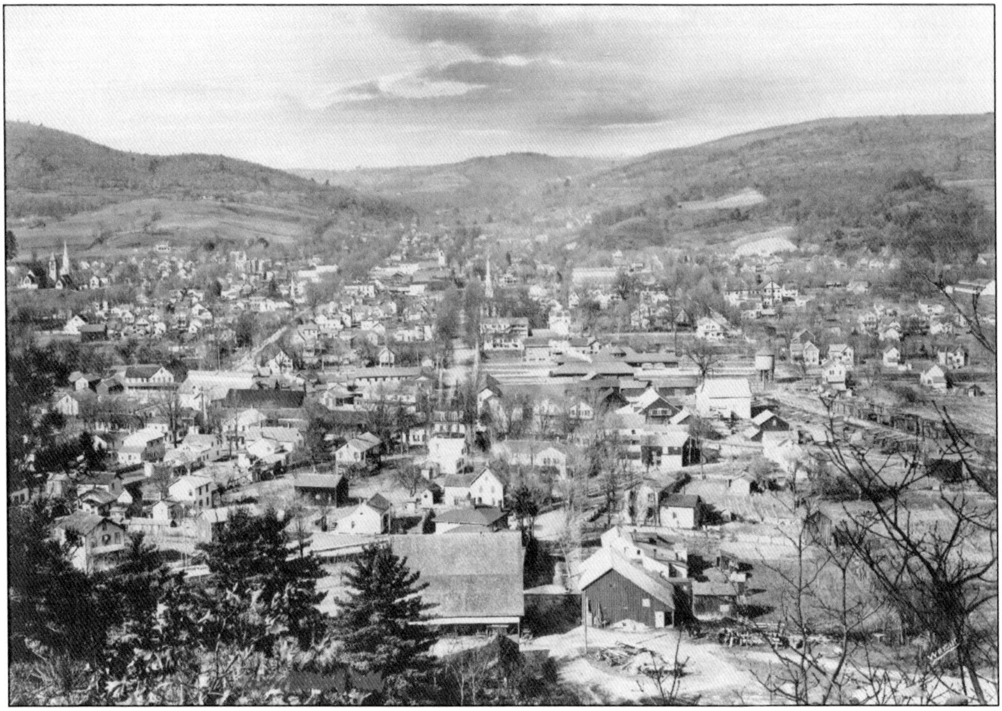

Taken by photographer V.T. Wright (note name, lower right), this early 1900s bird's-eye view of Ellenville shows Canal Street running vertically through the center. From left to right, the steeples of St. John's Memorial Episcopal Church and St. Andrew's Roman Catholic Church are visible. Moving horizontally, the steeple of the Lutheran church and the bell tower of the Methodist church can be seen. In the center is the steeple of the Dutch Reformed church.

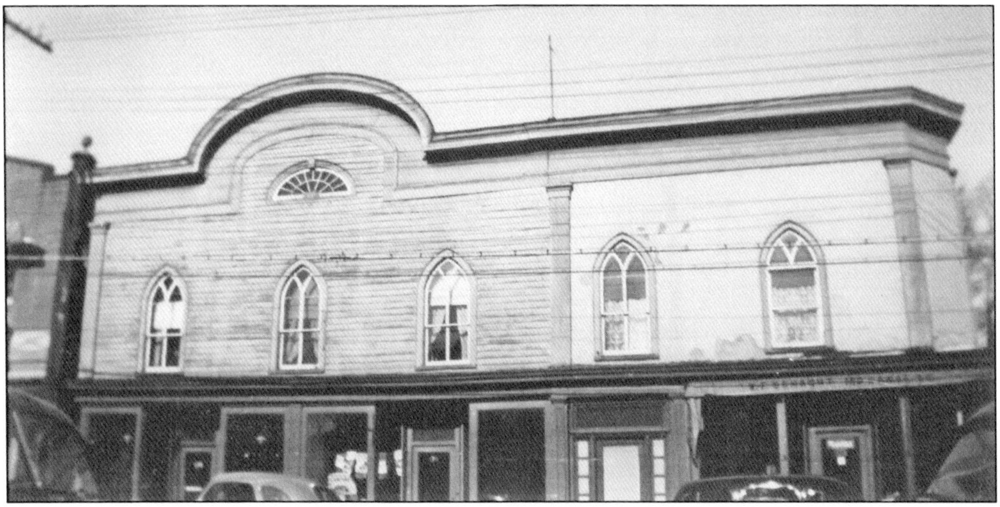

The Ellenville Methodist Episcopal Church was built in 1833 on the site of the current Methodist church on Canal Street. When the new Methodist church was built in 1858, George Warren purchased this building and moved it by oxen to the northwest corner of Maiden Lane and Canal; it became known as Warren Hall. Storefronts (later McAuliffe's Grocery) were downstairs, with a community room and apartments above. It burned down in 1959. Hosanna Assembly of God is there now.

The Reformed Church dates back to this area's original settlement when the first house of worship, made of logs, was built around 1735. A century later, Dutch and French Huguenots who petitioned for a new church formed the Protestant Reformed Dutch Church in 1840. The present Ellenville Reformed Church in the photograph at right was dedicated in 1852, replacing an earlier 1826 structure. Plans for expansion of the church's ministry began during the pastorate of Rev. Perry Van Dyke in 1931, after which a new pipe organ, seen below, was installed. The use of a pipe organ replaced the congregation's original melodeon (a small reed organ), which was followed by a cabinet organ, loaned each Sunday by Mrs. Fred Chapman, and then a seraphine (a cross between a reed organ and an accordion). Building on the work of its 24 founding members, Ellenville Reformed Church remains active today.

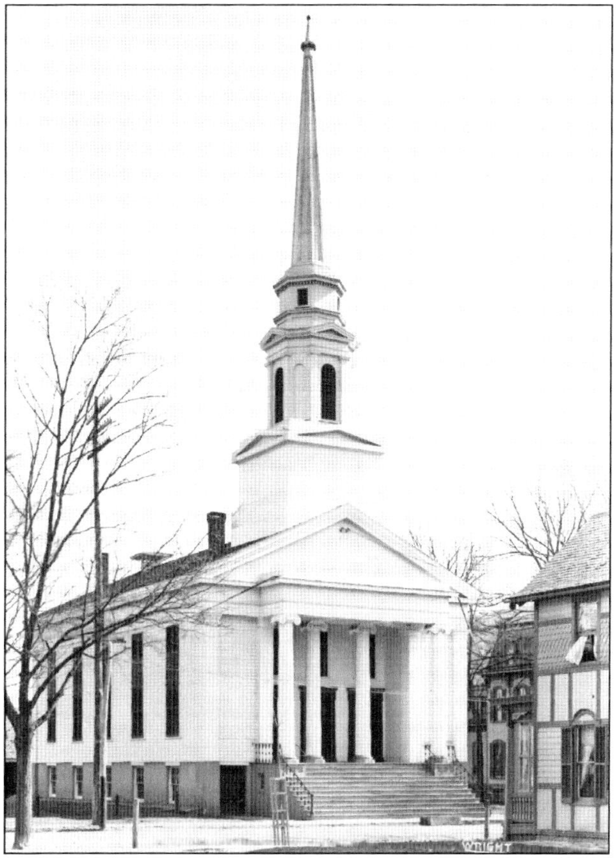

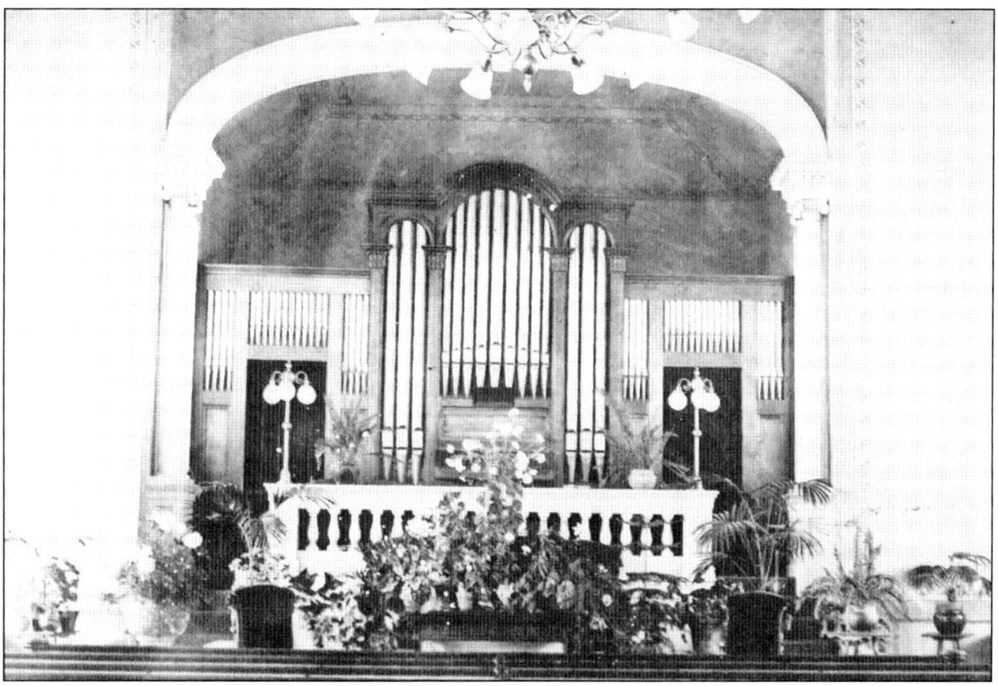

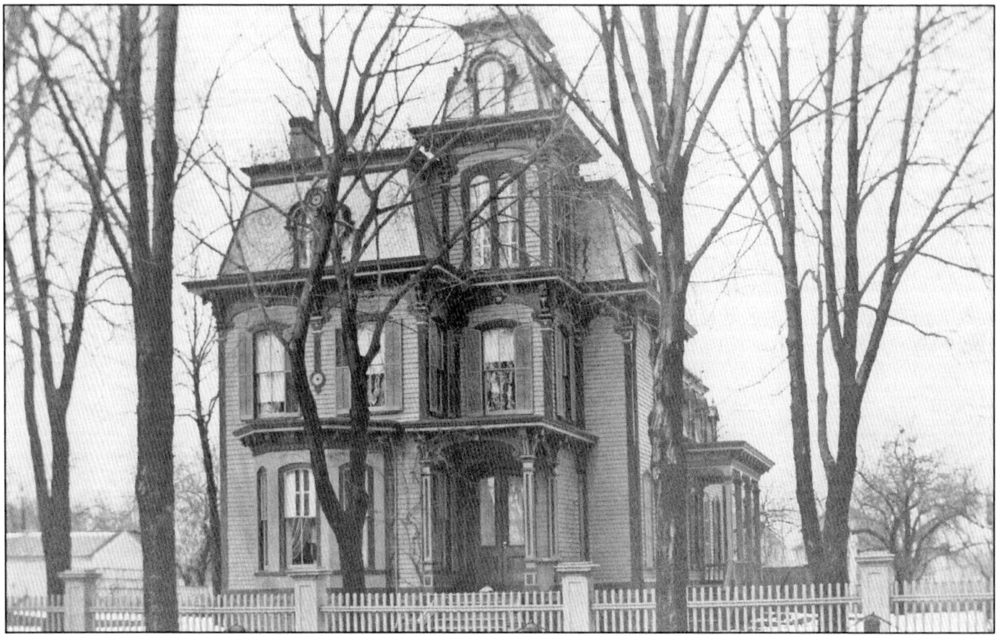

The Ellenville Dutch Reformed Church parsonage was built in 1874. This parsonage, next to the Reformed church on Canal Street, replaced an earlier parsonage on Center Street, east of Market Street. It was considered by many to be one of the finest examples of Victorian architecture in the area. Its columns, window dressings, roof, and siding details made it a showpiece in the village for over 100 years. It was taken down in 1983.

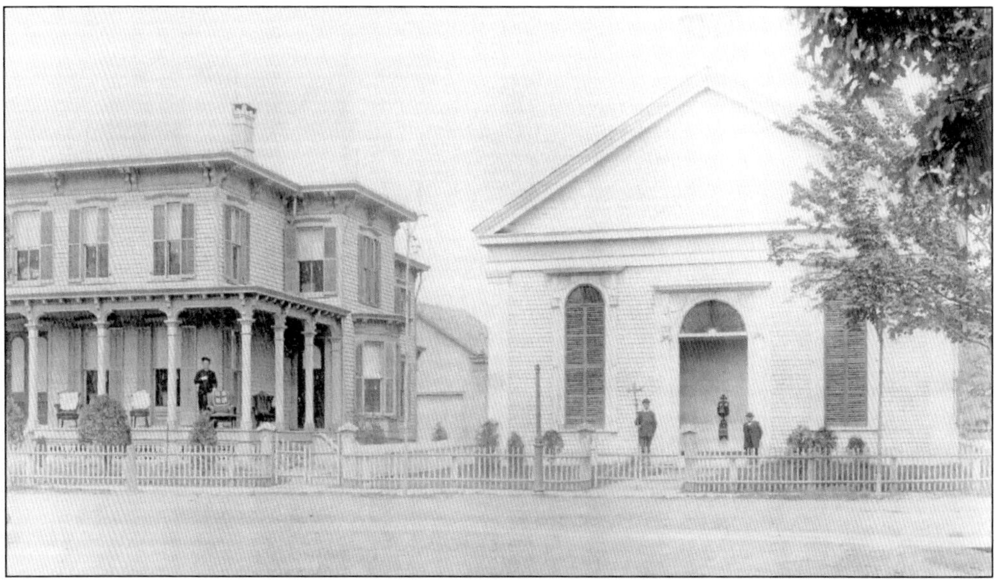

St. Mary's Catholic Church and its Irish Catholic congregation began when Fr. Michael Gilbride arrived in 1844. In 1852, St. Mary's bought the 1826 Dutch Reformed church building, moved it to Main Street, and refitted it for Catholic worship. The parsonage is on the left. St. Mary's centenary mass was celebrated by Cardinal Spellman, the first Roman Catholic cardinal to visit Ellenville. In 1974, Ellenville Savings Bank purchased the property; the building was demolished. (Courtesy of the Church of St. Mary's and St. Andrew's.)

The German Catholic church was first organized in Ellenville in 1849; its first church, called St. Mary's of the Assumption, was built in 1850. Two mission churches, one in Ulster Heights and one in Woodbourne, were part of this congregation. In 1881, the cornerstone of St. Andrew's Catholic Church was laid at its present location on South Main Street near Essex Street. Named after Father Andrew J. Sauer for his exceptional service as pastor, St. Andrew's became the spiritual home of Ellenville's German Catholic congregation. When St. Andrew's and St. Mary's congregations united in 1955, services were held at St. Andrew's. The congregation of the combined St. Mary's and St. Andrew's still thrives. The image below shows the early interior of St. Andrew's.

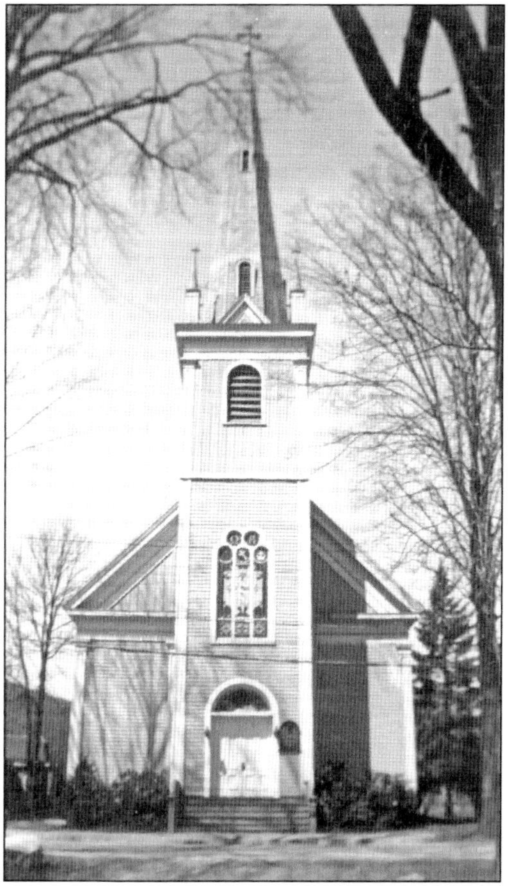

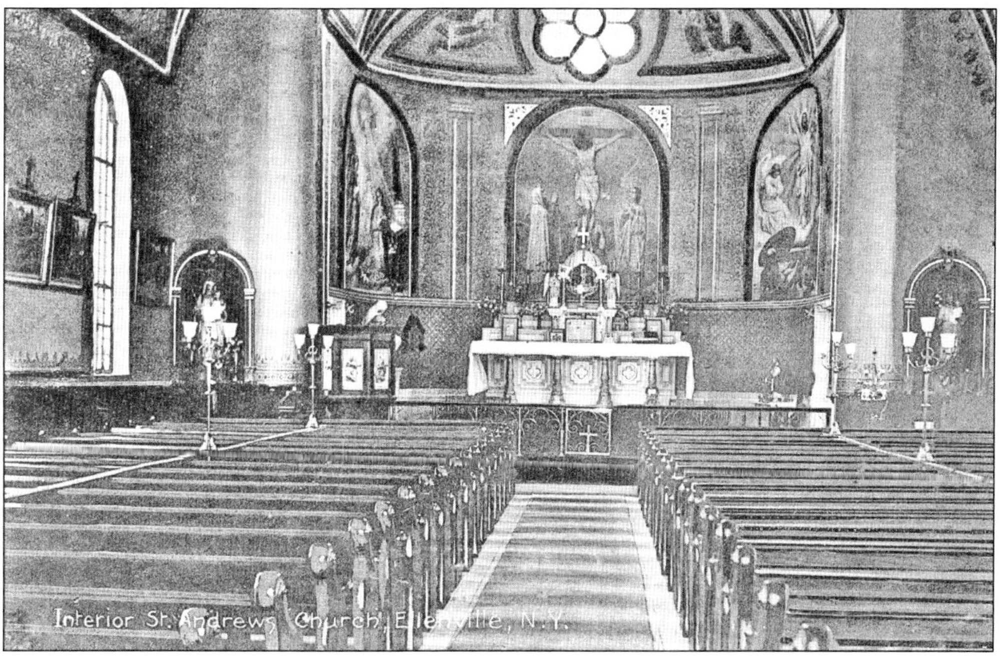

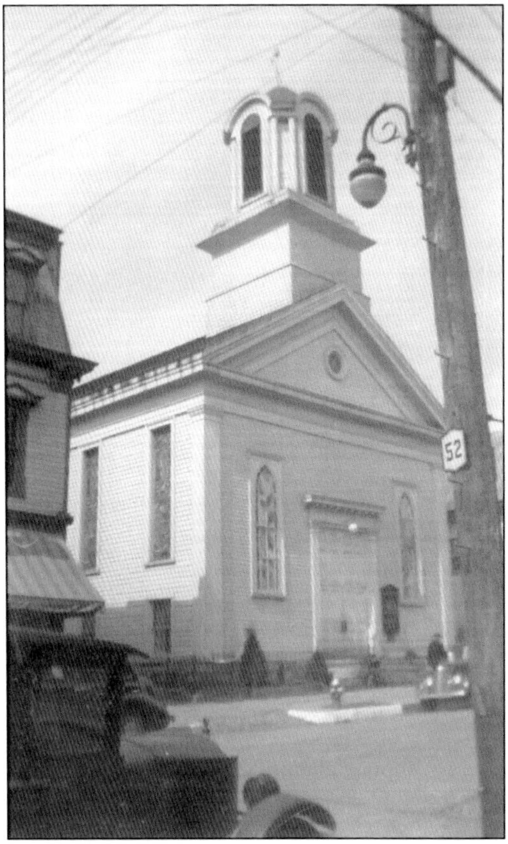

The current Ellenville Methodist Church was built in 1858. This building replaced the first Methodist church, which was built in 1833 at the same location. The church has been renovated and the Sunday school is located in a rear addition. It was centrally located in the early village, and businesses grew up around it. Since the early 1830s, when a large Methodist preaching circuit was established in the area, many businessmen and prominent village citizens have been involved with this church. An early parsonage was located on the east side of Main Street, and in 1869 was moved to 9 Cape Avenue to become part of the Decker-Delany home; this building still stands. In 1870, the brick Victorian home was built across the street and used as the Methodist parsonage until recent years. Currently, the home with its mansard third floor is the location of Step One.

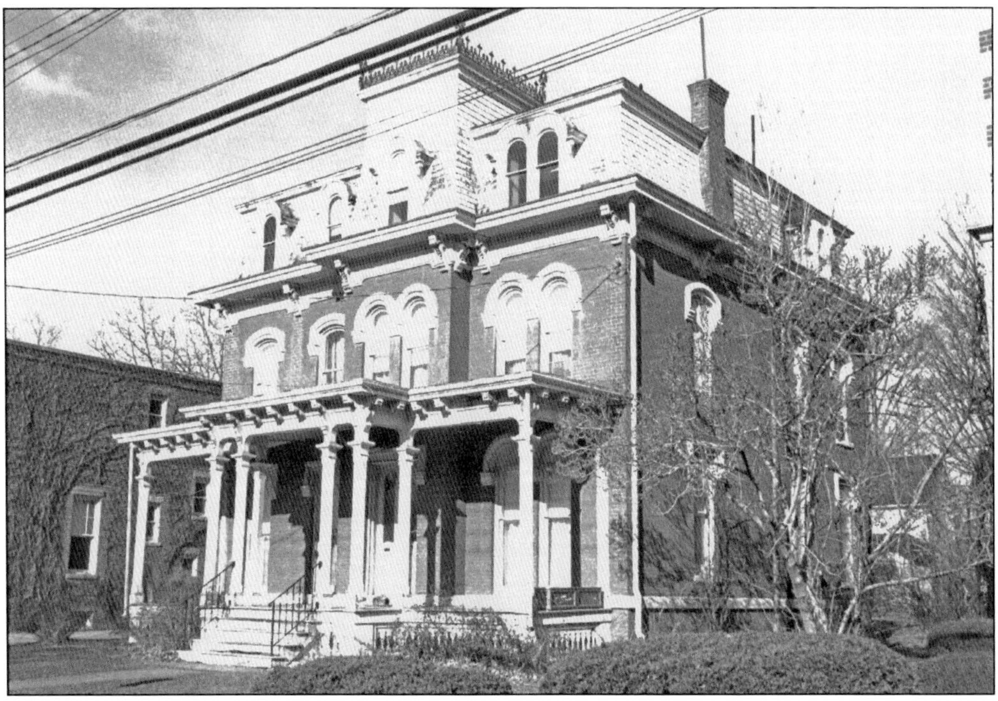

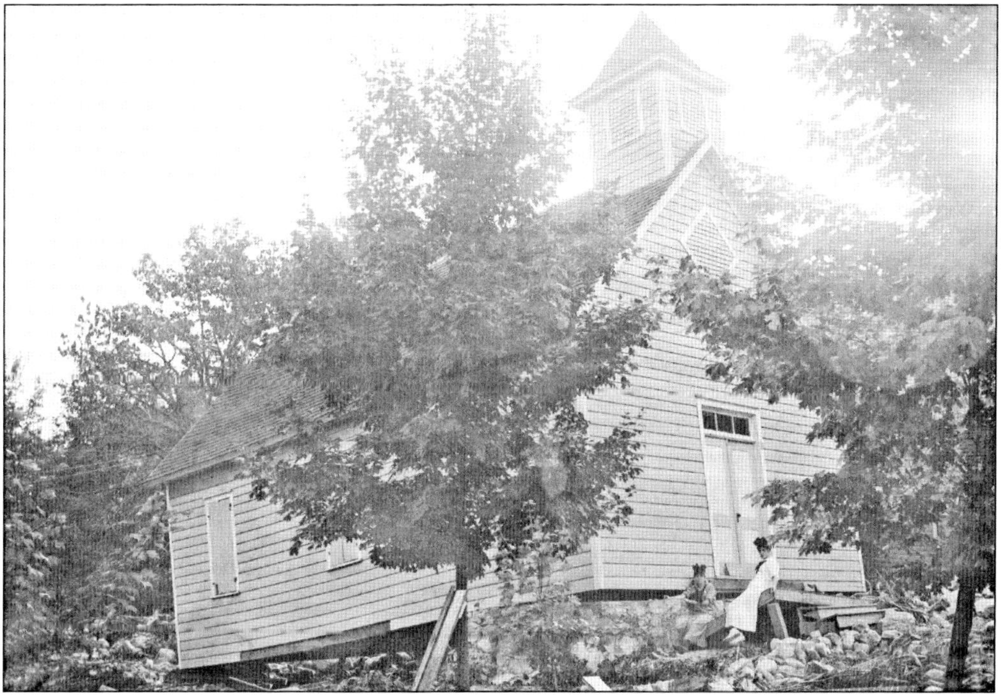

This Methodist church was on the upper end of Chapel Street. Built in 1900 and damaged in 1915 by a flood, the building still sits at its original location. The church was first used as a missionary chapel of many faiths before becoming a Methodist mission. After the 1915 flood, it was no longer used as a church, and became a private residence.

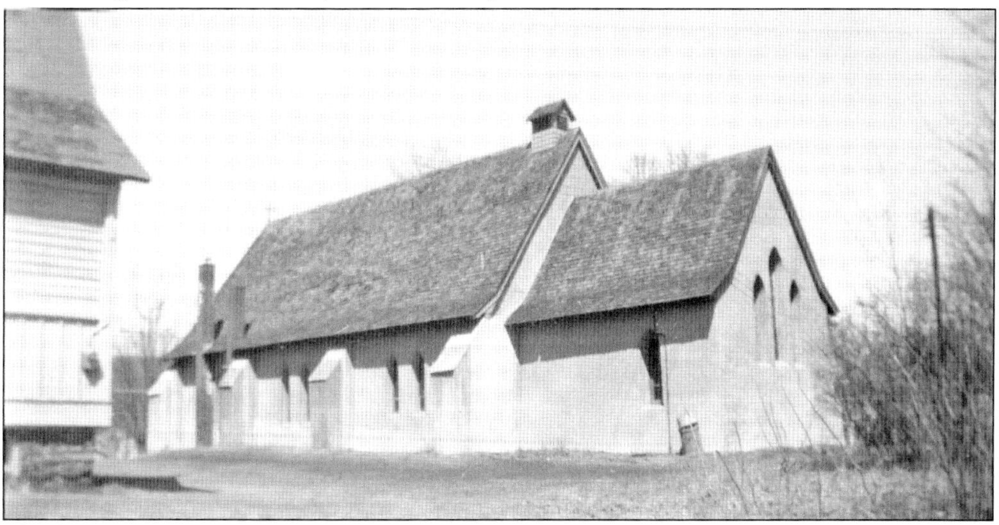

The first Episcopal services were held in Ellenville in 1849 under the leadership of Rev. Samuel Hawksley, a priest in Newburgh who also established missionary churches in Milton and Stone Ridge. The newly formed congregation laid the cornerstone for its first church building, St. Paul's Chapel, in 1866. St. Paul's was then replaced by St. John's Memorial Church in 1874 and used primarily as a parish hall and community area, including as rehearsal space for local marching bands. After falling into disrepair, St. Paul's was restored in 2003 and now serves as the home of the Music Institute for Sullivan and Ulster Counties.

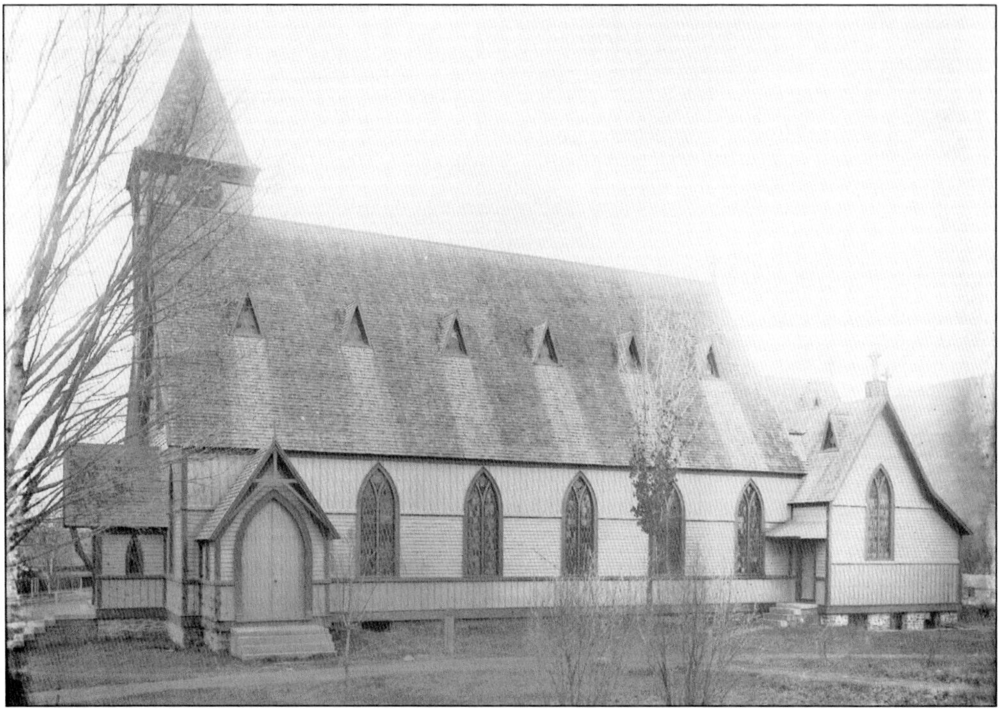

Consecrated in 1874, St. John's Memorial Episcopal Church was built by Manhattan banker and broker Elias Cornelius Humbert in memory of his 16-year-old son, Cornelius "Neil" Chandler Humbert, who died of a sudden illness. The consecration service, officiated by Bishop Horatio Potter, was followed the next day by a recital featuring Homer Bartlett, an Ellenville boy who later became a famous organist and composer.

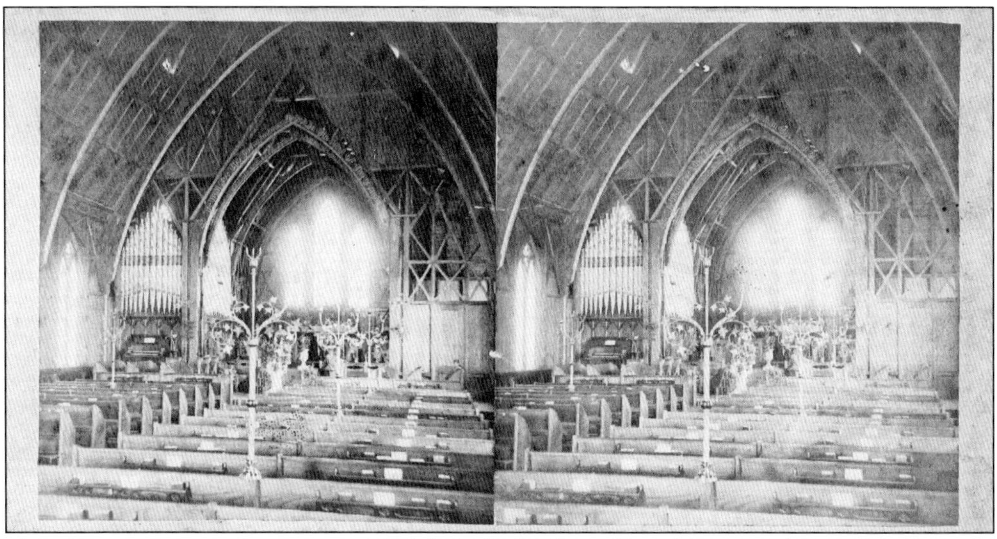

These stereoscopic interior views of St. John's shows the arching buttresses that evoke the image of a ship's hull, an architectural component characteristic of many churches built in the English tradition. The buttresses are adorned with passages from Holy Scripture. Not visible is Cornelius Humbert's name inscribed in the stained-glass window above the altar. The pipe organ, on the left, is still in use today.

The congregation of Christ Lutheran Church formed in 1850 as the German Evangelical Lutheran Church of Ellenville; it was soon thereafter named the Second Reformed Dutch Church. In 1861, under the leadership of Rev. E.C.H. Luebkert, it was reorganized as the First German Evangelical Lutheran Christ Church at Ellenville. Members included leading citizens of the village. The present church was built in 1862 on a lot purchased from Father Wigaham in the middle of Ann Street. In 1905, that church was then moved to its present location on the southwest corner of Ann and Center Streets. A fire partially destroyed this Greek Revival church in January 1912; the congregation quickly recovered and rebuilt the church by April of that year. The image below is a studio photograph of the congregational choir, around 1903.

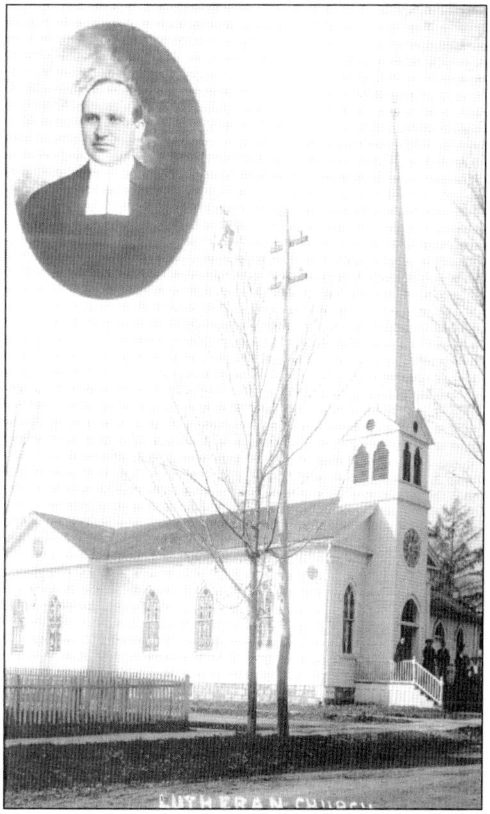

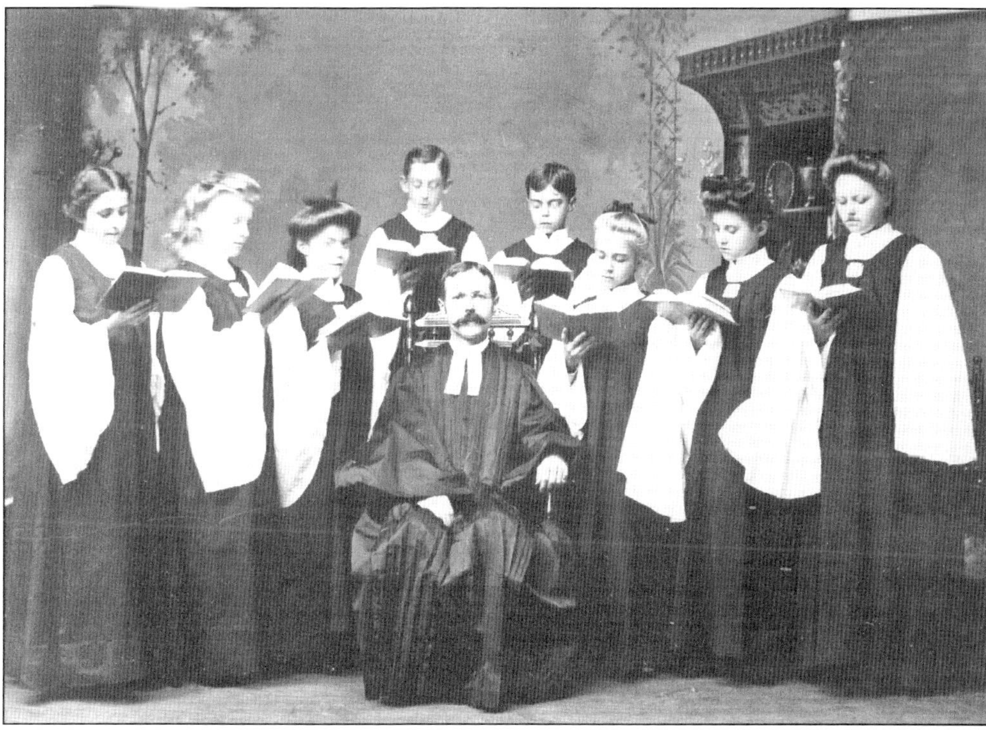

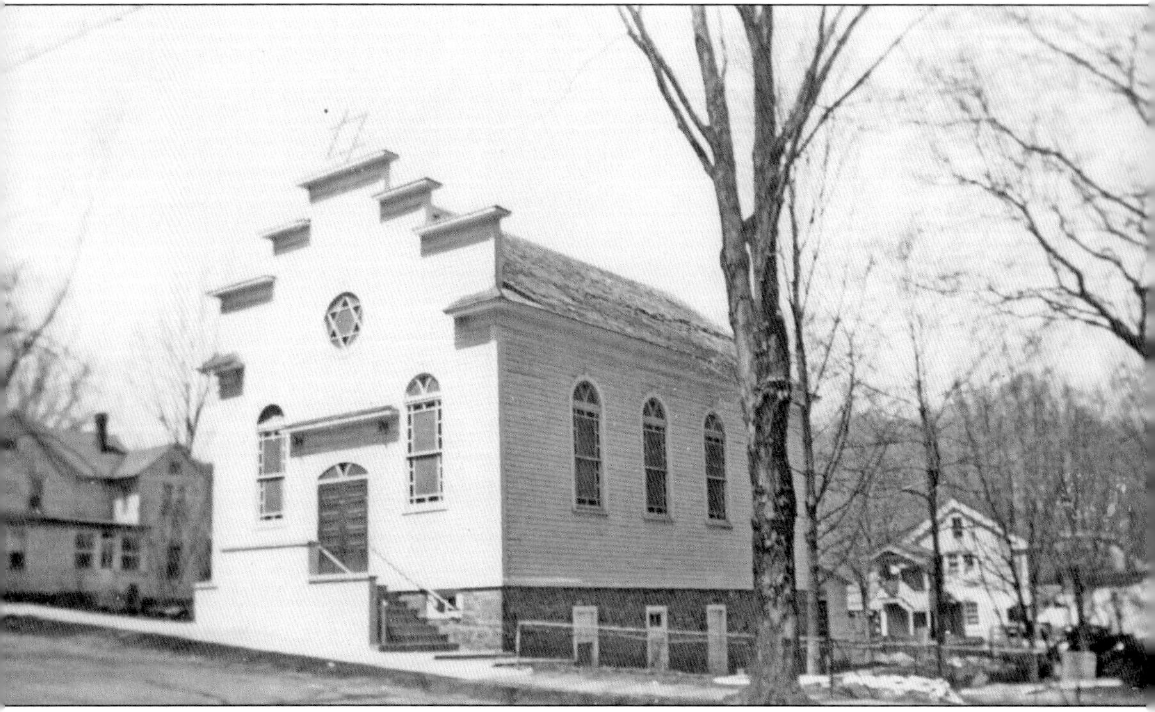

Dedicated in 1910, the Hebrew Aid Society Synagogue was one of the oldest synagogues in the Catskills. The congregation, founded as the Ellenville Hebrew Aid Society (EHAS) in 1907, purchased this Center Street property from the Ellenville Tannery. Kalman Goldman was the founder and first president of the EHAS, and Rabbi Leib Katz came to Ellenville in 1906 to lead the congregation. In 1908, Goldman bought land in Wawarsing for a Jewish cemetery that became property of the synagogue one year later. EHAS later became Congregation Ezrath Israel.

Seven

THIS, THAT, AND THE OTHER

Ellenville's distinguished history in the Hudson River valley has been marked both by the everyday influences and forces of community life and by unique events, such as the appearance of mastodon bones found in a local pond and US presidential visits. Ellenville has survived floods, fires, wars, economic booms, and national depressions, all of which affected the nature of the village's economic life and the personal lives of its residents. Many Ellenville citizens became prominent figures locally and some on the state and national levels. This concluding chapter offers a cross section of events that helped form the village of Ellenville's character and just a few of the people that shaped the village into a community.

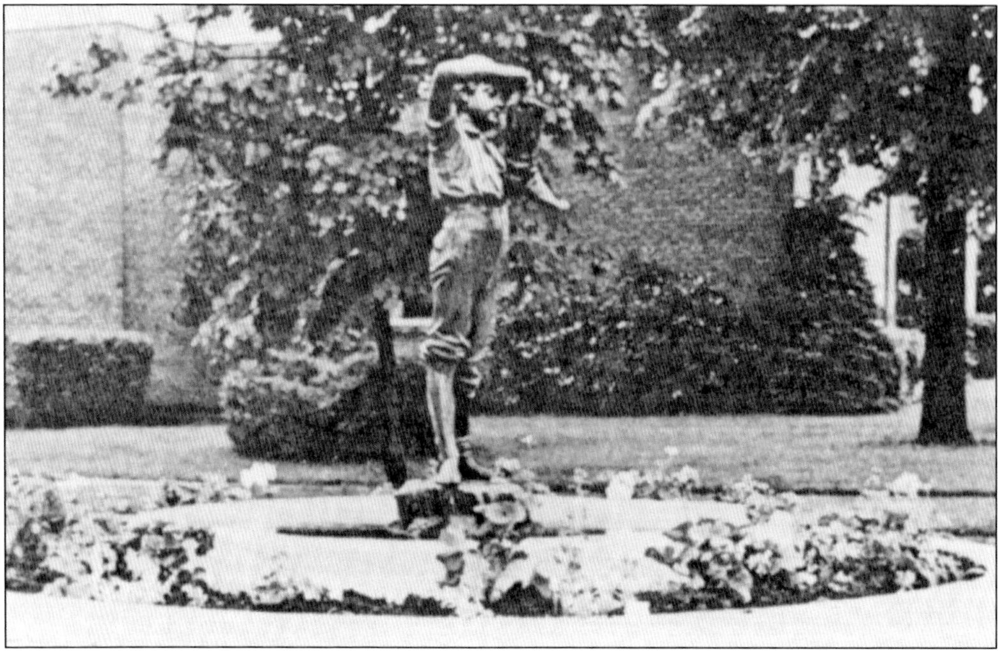

The *Boy with the Boot* has been a central figure in Ellenville since 1925. The landmark resided in a fountain at the head of Liberty Street on land given to the Scoresby Fire Company by Walter Cox. The statue currently in Liberty Square is a reproduction of Scoresby's "Boy," which now resides at EPL&M. Many of these statues can be found throughout the United States and overseas.

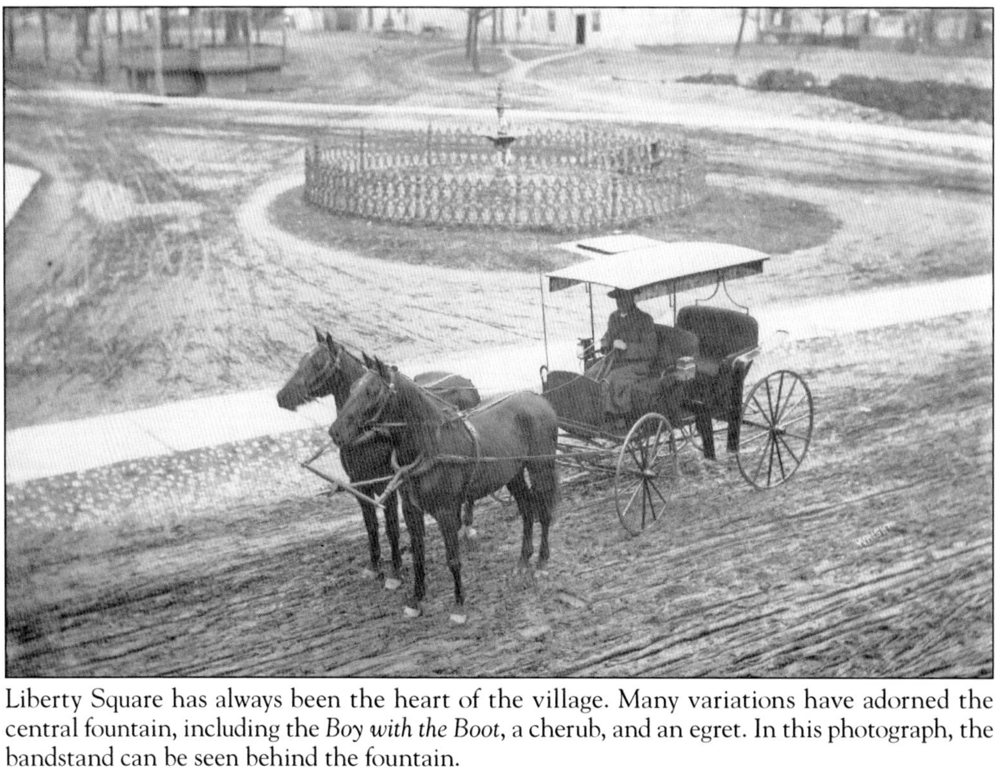

Liberty Square has always been the heart of the village. Many variations have adorned the central fountain, including the *Boy with the Boot*, a cherub, and an egret. In this photograph, the bandstand can be seen behind the fountain.

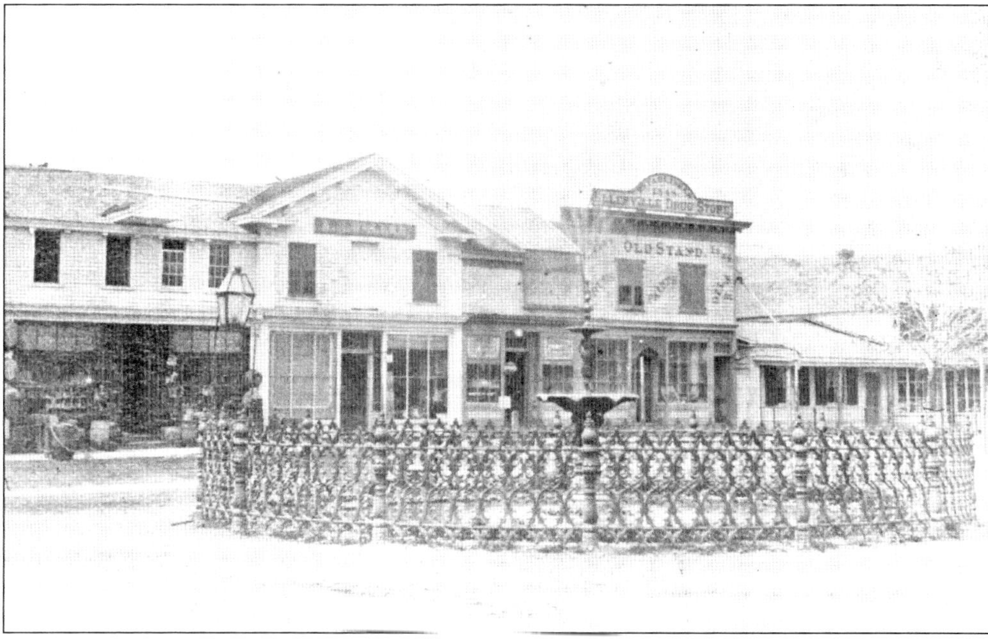

This location at Liberty Square on the southwest corner of Canal and Market Streets was the site of the first stores and homes in Ellenville. Considered to be the center of town, this area was always the hub of activity. These brick buildings, erected by prominent businessmen, proudly display the names Albert and Rothkopf. They were constructed to replace the wood buildings of the mid-1800s that were destroyed by fire in 1931. These fine buildings still stand today and have housed many stores and offices over the years.

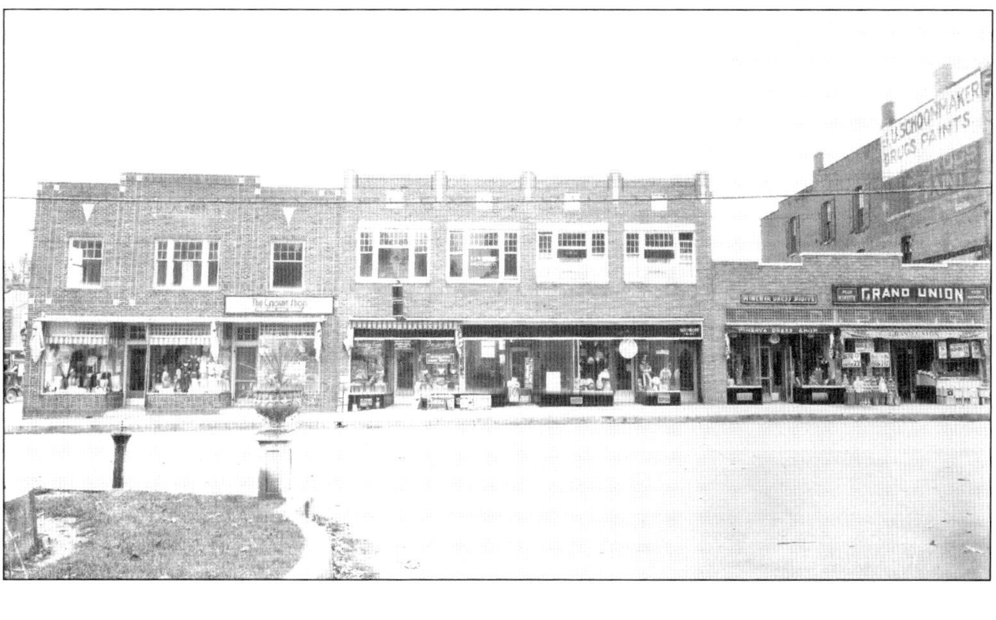

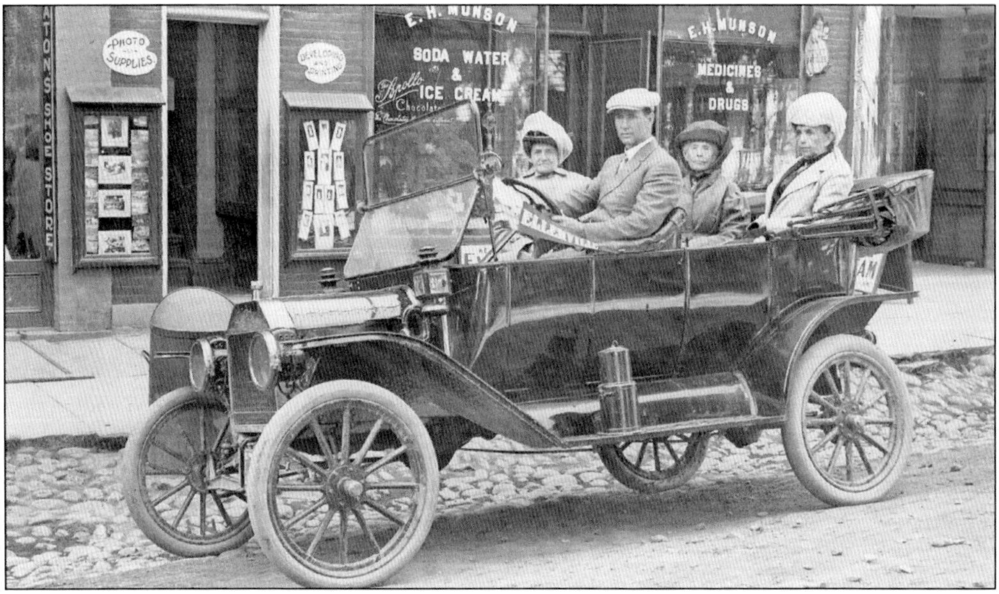

A Ford Model T Touring Car displaying an Ellenville banner is parked in front of Edgar H. Munson's drugstore at 155 Canal Street around 1910. Eaton's Shoe Store was next door, and V.T. Wright's photography studio was upstairs. In 1908, the Automobile Club of Ulster County met and dined at the Wayside Inn. A newspaper notice recommended that drivers "not form in line, as the dust would be intolerable."

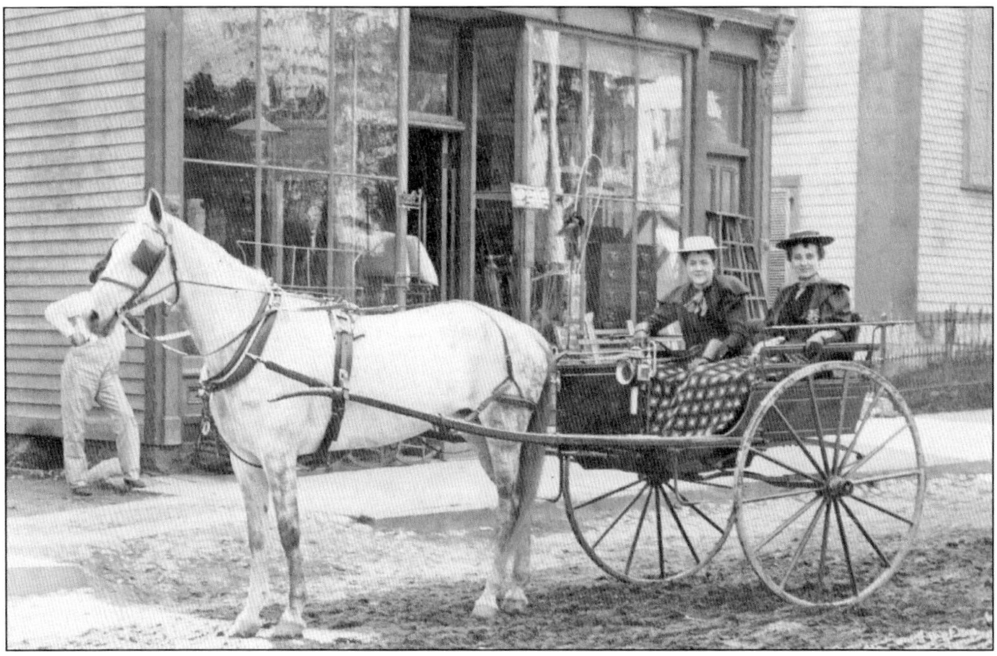

This single-horse-drawn buggy, called a sprung cart, is in front of a furniture and undertaking business at 227 Canal Street, which was owned over the years by Dutcher & Holmes, Dutcher & Briggs, Hoornbeek & Son, Hoornbeek & Terwilliger, and Irving Ostrander. It was common during the late 19th and early 20th centuries for a furniture maker to build coffins, and many included embalming and funeral services. Funerals were commonly held in the deceased's home.

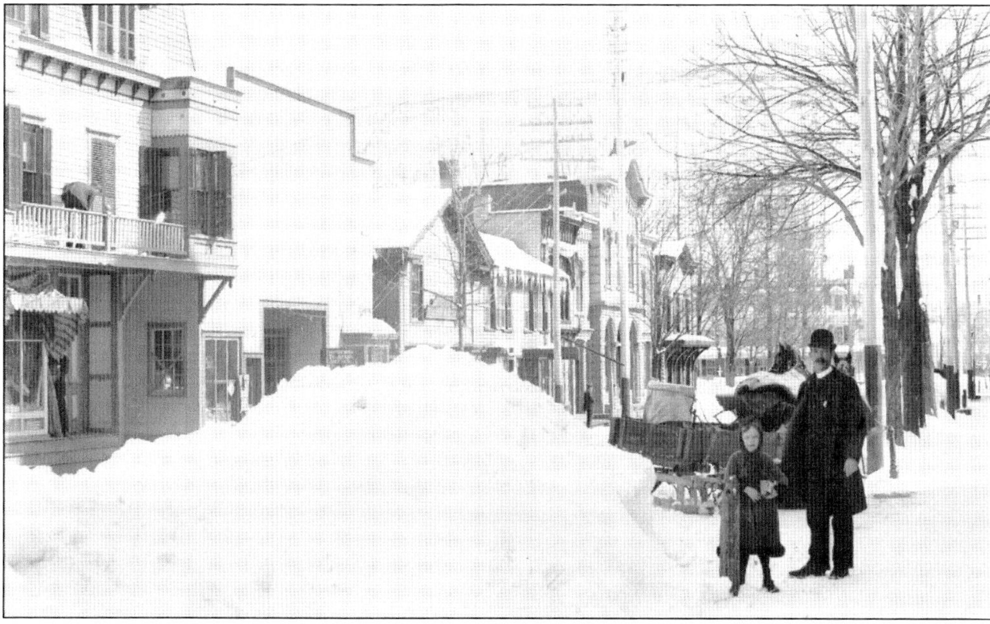

A man and child pose near a hitching post on Canal Street in the late 1860s. On the left is Beers & Company Hardware and Tin Shop, with the First National Bank farther down the block. The wooden buildings between will later be replaced with masonry structures housing the Ellenville Savings Bank and the Ellenville Post Office. Terwilliger House is in the background. Notice the horse and sleigh curbside in the photograph above. In the image below, a delightful mix of young village residents enjoy a winter outing in a horse-drawn sleigh and ham it up for the camera. At a time when streets were not cleared of snow (any snow removal was done by hand), horse-drawn sleighs were a common means of transportation. Today, a Rose & Douglas delivery sleigh is on display at Thornton's Hardware on Canal.

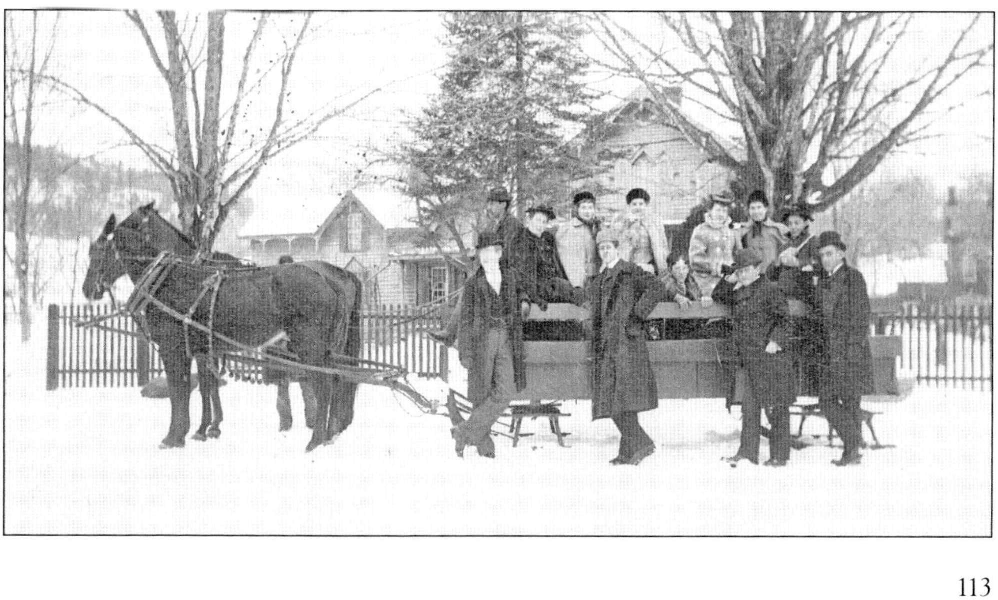

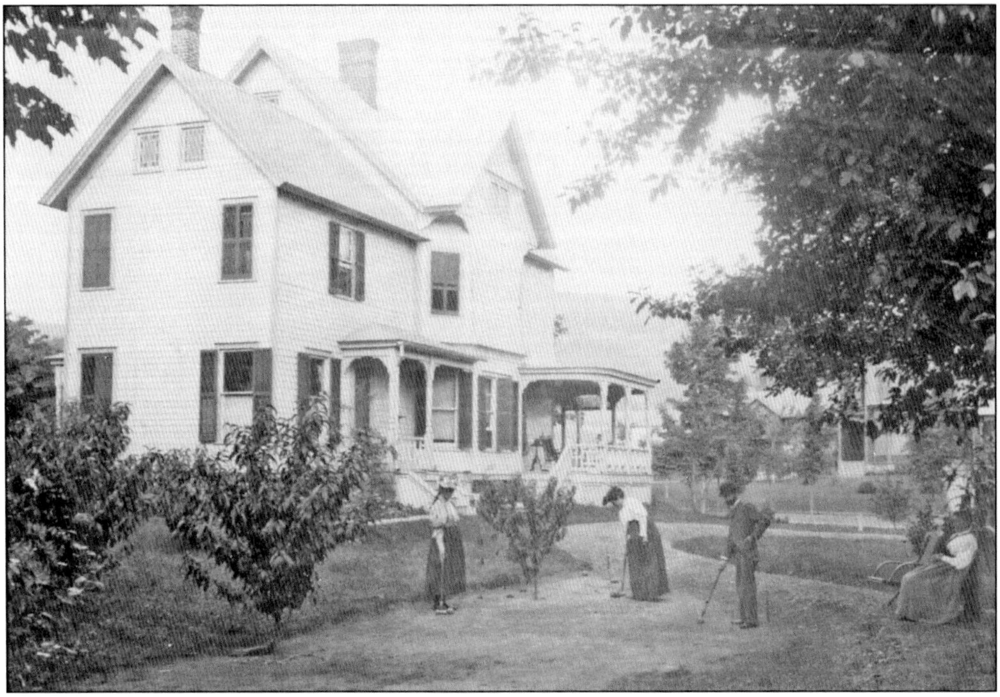

Played here at 156 Main Street, croquet was a popular pastime in the late 19th century. Originating in Great Britain around 1850, the game quickly caught on in the United States. This photograph was taken in the early 1890s, based on the leg-of-mutton sleeves, or gigots, sleeve seen on the women's dresses, which had recently come into fashion.

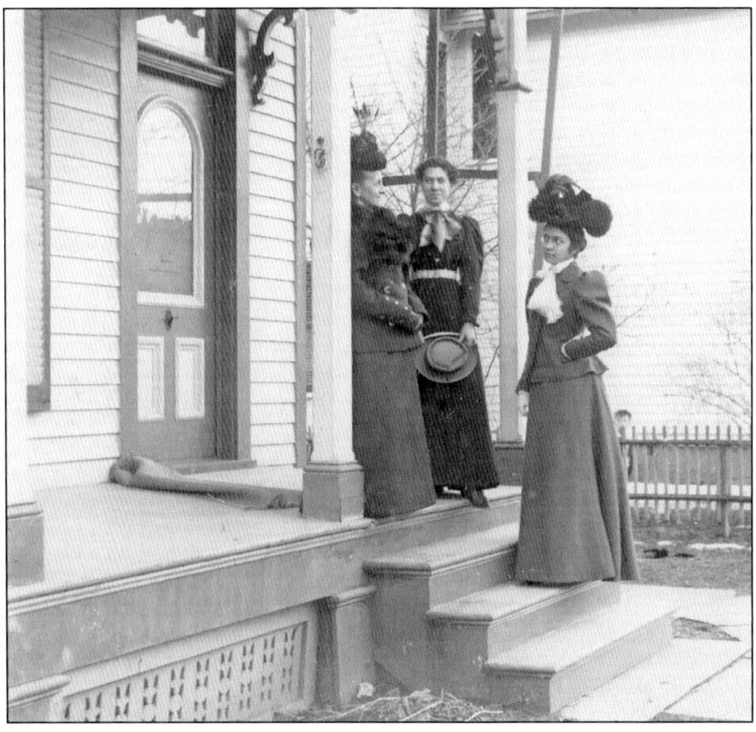

On the porch of this Maiden Lane home are, from left to right, Mary Robeson Smith, wife of Ellenville druggist Arthur Gridley Smith; Eva Van Campen, a fashion designer visiting from out of town; and Helen Deyo, daughter of W.H. Deyo, owner of Deyo Lumber. A lifelong resident of Ellenville, Helen married W.R. DuBois, a partner in DuBois Brothers Hardware. She lived to be 94 years old.

Area boys pose at Worcester Academy around 1895. William R. DuBois (left) partnered with his brother Lemuel in DuBois Brothers Hardware. George Young Jr. (second from left) received his bachelor of architecture degree at Cornell University, where he was dean of architecture after serving in the Army Signal Corps during World War I. Young designed the Scoresby Clubhouse. His brother Chester (second from right) also attended Cornell, returning to Napanoch and becoming a prominent farmer. Richard T. Childs (right), son of Ellenville banker George Childs, earned a degree at Rensselaer Institute.

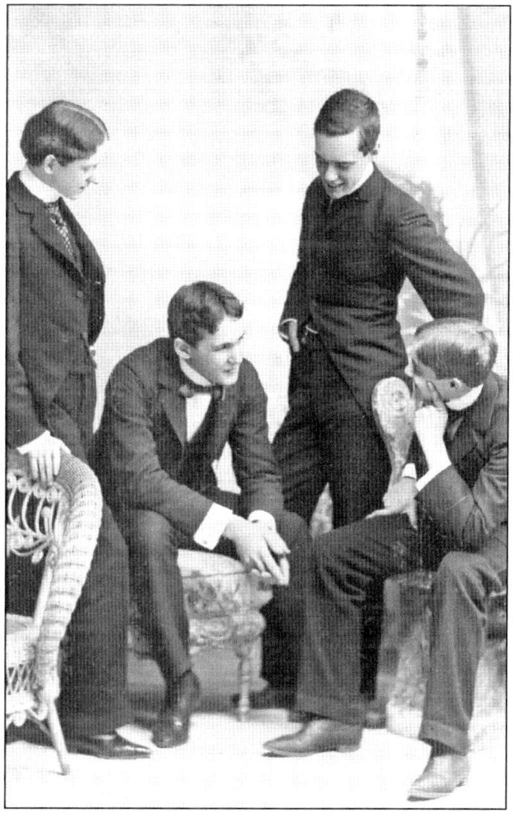

The 1905 census lists Augusta Clark, age 23, as living with her parents on Market Street and with a private school occupation. She might have operated what was known as a dame school, a form of early education used since 16th-century England, in her home. Clark married Ellenville attorney Raymond Cox in 1907. Students are, from left to right, (first row) George Childs Rose, Dorothy Vernon, and Clarence Earle Vrooman; (second row) Aimee Derby and Helen Campbell.

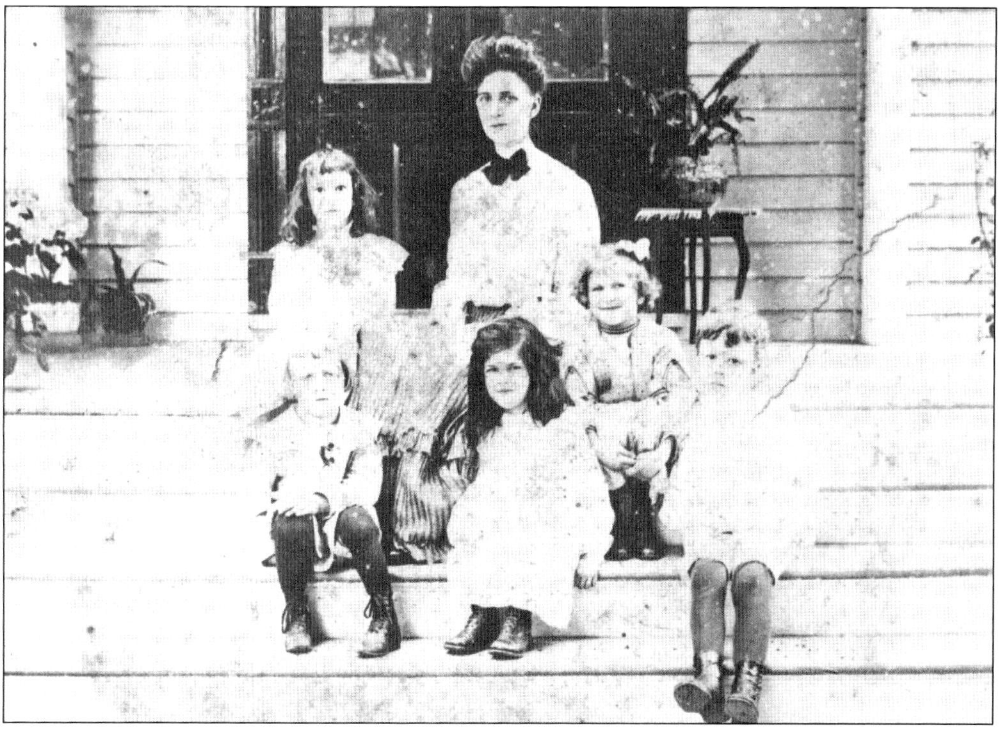

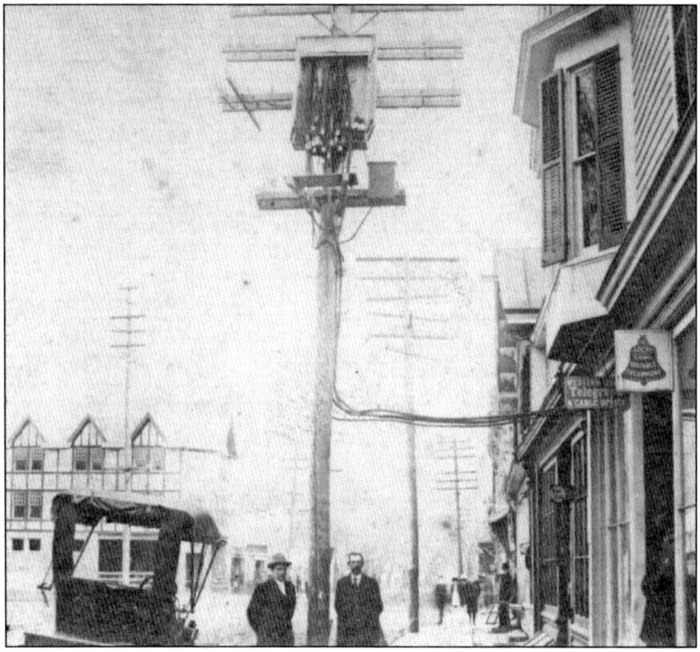

Ellenville was one of the first communities in the area to offer electric service to residents. The first telephone was installed to facilitate communication between canal locks. Telegraph systems operated from the D&H Canal building, the post office, and, later, on Canal Street next door to the telephone office, as seen in this 1911 image. Established in 1892, the Ellenville Electric Co. received power from a Napanoch generator; its 1913 building on Route 209 near Canal presents a recently restored original facade.

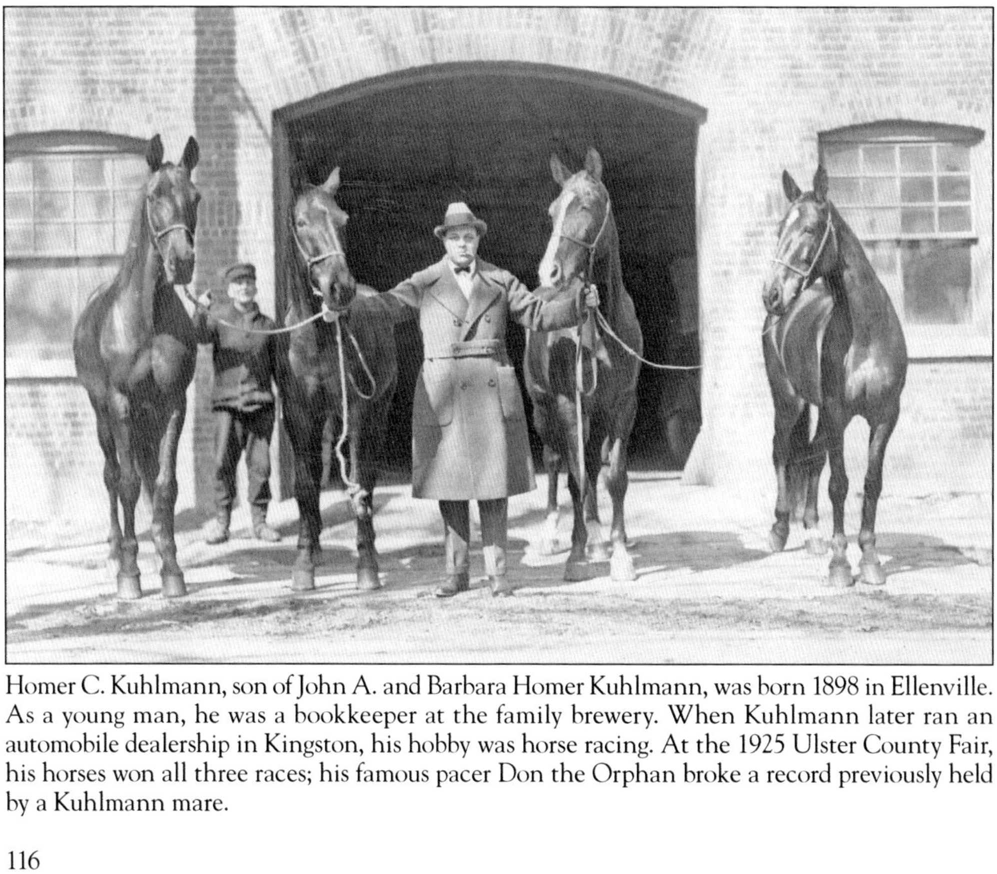

Homer C. Kuhlmann, son of John A. and Barbara Homer Kuhlmann, was born 1898 in Ellenville. As a young man, he was a bookkeeper at the family brewery. When Kuhlmann later ran an automobile dealership in Kingston, his hobby was horse racing. At the 1925 Ulster County Fair, his horses won all three races; his famous pacer Don the Orphan broke a record previously held by a Kuhlmann mare.

Girls pose as Little Bo Peep, Mother Goose, and Red Riding Hood in V.T. Wright's photography studio; Wright's daughter Edith is in the center. In 1918, Edith married S. Maxwell Taylor, who worked in partnership with his brother Ben at the *Ellenville Journal*. Edith was active in the Kingston YWCA and 20th Century Club, acting in and directing plays for charity.

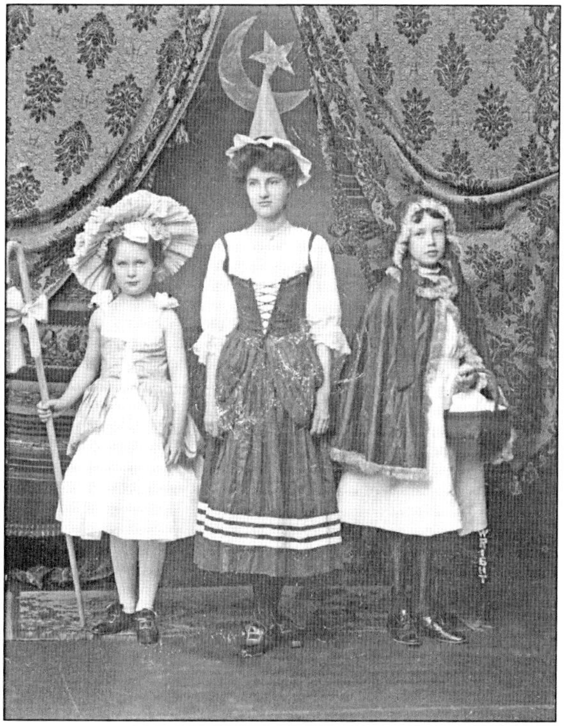

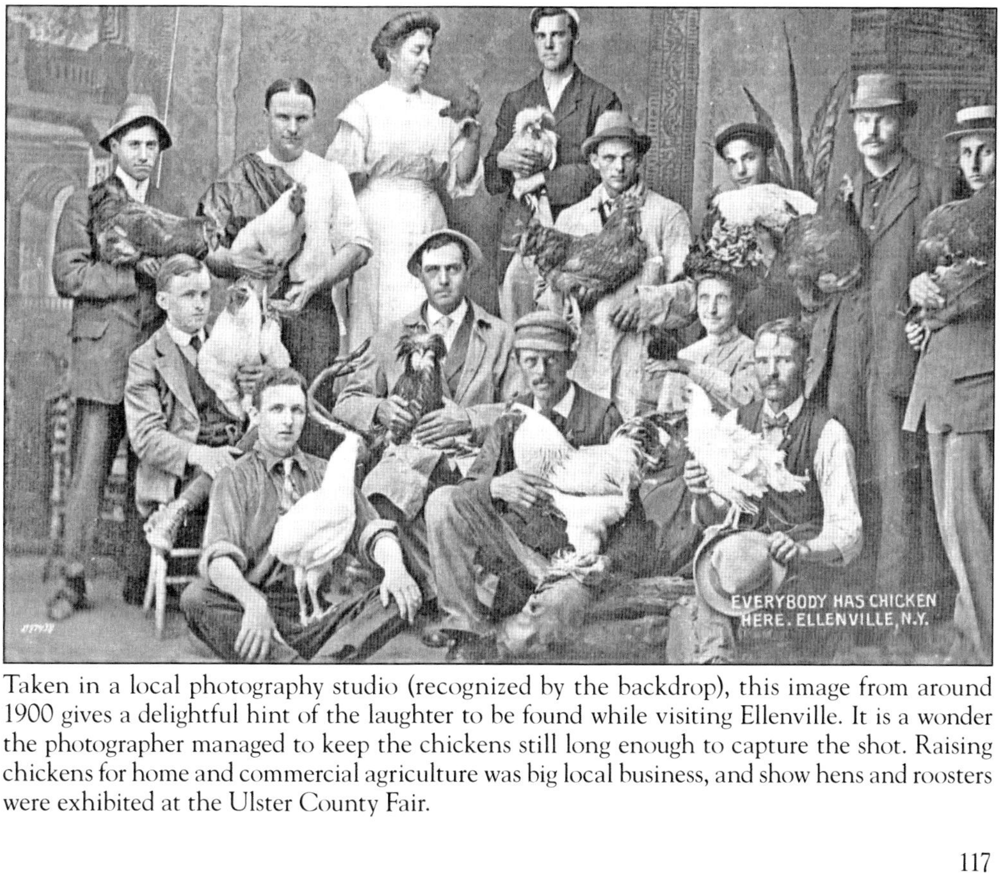

Taken in a local photography studio (recognized by the backdrop), this image from around 1900 gives a delightful hint of the laughter to be found while visiting Ellenville. It is a wonder the photographer managed to keep the chickens still long enough to capture the shot. Raising chickens for home and commercial agriculture was big local business, and show hens and roosters were exhibited at the Ulster County Fair.

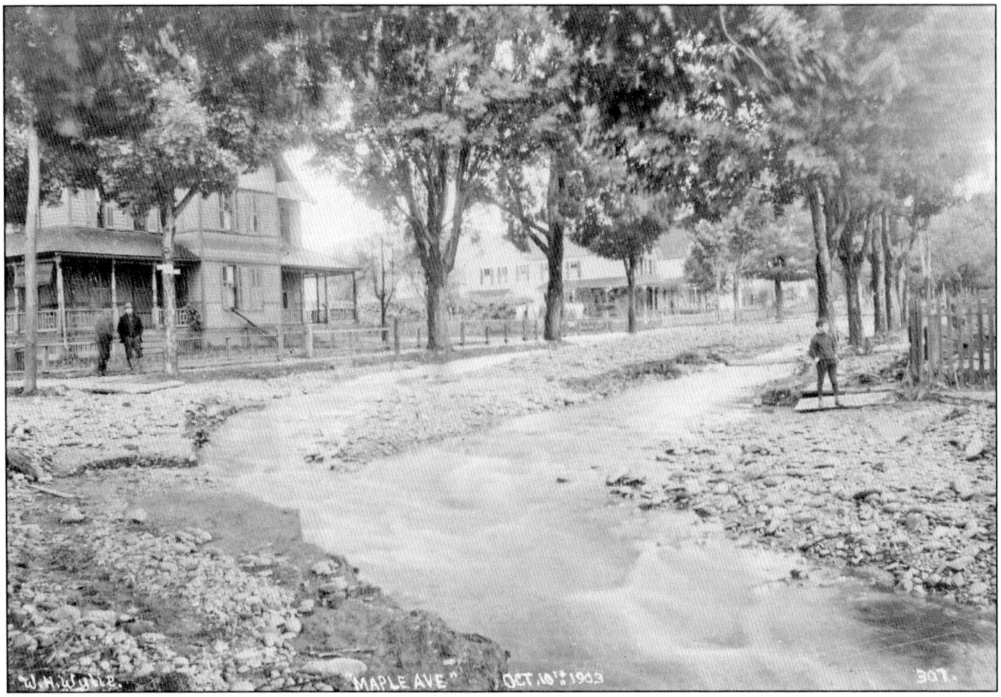

The early history of Ellenville includes a number of floods that caused significant damage. One of the earliest recorded accounts is dated 1852, when Mountain Brook, running down the Shawangunk Ridge east of the village, overflowed its banks after a cloudburst; this occurrence would repeat itself in 1915. Other floods over the years include the Beerkill and Sandburg Creeks. A flood in 1869 brought destruction of dams and buildings, flooding of streets and fields, and severe damage to the new Ellenville Driving Park. The image above shows the devastation of Maple Avenue in 1903, when a dam break in Ulster Heights contributed to the effects of rain. That year's flood swept away three bridges, including a new iron bridge over the Beerkill.

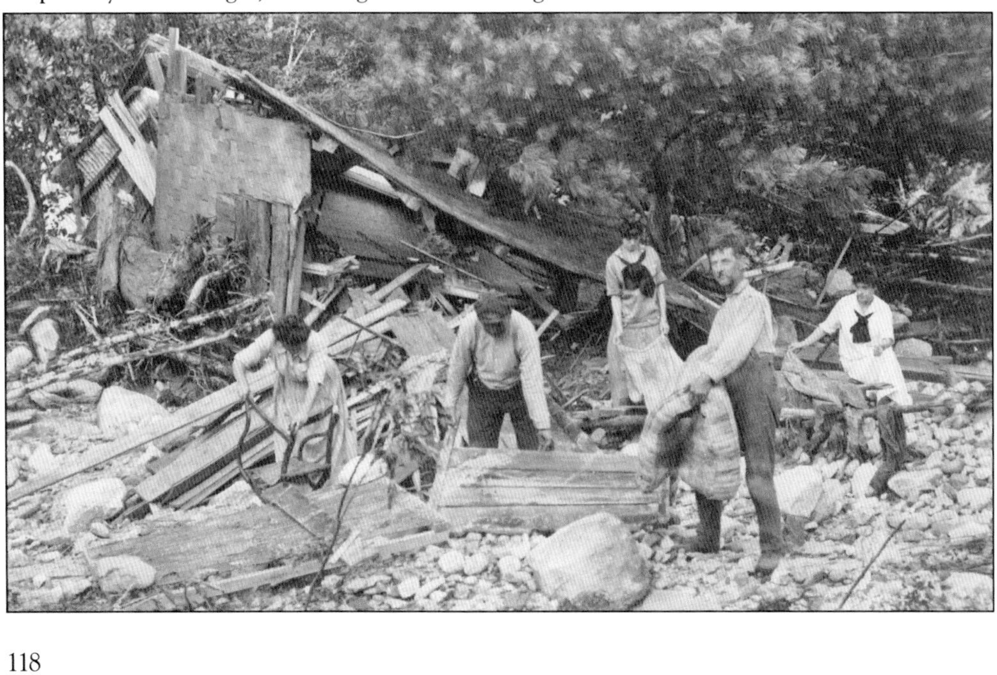

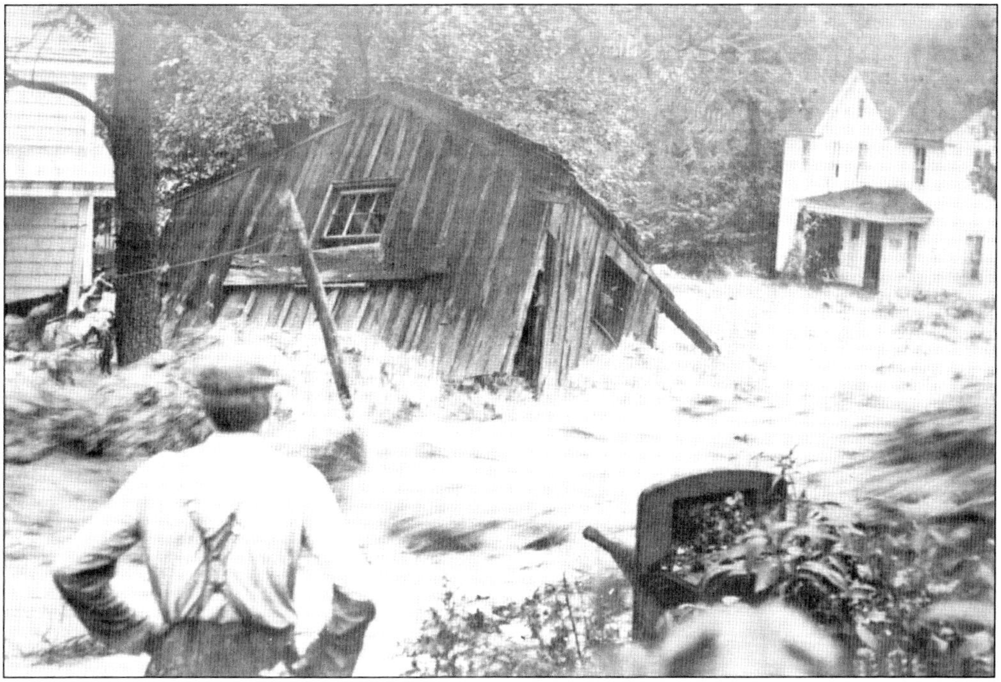

In August 1915, a heavy rainstorm struck Ellenville and vicinity. Up the mountain to the east near Cragsmoor, the usually quiet Mountain Brook (also called North Gully Brook) swelled beyond capacity and broke free of its banks. The raging water carried trees, boulders, and other debris down Chapel Street, as shown in the photograph above, dislodging several houses and the Methodist church from their foundations. The stream took out barns, fences, yards, and gardens, leaving gullies and piles of rocks in its wake. Another result of the 1915 flood was the interruption of railroad service between Ellenville and Kingston; hundreds of feet of O&W track were demolished by the water, as can be seen in the photograph at right.

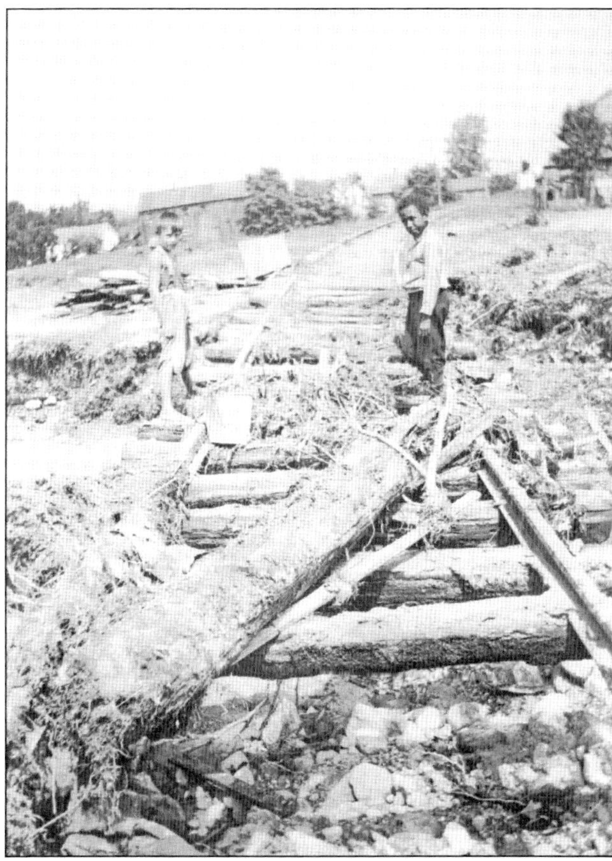

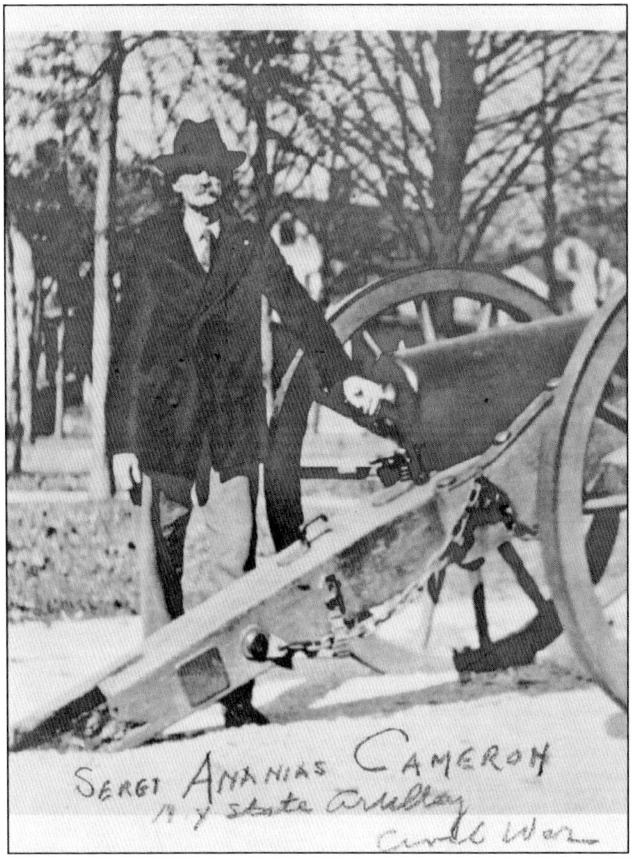

Born in Ellenville in 1848, Ananias Cameron enlisted as a private in Company B of the 15th Heavy Artillery Regiment of New York Volunteers in 1864, serving in the Army of the Potomac until the end of the Civil War. Cameron was wounded at the Second Battle of the Weldon Railroad in Petersburg, Virginia. Returning home to Ellenville, he became a member of GAR Ward Post No. 191. Ward Post was named in honor of Capt. Pelatiah Ward, Company E of the 20th Regiment of the New York State Militia. Ward was a pastor at the Ellenville Methodist Church; he was persuaded to lead a regiment by local enlistees. Ward was fatally wounded at Manassas, Virginia. The image below, from around 1906, is of GAR members on a float decorated for the Ulster County Fair, with Cameron standing on the far right. EPL&M has his handgun.

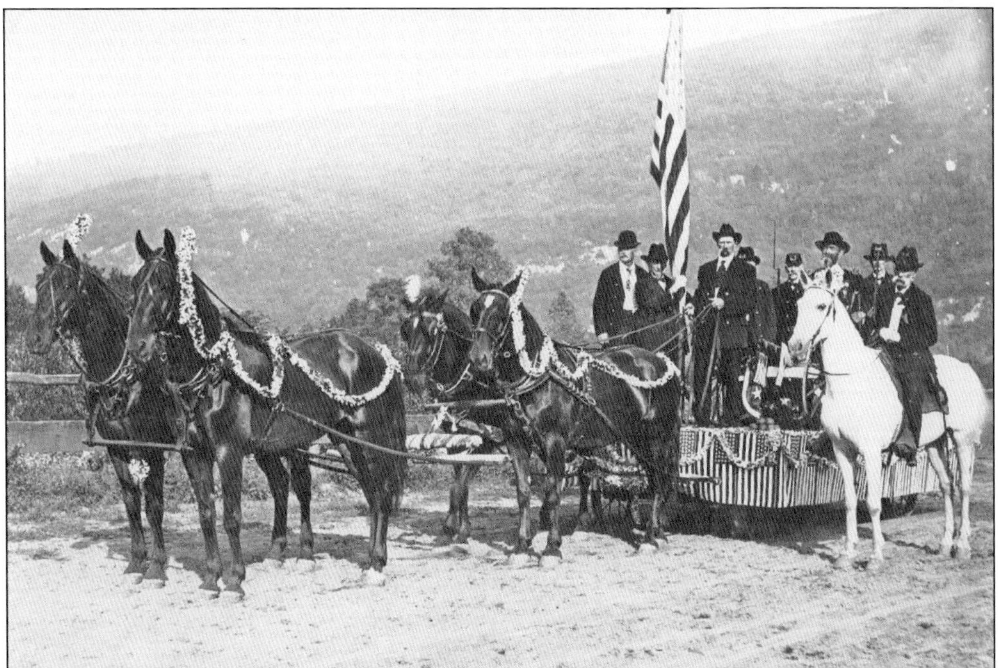

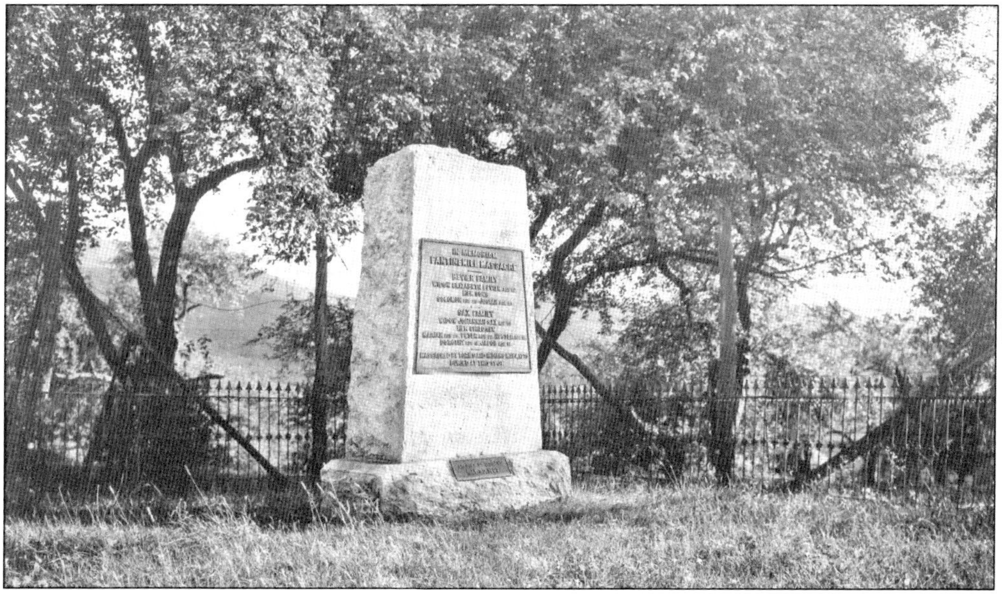

The Fantinekill Monument on Route 209 in north Ellenville marks the graves of Bevier and Sax family members killed in the Fantinekill Massacre of 1779. During the American Revolution, Native Americans and Tories (who paid them for white scalps) attacked the settlement. Made of Shawangunk stone, the monument was dedicated in 1903. Ellenville marked the dedication day with a parade from Liberty Square to the site; speakers included prominent citizen and historian the Honorable Thomas E. Benedict and state senator John J. Linson. Other local monuments include the World War Veterans Monument in Liberty Square and the Soldiers and Sailors Monument in Fantinekill Cemetery. The Old Ellenville Cemetery has graves dating back to Revolutionary days.

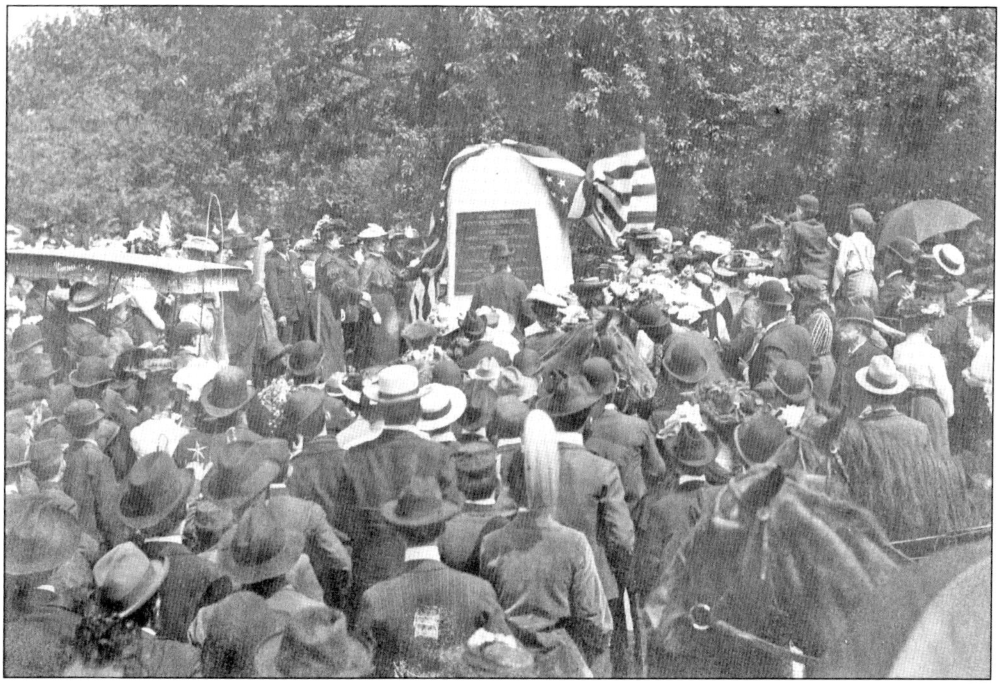

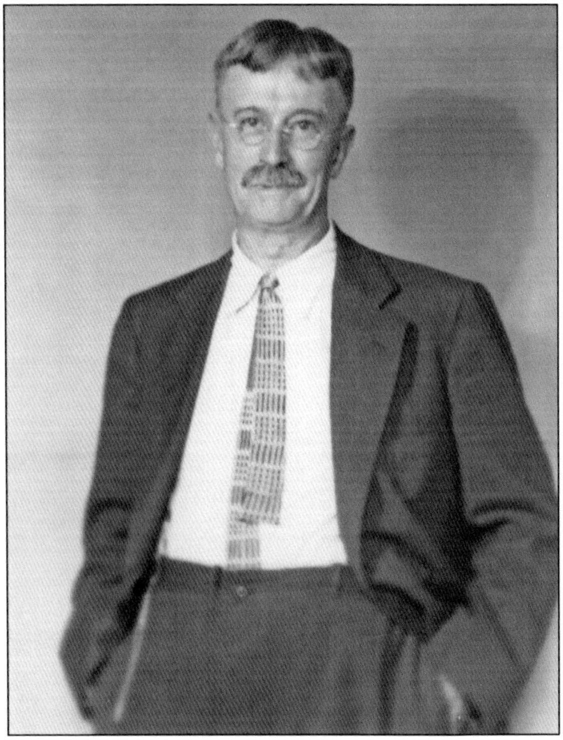

Born in Brooklyn in 1869, P. Edwin Clark was a renowned surveyor in this area in the early 20th century. A Cooper Union School of Engineering graduate, Clark married Lillian Scoresby of Ellenville. Active in the community, he was president of the Ellenville Board of Education as well as a member of the Noonday Club and the Scoresby Hose and Hook & Ladder Company. Below is a page from one of Clark's meticulous field books; this sketch is for a "survey for the Hartshorn Place, Ellenville, NY, for the WCTU loc. of proposed Geo & John R. Hunt Memorial Bldg." From his sketches, Clark developed survey maps. EPL&M is fortunate to have an extensive special collection of Clark maps and ephemera.

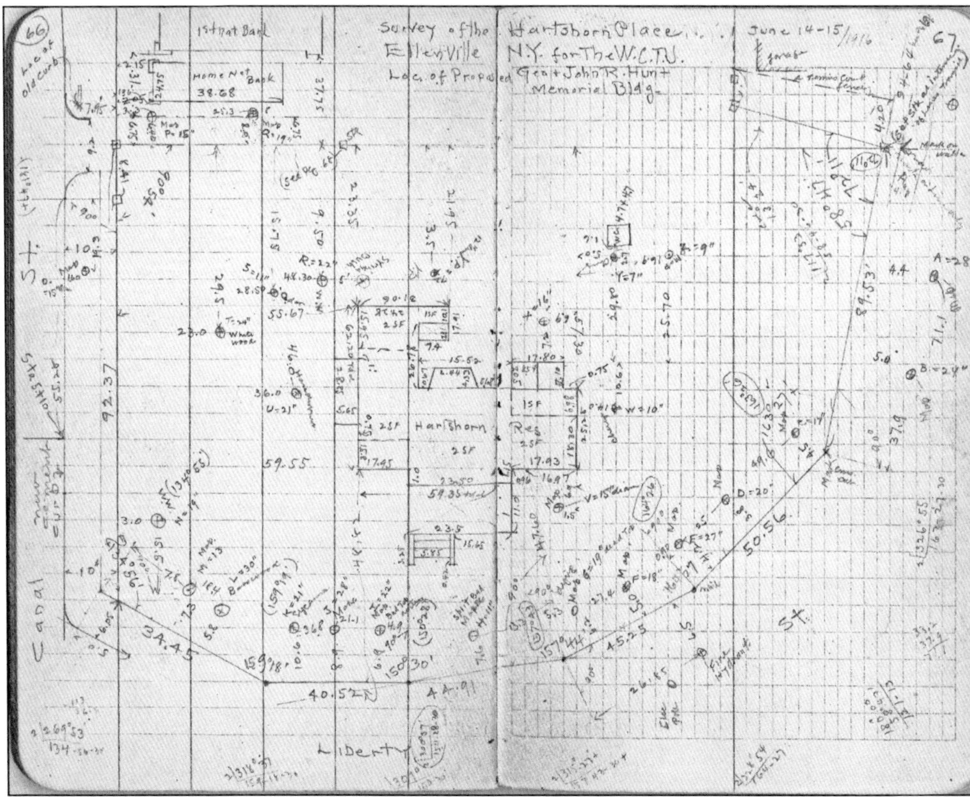

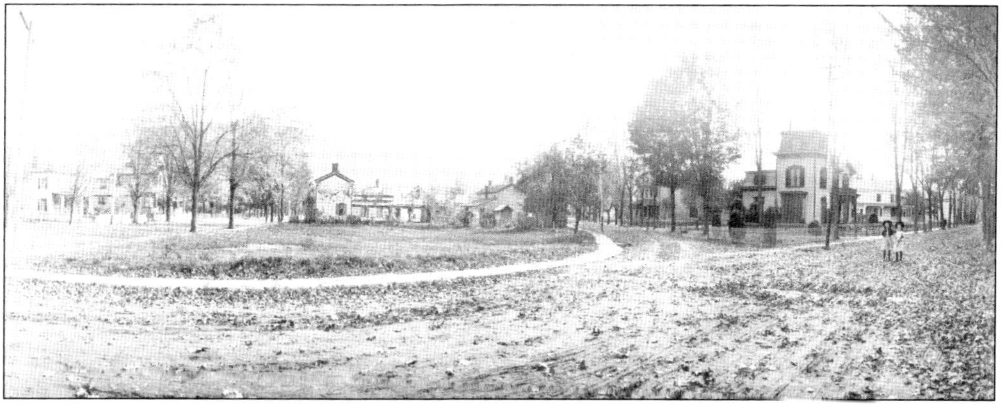

This 1916 photograph shows the intersection of present-day Route 209 and Liberty Street. The lot on the left is where the Scoresby Fire Company will build its clubhouse, and the home on the right is the Walter S. Cox house. Cox donated part of his lawn to the Scoresby firemen for a small park; they used it for their *Boy with the Boot* statue, which stood there welcoming visitors to Ellenville for more than 50 years.

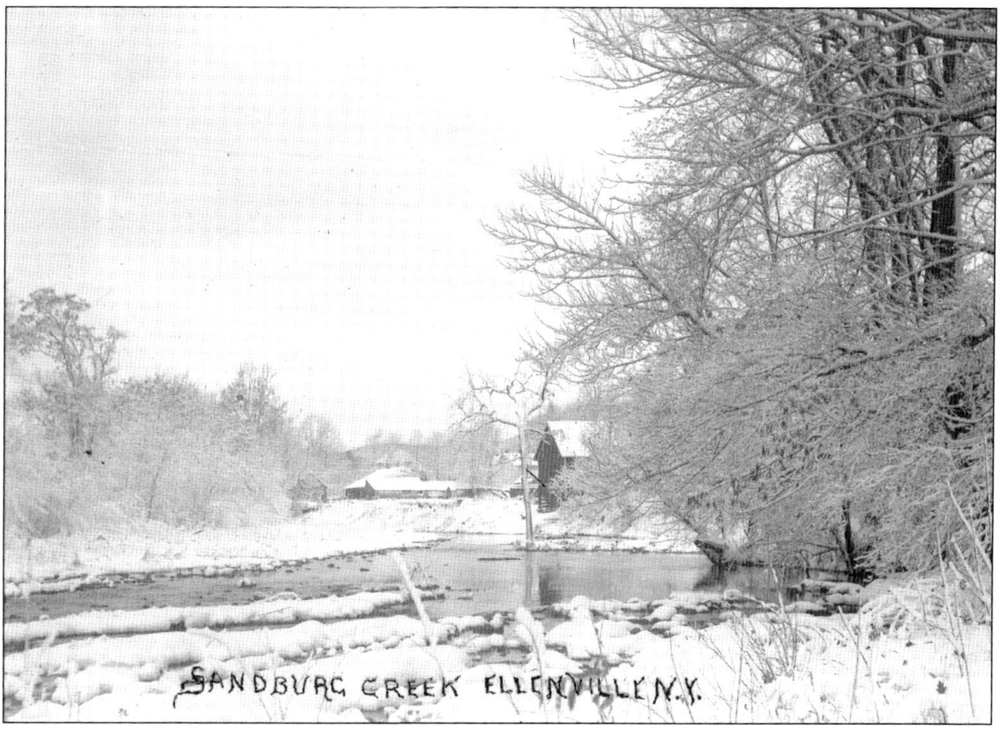

Sandburg Creek travels north along the base of the Shawangunk Mountains. It joins the Beerkill near Berme Road, and they flow together into the Rondout Creek, a tributary of the Hudson River. The Sandburg, Beerkill, and Rondout Creeks were all feeders to the D&H Canal. This image from a glass-plate negative shows the Sandburg in winter, around 1900. It is still a favorite location for trout fishing.

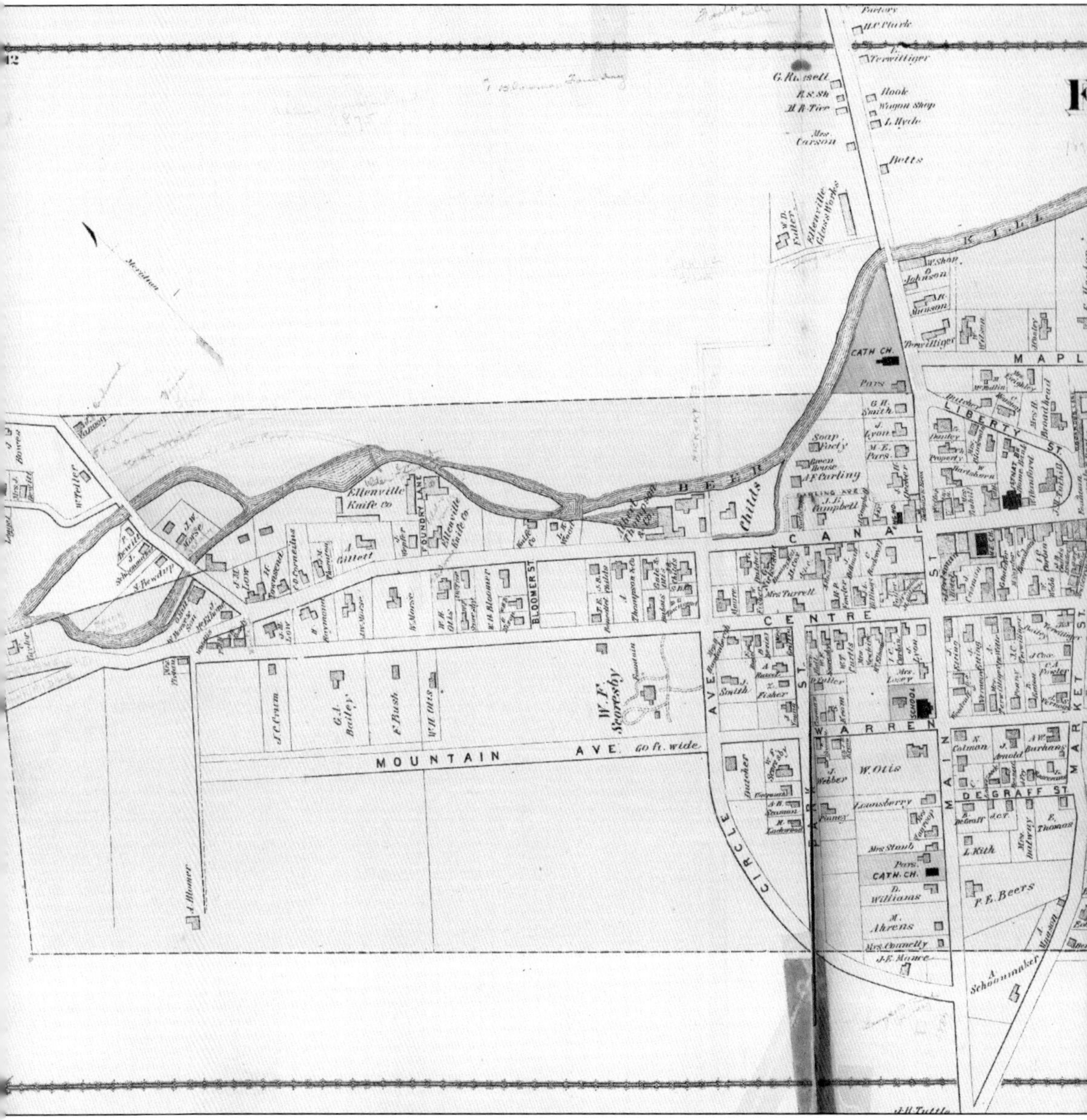

The backbone of today's village can be seen in this map of Ellenville, published in 1875, as can the importance of the "Good Beer Kill" and Sandburgh Creeks. The D&H Canal and the New York & Oswego Railroad are on the right at the east end of Ellenville. Along with street names, many of which remain today, family homes and businesses are identified. The map is in the *County*

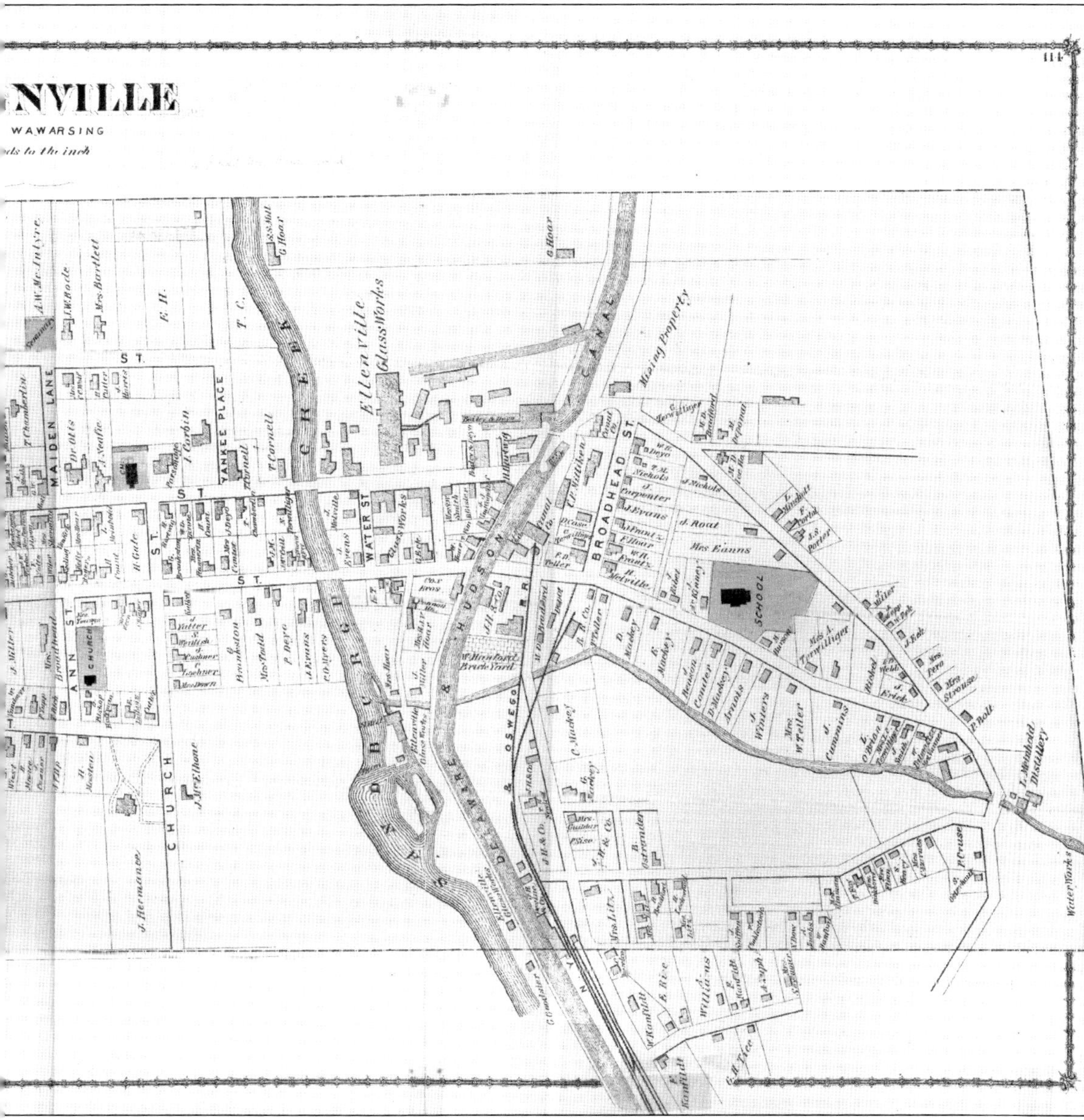

Atlas of Ulster New York, page 12, published by Walker & Jewitt of New York. A copy of this map can be viewed on the Ulster County clerk's website. An 1887 map, drawn and published by L.R. Burleigh of Troy, New York, is available online from the Library of Congress website.

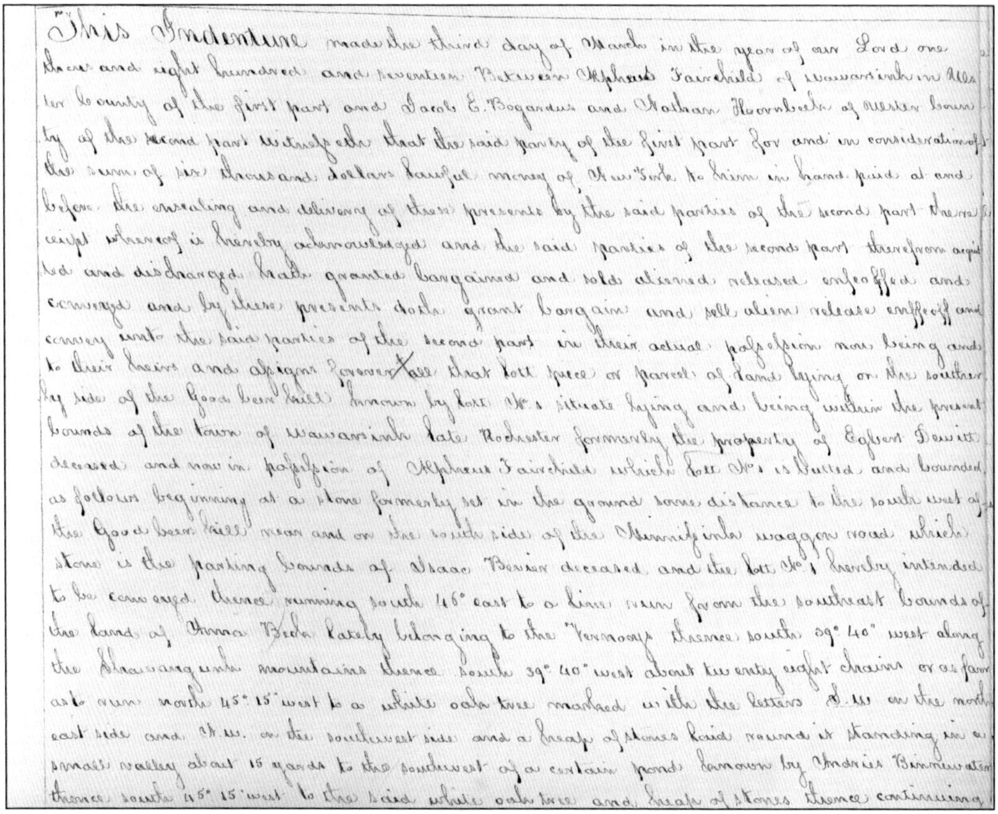

This Indenture made the third day of March in the year of our Lord one thousand eight hundred and seventeen Between Alpheus Fairchild of Wawarsink in Ulster County of the first part and Jacob E. Bogardus and Nathan Hoornbeck of Ulster County of the second part witnesseth that the said party of the first part for and in consideration of the sum of six thousand dollars lawful money of New York to him in hand paid at and before the ensealing and delivery of these presents by the said parties of the second part the receipt whereof is hereby acknowledged and the said parties of the second part therefrom acquitted and discharged hath granted bargained and sold aliened released enfeoffed and conveyed and by these presents doth grant bargain and sell alien release enfeoff and convey unto the said parties of the second part in their actual possession now being and to their heirs and assigns forever All that lott piece or parcel of land lying on the southerly side of the Good beer kill known by lott No 1 situate lying and being within the present bounds of the town of Wawarsink late Rochester formerly the property of Egbert Dewitt deceased and now in possession of Alpheus Fairchild which lott No 1 is butted and bounded as follows beginning at a stone formerly set in the ground some distance to the south west of the Good beer kill near and on the south side of the Minisink waggon road which stone is the parting bounds of Isaac Bevier deceased and the lott No 1 hereby intended to be conveyed thence running south 46° east to a line run from the southeast bounds of the land of Anna Beck lately belonging to the Vernooys thence south 39° 40" west along the Shawangunk mountains thence south 39° 40" west about twenty eight chains or as far as to run north 45° 15' west to a white oak tree marked with the letters I. W on the north east side and N.W. on the southwest side and a heap of stones laid round it standing in a small valley about 15 yards to the southwest of a certain pond known by Andries Binnewater thence south 45° 15' west to the said white oak tree and heap of stones thence continuing

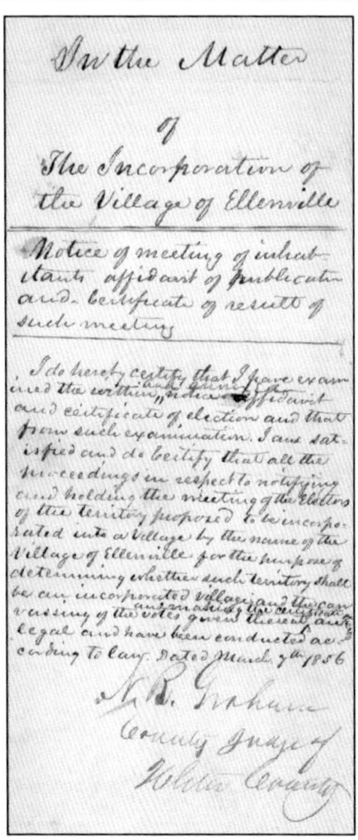

In the Matter of The Incorporation of the Village of Ellenville

Notice of meeting of inhabitants affidavit of publication and certificate of result of such meeting

I do hereby certify that I have examined the within notice affidavit and certificate of election and that from such examination I am satisfied and do certify that all the proceedings in respect to notifying and holding the meeting of the Electors of the territory proposed to be incorporated into a Village by the name of the Village of Ellenville for the purpose of determining whether such territory shall be an incorporated village and the canvassing of the votes given thereat are legal and have been conducted according to law. Dated March 7th 1856

N.R. Graham
County Judge of
Ulster County

A deed between Alpheus Fairchild of Wawarsing of Ulster County and Jacob E. Bogardus and Nathan Hoornbeek of Ulster County conveys the sale for "the sum of six thousand dollars lawful money of New York" of a portion of land (formerly the property of Egbert Dewitt) "lying on the Southerly side of the Good beer kill . . . to the Southside of the Minisink wagon road." This land would become the village of Ellenville. (Courtesy of the Ulster County Clerk's Office.)

A legal notice of February 5, 1856, states the meeting time and place "for determining whether such territory [Ellenville] shall be an incorporated village." Boundaries for the proposed village are outlined in great detail, "to wit: Beginning at a stone set in the ground . . . to . . . four links Westerly from a Butternut tree . . . three feet east . . . of a small shed near the Grist Mill . . . across . . . the Southerly bank of the Good Beerkill . . . ten links to an ash tree on the . . . bank of the Sandburgh . . . to the Anna Beck line . . . in the Sahawangunk mountain." Pictured at left is the document signed by N.R. Graham, county judge of Ulster County on March 7, 1856, affirming Ellenville's sovereignty. (Courtesy of the Ulster County Clerk's Office.)

Bibliography

Anderson, J.C. *Summer Homes Among the Mountains on the New York, Ontario & Western Railway.* New York: New York, Ontario & Western Railway, 1891, 1901 and 1905 editions.

Child, Hamilton. *Gazetteer and Business Directory of Ulster County New York for 1871–2.* Syracuse, NY: Hamilton Child, 1871–2.

Directory of the NY Ontario & Western Railway from Cornwall to Norwich, and Branches for the Year 1890 Second Issue. Newburgh, NY: Thompson & Breed, 1890.

Dumond, Marion M. "Forward, Into the Past." *Wawarsing.net Magazine.* Ellenville, NY: Ellenville Wawarsing Chamber of Commerce, December 2002–September 2006.

Ellenville Days and Ways. Ellenville, NY: Rondout Valley Publishing Company, 1968.

Ellenville (New York) Journal. 1849–1919.

Ellenville (New York) Press. Ellenville, New York. 1849–1863.

Hine, C.G. *The Old Mine Road.* New Brunswick, NJ: Rutgers University Press, 1963.

Kingston (New York) Daily Freeman. 1895–1913.

Laurito, Carol W. *A History of the Ulster County Fair; the First 100 Years.* New Paltz, NY: Ulster County Agricultural Society, 1987.

Sanderson, Dorothy H. *The Delaware & Hudson Canalway; Carrying Coals to Rondout, 2nd edition.* Ellenville, NY: Rondout Valley Press, 1974.

Terwilliger, Katharine T. "Before Today's Headlines." *Ellenville Journal.* Ellenville, NY: Rondout Valley Publishing Company, January 1969–December 1971.

——. *Wawarsing, Where the Streams Wind.* Ellenville, NY: Rondout Valley Publishing Company, 1977.

Terwilliger, Katharine T. and Marion M. Dumond. *An Old House Sampler: Some Old Houses in the Town of Warwarsing.* Ellenville, NY: Ellenville Public Library & Museum, 1986.

Wakefield, Manville B. *Coal Boats to Tidewater, 2nd edition.* Grahamsville, NY: Wakefair Press, 1971.

———. *To the Mountains by Rail.* Grahamsville: Wakefair Press, 1970.